T0117027

OUR TIME

A High School Baseball Coach's Journey

Scott Illiano

iUniverse, Inc.
Bloomington

Our Time
A High School Baseball Coach's Journey

Copyright © 2011 Scott Illiano

All rights reserved. No part of this book may be used or reproduced by any means,
graphic, electronic, or mechanical, including photocopying, recording, taping or by any
information storage retrieval system without the written permission of the publisher
except in the case of brief quotations embodied in critical articles and reviews.

iUniverse books may be ordered through booksellers or by contacting:

iUniverse
1663 Liberty Drive
Bloomington, IN 47403
www.iuniverse.com
1-800-Authors (1-800-288-4677)

Because of the dynamic nature of the Internet, any Web addresses or links contained in
this book may have changed since publication and may no longer be valid. The views
expressed in this work are solely those of the author and do not necessarily reflect the
views of the publisher, and the publisher hereby disclaims any responsibility for them.

Any people depicted in stock imagery provided by Thinkstock are models,
and such images are being used for illustrative purposes only.

Certain stock imagery © Thinkstock.

ISBN: 978-1-4620-2756-9 (sc)
ISBN: 978-1-4620-2757-6 (hc)
ISBN: 978-1-4620-2758-3 (e)

Library of Congress Control Number: 2011909304

Printed in the United States of America

iUniverse rev. date: 10/21/2011

This book is dedicated to every student who I have taught and every player who I have coached. You have given me more than words could ever describe, inspired me, and changed my life for the better.

To my assistant coaches: Jim Whalen, Steve Trongone, John Regan, Tom Lancaster, and Ray Renshaw, I am grateful for who you are and what you do.

To the memory of Tina Lane, whose friendship and influence made this book possible.

Finally, I dedicate this book to my parents whom I could never thank enough for what they have provided. It is their love, upbringing, guidance, and support that have given me everything that I have in this world. To my brother Dan whose knowledge and wit serve as a pillar of strength, and to Rosanne Renda, who I know for certain has made me a better man. I love you all.

Contents

Foreword

by Mark Ruggiero
West Essex High School, Class of 2006

In life, it is easy to rationalize taking the easy way out of a difficult situation. For example, if a big test is coming up in school and the teacher did not provide you with enough study material, you might just chalk it up to your teacher's lack of competence when you receive a poor grade. Or, perhaps, a deadline is approaching at work and you did not receive certain reports that you needed in time. When the project doesn't get finished, you explain to your boss that there was nothing you could have done because one of your assistants did not provide you with the necessary resources. In both situations, the end result is the same: you failed to succeed. So, while you rationalized a reason for why you failed so that you could feel better about yourself, the consequence of your failure remains. In the game of baseball it is just as easy to make similar rationalizations. After all, baseball, in many ways, is a microcosm of life.

When back-to-back snowstorms made the fields at West Essex High School unplayable for two straight weeks in March during the 2006 preseason, it would have been easy for Coach Illiano to wrap up practices early and cut short instruction because we were locked up in a tiny gym. In fact, I know plenty of players in other high school programs, even in college programs, whose coaches had their teams do nothing more than conditioning exercises and batting practice before sending them home, because they believed that there was only so much that could be accomplished indoors.

Not at a program like West Essex! We prepared for every situation that could ever arise on a baseball field, even though we were cooped up in the stuffy gym for weeks. Coach Illiano's goal was for us to be the hardest working and most prepared baseball team in the state of New Jersey. He took pride in our attempts to be "game ready" the moment we stepped out of the gym. In Coach's program, there were no excuses. The bottom line was that if there was something standing in the way of what you wanted, you needed to work hard and find a way to get it done. Find a way to do well on your test, find a way to meet your deadline, find a way to successfully prepare—no matter what.

We were high school kids, and many of us were too blind to see that this was exactly what would make us great. This was what would keep us ready to react to any situation we faced, and, most importantly, this was an attitude we would take with us for the rest of our lives.

On one bitter March afternoon, the 2006 West Essex Knights baseball players were dressed in layers on a bus heading to a preseason scrimmage.

I sat in my spot on the bus waiting for our departure, while a few players scrambled to make sure we had all of the equipment. I leaned my head against the cold, frosted window, more tired than excited. This was my third year playing varsity, so I had been through this drill before. The scrimmages were interesting, because they gave us a chance to get an early look at what we had as a team, but overall, they were usually cold, damp, and lacking in excitement. Just as I began to let my mind wander, I heard a voice call to me, "Yo, Mark."

It was Lawrence Caprio calling my name from the seat behind me. Everyone knew him as L. J., and he was a fellow senior who had been one of my best friends for as long as I could remember. L. J. played right field and could run like a deer, but he could be more accurately defined by his ferocity as a competitor.

L. J. asked me what my outlook was for the upcoming season. We discussed our lineup and pitching rotation for a minute and agreed that, as usual, our team had some potential. Then L. J. asked me, "What are our chances in the GNT?"

The GNT, or the Greater Newark Tournament, is the oldest and arguably the most prestigious tournament in New Jersey—and notoriously dominated by perennial powerhouse Seton Hall Prep.

I considered the notion for a second. Getting through that tournament was the equivalent of working your way up through the depths of hell—only to be told once you reached the top that you must then climb Mount Everest, as it was inevitable that the mighty Seton Hall Prep would be waiting for you in the championship game.

For whatever reason, the first time I truly understood the gravity of the GNT, I was hooked. Maybe it was something about seeing thousands of screaming fans pull for a bunch of high school kids as they lifted an entire town, or perhaps it was hearing the glorious stories of old Greater Newark Tournaments and the rich history of years past.

Many of our coaches, parents, and grandparents had their own version of a GNT tale. My father's side of the family hailed from Montclair, New Jersey, so they naturally passed down lore of how the 1942 GNT championship game was rained out, causing legendary Montclair High School Coach Clary Anderson to miss the rescheduled championship game because he had to leave for the navy. There were stories of classic battles between undefeated rivals from storied programs such as Union, Westfield, Newark Eastside, and Parsippany through the '60s and '70s. In the '80s there were epic struggles and storybook runs through the GNT by revered teams, such as Columbia, Glen Ridge, and Cedar Grove. A fierce rivalry between Seton Hall Prep and Nutley High School featured heroics that will be fabled for years to come.

The names of the heroes who starred in these stories will live forever in GNT lore. Guys like Elliot Maddux and Al Santorini, who were both from Union, made it to the major leagues. Maddux played for the Yankees, while Santorini played for the Braves after being drafted eleventh overall in 1966. Parsippany's Richie Zisk spent thirteen seasons in the big leagues during the '60s and '70s. In addition to Zisk, Parsippany also had Joe Orsulak, who played for the Orioles. The list of major leaguers who starred in the GNT includes our own West Essex alumnus Scott Bradley, who played in the late '70s and spent eight years in the big leagues with the Yankees and Mariners. Montclair's Guy Keriazakos played for the White Sox in the '50s. Hanover Park's Harry Fanok spent two seasons with the Saint Louis Cardinals; he had arguably the hardest fastball of all time. The list goes on and on, as do the stories.

More recently, Montclair Kimberly's Frank Herman of the Cleveland Indians and Seton Hall Prep's Joe Martinez of the San Francisco Giants have been analyzed by Buck Showalter and John Kruk on ESPN's *Baseball Tonight*, but we remember them as local high school kids who carried their teams through the GNT.

Each year, alumni of this great tournament gather to watch members of the latest era fight their way to victory and to reminisce about memorable GNT moments and even argue questionable calls that were made decades ago. They recount endless moments that will never be forgotten, like the 2003 GNT semifinal, when Seton Hall Prep's Eric Duncan, a first-round draft pick of the New York Yankees, lifted his team with a mammoth drive that he hit off future Cleveland Indians hurler Frank Hermann, or the tale of the 1965 GNT semifinals, when Greg Chlan of Westfield threw a twelve-inning complete game to beat Al Santorini, who was 20–0 in his high school career prior to that game. There are more of these stories than you could ever imagine.

I grew up watching countless classes of West Essex baseball players take their best shot at winning the GNT. They all came up short.

My dream was to reach the Greater Newark Tournament championship. There would be countless roadblocks standing in the way of getting there, but it would be up to me to navigate these adversities by preparing, working hard, concentrating, and making sound decisions. This foundation is an outline of what it takes to be a successful ballplayer. And with strong leadership, if an entire team can buy into these principles, anything is possible. The trick is finding a way to have an entire team believe in the system—and to believe in each other.

The journey through the 2006 baseball season was a roller-coaster ride that taught me more about life than any experience I have ever had. The guys on the team were a raucous bunch, with hearts the size of mountains. I couldn't be more proud to be a part of such an exceptional collection of personalities. Each individual brought a unique element to the team that culminated in endless entertainment and laughter. And each member of the program was challenged to put aside his distractions in order to solidify us as a team and overcome insurmountable adversity.

It's amazing how caught up people get in high school sports—often to the point that it practically becomes life or death. As a player, you feed right into it and embrace the notion. You become so focused and wrapped up in the moment that you would lay your life on the line to succeed and beat the guy across from you. I was used to feeling as if I were the only one who thought of it like that, or just one of a few, but when I gazed at all the guys around me on that '06 team and looked into their eyes, I was certain that they were feeling the same thing. You couldn't put your finger on exactly what it was, but it was as real as anything. Some kids grew up fantasizing about that big "at bat" in the bottom of the ninth to win the game, but kids like me, we ached for that moment. We lived for it, and dreamt about it, we talked about it, and we argued who was better suited for it.

The 2006 season was my last chance to take a shot at the GNT championship.

L. J. had asked about our chances in the GNT.

The way I saw it, we had an opportunity to do something bigger than anybody could have ever imagined. And we had just the type of guys capable of pulling it off.

We just needed to find a way.

Introduction

"Three frogs were sitting on a log, and one decided to jump off. How many are left?" asked Dr. Rob Gilbert, a sports psychology professor at Montclair State University. The audience responded in unison, "Two!" Gilbert explained that this was a trick question—just because you decide to do something doesn't mean that you ever do it. You must take action. Three frogs still remained on the log. Gilbert pointed to a formula (K-A = 0) that he had written on the board. "Knowledge minus action equals nothing," he explained. Over time, I often thought of this anecdote as well as his formula, but it was in the staff room at West Essex High School where I have served as the head baseball coach for the past sixteen years and a special education teacher for the past fourteen years that I thought of it the most.

As my colleagues and I would share our experiences as teachers and coaches in the field of education, we often thought that many of our daily occurrences sounded more like events that were scripted out of Hollywood rather than events that we had actually experienced firsthand. I can't even remember just how many times I heard the phrase, "We should write a book."

One day a colleague of mine said, "Scott, really, you should write a book." That's when I heard Gilbert's voice, "Three frogs sitting on a log ..." Realizing the enormous gap between saying you should write a book and writing one, I decided to take action.

This is the story of a baseball team. These events are true. Some of the names are not. Some parents, certain administrators, a few kids, and a handful of others have been changed.

I suppose that if this story were fiction I may not have been able to write it. It has been written simply because I have lived it. It will reveal how I arrived at West Essex, what inspired me to become a teacher and a coach, and I will describe the evolution of my teaching and coaching philosophy. As I describe my journey, there will be a few recurring themes along the way. One of them is the ever present issue of dealing with sports parents. While I have been privileged to teach baseball to many outstanding adolescents, I have also met many wonderful, supportive parents along the way. In the process, I have also encountered some disgruntled parents who seemed willing to do anything in their power to tear down and destroy an entire program for the purpose of building their own child's self-esteem.

A second theme is a premise that I hold dearly and believe to be the true essence of sports—the best team does not always win. The team that plays the best does. While Las Vegas oddsmakers can always tell us who the better team is, they never really know who will perform better, especially when the power of the human spirit and the inevitability of human error are involved in competition. The incredible power of the human spirit is amazing to me and represents the real heart of athletics. When it is combined with a variable as unpredictable as human error, we then realize why sports are so consuming to us.

An additional theme will require some thought on behalf of the reader and will come in the form of an underlying question—when does a coach become a coach? Is it the moment an athletic director reaches across the desk, offers his or her hand, and says, "Congratulations, you've got the job?" Is it after that first win? That first championship? Is it somewhere else along the way, or is it when all those nagging questions in the back of your mind finally stop nagging?

Faced with the issues outlined above and a multitude of others, I will share my journey and provide you with an intimate look at the life of a coach in a public high school. Some of these issues may surprise you or even shock you, but I feel compelled to share them, not only because these occurrences actually happened, but because there is so much that can be learned from them. I know that who I am today has less to do with any ball game and has everything to do with the lessons that I learned from my own mistakes, my own failures, and my willingness to deal with such volatile issues. What I have learned from my experience as a coach has helped to mold and shape me into the type of person and professional that I always aspired to be. Some of these issues may seem extreme, but I am certain that they are similar in theory to what most any other modern-day coach in another community is currently facing.

Come and take the journey with me. I will take you behind the scenes and bring you into my own home, inside our coaches' office, into our locker room, out onto our practice field, and also inside our dugout. I will explain some of the methods that I used in order to prepare my team. You will learn how I interacted with my players both individually and as a group. You will hear locker-room speeches as if you were actually there and learn how I attempted to motivate my players depending on each situation. I will explain how certain factors can negatively influence a team, easily spread throughout a program, and ultimately lead to a team's demise. I'll also share what components I believe are essential for winning teams. Along the way, you will also learn how close I once came to just walking away from it all, without ever turning back. You will read about a conflict that I had with a sportswriter and about how I once feared that I had just coached my last game.

This story may sound surreal at times. In fact, I often feel it necessary to preface it by stating, "This is a true story." I will describe how in 2006, a rash of injuries, biting cold temperatures, poor practice space, enormous pressure, and fierce competition, particularly from Seton Hall Prep, a national power with several Division I scholarship players and a pitcher less than three years removed from his first major league start, all lined up against twenty kids and four coaches who shared a dream and a whole lot of heart. Please join me as we travel together.

PART I

CHAPTER 1

A Tiny Three-by-One-Inch Ad
Can Alter Your Life Forever

I suppose if I had gotten the job I wanted at Montgomery
Ward, I never would've left Illinois.

—Ronald Reagan
Fortieth President of the United States

"CORNER!" RANG OUT FROM the hallway. My mind was somewhere back in
Melbourne, Florida, where I had recently attended a tryout with the Florida
Marlins. It was March of 1994.

I'm not sure which came first: the smell of the sizzling fajitas or the
beckoning sound of *"Corner!"*

Screaming "corner" was a mandate from the higher-ups at a well known
chain restaurant where I worked so the waiters and waitresses could avoid a
collision while carrying fajitas. The management had insisted that servers sprint
the fajitas out to the customer's table so the sizzle could be appreciated—but
we'd better not bump into anyone along the way!

"Corner!"

"Eighty-six the quiche."

"Ixnay this."

"Ixnay that."

"What station are you? Early or late?"

"Pick up forty-eight; I'm in the weeds!"

How much of this could I really take? How much longer could I listen

1

to the lingo and put up with obnoxious customers? How much longer could I tolerate the two-headed managers? You know the kind. They had one set of rules for me and another set for the female waitresses. These restaurant managers had a key principle that they adhered to in their management style: the prettier they thought you were, the fewer rules you had. Amy and Lisa, for example, had carte blanche, while I would have to make sure there wasn't a drop of ketchup on the bottom of the Heinz caps before getting signed out for the evening.

"Hey, Scott!" Collin, the manager, screamed out.

"Yeah, Collin," I answered.

"Scott, I don't think that seventy-year-old woman really asked for the Ranger game to be put on the TV near your section. If your food's not up yet, go run someone else's."

"You really think she's seventy, Collin?" I quipped.

"At least!" he yelled in disdain.

"Well, she might be seventy, Collin, but she was just saying 'Mess is flyin' out there tonight.'"

"Mess" of course was Mark Messier. The New York Rangers were my team, and as a long-suffering fan, I believed in "The Curse." Legend had it that the Rangers' founder, Tex Rickard, had burned the deed to the old Madison Square Garden inside the Stanley Cup back in 1940. From that point on, they were supposedly jinxed, and I, for one, believed it. But there was something different about Messier. He wasn't like all those other big-name guys who would eventually turn into a bust. He had a look about him—and a tone in his voice. He talked openly about "slaying the dragon," which was his assurance he would end the curse. And, boy, could he play! For the first time in my life, he made me think that the Rangers actually could win. Messier's belief that curses simply didn't exist had a profound impact on me for years to come.

At my tender age of twenty-two, part of my motive for waiting tables was to pay for my mini-season ticket plan at the Garden. If this were to be the Ranger's year, I wasn't going to miss it. My other motive was that I had graduated from Ramapo College in December, and I didn't have a clue what I really wanted to do. Slowly, I was putting together a résumé. I convinced myself that I was entitled to enjoy the spring, and then I would get serious about finding a real job. In the meantime, I would keep hanging out with my friends, chase after girls, and follow the New York Rangers.

Some of that was my way of dealing with what had just happened in Melbourne.

Former University of Florida and current New York Yankees organizational guru, Pat McMahon, once said, "The game is always taken from you before you are ready."

The game was about to be taken from me. Hundreds of players had attended the Marlins' tryout in Melbourne. We had all run the sixty-yard dash and thrown from our positions. Only twenty-two players advanced to the next phase of the tryout. I was included in that group.

One of the coaches called us in and said, "Some of you are really close to getting signed, right here and now, depending on what you show here!"

I was pumped!

We then took batting practice on the field. I had a pretty good round, spraying several line drives into the gaps of the outfield. After batting practice, we were divided into teams and played a game. At the end of the game, two players were signed, while the rest of us were sent packing.

I had done well in every phase of the tryout—running, throwing, batting practice—and also collected a few hits in the game. The coach pulled me aside and explained the difference between "performance and potential." He complimented me on my performance but explained that they did not project my potential. He also explained that on the flip side, another player may not have had a great performance during the tryout, but they might see something in him that made them project his potential. That was it. They didn't project that I would ever make it to Joe Robbie Stadium, the home of the Marlins. My career was over.

I had played baseball my whole life. When you're on your way up, there is always hope. Then, when you get cut at a tryout and you have already played the four years allowed as a college student, it suddenly becomes a very personal moment. I took my bag and headed down the road to hail a cab. As I walked out, I saw a young Carl Everett and asked him to sign a ball for me. Reluctantly, he did. Then, I saw Gary Sheffield back a sparkling red Mercedes Benz into his parking spot.

I wish I was one of those guys. Must be nice! I said to myself.

When my cab dropped me off at my hotel, I opened the door, dropped on the bed, and cried my eyes out. Why? Because, whether I was ready or not, a game that I had given my life to had been taken from me. Like it or not, there were no more games left to be played. So what next?

My degree was in business marketing. Word on the street was that if you wanted to go anywhere in marketing, you would need a master's degree. I figured I'd have to go back to school.

Entry-level salary at that time was around thirty to thirty-five thousand dollars, but to me that was a lot of money. I think what I wanted then, more than a career, was a car. I wanted a nice new car with power everything. With thirty thousand dollars I could afford a brand-new BMW as long as I kept living in my mother's basement—at least that was how my twenty-three-year-old mind figured it. Waiting tables would hold me over for the moment, and pretty soon I'd begin sending out résumés.

Within a few months I would have a full-time job, as well as my new car.

My alarm sounded. I woke to the smell of bacon drifting throughout the house. There was nothing better than my mom's turkey bacon on a Sunday morning, especially after a long night in Hoboken. I overheard my brother and father talking.

"Yeah, Dan, the Yankees are on TV in spring training today," my father said.

"I think they're gonna be good this year. They gotta win one before Mattingly retires, ya know," my brother Dan replied.

I walked into the kitchen.

"Hey, Scott, what time did you get in last night?" Dad asked.

I gave my patented, "Oh, one."

Whenever my parents asked me, "one" was the time I got home, whether it was one, three, or later. That's what I always said, and over time, it became a bit of a joke.

"What time do you have to be at work?" my dad asked.

"My shift starts at three," I answered.

As I thumbed through the Sunday *Star-Ledger,* my mother handed me a turkey bacon, egg, and cheese sandwich.

"I don't think you got home at one, Scott," she said. *"Scott!"* she repeated. I was in a deep stare.

"Look at this. West Essex needs an assistant baseball coach," I exclaimed.

"What?" my dad asked as I held up the paper.

There it was: a tiny three-by-one-inch ad that read, "Wessex Needs Baseball Coach."

"That's odd; high schools start up on the eighth of March. How could they be looking for a coach when they're already three weeks into the season?" I asked.

"Maybe something happened," my mom answered.

"I'm going to call first thing tomorrow morning," I stated. I figured I'd rather coach baseball every day than put myself through the torture of waiting tables three nights a week.

As I clipped out that tiny little ad, I didn't know what my chance was of getting the job. And so I could not have known that it would change my life forever.

4

Within a few days, I was granted an interview. I went to West Essex with the mere hope of not having to wait on tables anymore.

West Essex was located in North Caldwell, New Jersey, which bordered my hometown of Cedar Grove. On the short drive over, I pondered how badly we used to beat them when I was in high school. They weren't very good back then.

As I walked toward the entrance, I looked up at the white letters on top of the building that read "West Essex Senior High School."

Have they ever won a GNT? I asked myself.

"Wow! In all these years, I don't think they've ever won the GNT," I answered out loud.

The GNT was the Greater Newark Tournament. It was the oldest and most prestigious tournament in the state of New Jersey. We had won it back in 1988 when I was a junior at Cedar Grove High School. I don't know why, but all I kept thinking while looking up at those white letters was that if this school hadn't won a GNT championship, I would like to help them do so.

I went inside and interviewed with Athletic Director Tom Pengitore. Then I met with the head coach, Mike Christadore. Mike was a straight shooter, a disciplinarian who stood for the right thing.

During the interview, we seemed to hit it off, but when more than a week went by, I assumed that they had hired someone else with more experience. I'd just keep waiting on tables, I figured.

About ten days later, Mike called me.

"Scott, you're it. You're hired. You gotta come in and see Peng," he said.

I pumped my fist in the air.

"Um, okay, thanks. I'll be right down."

When I arrived, Tom Pengitore, who went by the name "Peng," explained a small stipulation to the position.

"The school really needs substitute teachers. They want me to bring in someone who can sub. Are you okay with that? We'll get you fingerprinted and all that," he said.

"Yeah, sure," I answered.

Before I knew it, I was substitute teaching too—and loving every minute of it.

It's amazing to me how life works sometimes, especially when you don't get what you want. I had wanted to play for the Florida Marlins. Instead, after having such a positive experience coaching and substitute teaching that spring, I was completely sold. This was what I wanted to do! The BMW could wait. I was going to go back to school to study to become a teacher. I imagine that if I had toiled around in the minor leagues for a few years I might have ended up in teaching at some point, but probably not in the same place. Getting sent home by the Marlins put me on a fast-track course to develop as a person and a professional, and it presented me with opportunities that might not have been there at a later time.

My schedule was full. I would substitute teach during the day, coach after school, and attend Montclair State University at night as a student in the education department's Teacher of the Handicapped Program. A year later, I became a full-time teacher's aide and worked side by side with established teachers in a variety of subjects. The learning experience was tremendous. I developed a philosophy that the best teachers are the best learners. Furthermore, the best learners would be borrowers, or thieves, of great information.

After two years serving as Mike Christadore's assistant coach, an unexpected opportunity arose. Christadore was a teacher in the business department and a fantastic one at that. Toward the end of the 1995 school year, he learned that although he was a well-respected teacher who had earned tenure, there would be a reduction in force within the business department. Since he had the fewest years of service within the department, he would not be rehired for the following school year. Within weeks, he had taken a full-time teaching position at another school. Realizing how difficult it would be to run a baseball program while teaching outside the district, he decided to resign as head baseball coach.

I didn't expect this opportunity to come up so early in my career. I immediately sent in my cover letter and résumé with the hope of being hired as the next West Essex head baseball coach.

The process seemed to take forever. I was still only twenty-four years old, and I supposed that some members of the board of education and administration had questions about my age and lack of experience. However, Tom Pengitore was in favor of hiring me. He had seen something in me that made him feel confident that I was ready—in spite of my youth and in spite of the fact that I was not yet a full-time teacher within the school.

As the weeks and months went by, I hadn't heard any official word as to whether or not I would get the job. I kept hoping and praying, but it was January of 1996, and I had yet to even interview for the position. Finally, during winter recess in February, Pengitore said he would like me to meet with him and the school principal, Jim Corino.

Both meetings went well. When I met with Corino, he informed me that he was willing to support Pengitore's endorsement of me, and that I would be formally approved as the new head baseball coach at the next board of education meeting.

As I walked down the path to my car, I was walking on air. I couldn't believe it. I had officially become the West Essex head baseball coach.

I had worked very hard to become a head baseball coach. This team, pictured here in April, 1996, was the first one I could call my own.

I continued to serve as a teacher's aide during the day, coach after school, and attend graduate school in the evenings. Finally, after two and a half years, I earned my teaching certificate. Coincidentally, two teaching positions in the special education department at West Essex opened up at that time. I was hired for one of them. Luckily, the school also had an assistant ice hockey position, which I was hired for as well. I was eagerly preparing for these opportunities and striving to learn more as I went.

At or around this time, on the campus of Montclair State, was when I first met Dr. Rob Gilbert, a renowned sports psychologist and one of the most influential people in my life. Dr. Gilbert had a regular hotline message called *Success Hotline*, and his creative and witty motivational messages were updated daily for free. I couldn't believe it. Each day I would call and jot notes down in my "success" notebook. To this day, I still call his hotline, and I have stacks of notebooks to prove it.

By calling Dr. Gilbert's hotline, I would also learn of other free hotlines such as David Denotaris's *Do You Have a Minute?*, Ed Agresta's *Power Thoughts*, and Coach Mike Tully's *Pep Talk*. Of the thousands of motivational messages that I heard, two of Dr. Gilbert's simple premises would serve as a guide for my future: 1) You already have all the ability that you need inside you. All you need is the proper training. 2) Success leaves clues! Find out what successful people are doing and imitate them. Do whatever it is that they do.

I would take those two premises to heart—in my teaching, in my coaching, and in my studies—and some might say that I became eccentric over them.

I would religiously drive to Cherry Hill, New Jersey, for the Be the Best You Are Baseball Coaches Clinic. I met Skip Bertman (Louisiana State University), Pat McMahon (New York Yankees), Rick Jones (Tulane), Rod Delmonico (Tennessee), Trey Hillman (New York Yankees), Gary Denbo (New York Yankees), Ron Polk (Mississippi State), Jim Wells (Alabama), Rick Peterson (New York Mets), Mike Martin (Florida State), Fred Hill (Rutgers), Bill Springman (Minnesota Twins), and too many others to name. I wrote so many notes that my hand hurt. The old adage that the shortest pen is better than the longest memory became a way of life for me.

I would ask so many questions that I'd find myself apologizing for taking too much of their time. By the end of these clinics, my brain felt just like it did during a week of midterms in college. I attended seminars. I ordered VHS tapes and DVDs, read coaching books from cover to cover, taped shows or interviews of people whom I admired. If Joe Torre or Rick Peterson were on WFAN's *Mike and the Mad Dog* show, I'd have my notebook out. I was a junkie, who couldn't get enough good information or quotes about coaching or the game of baseball. I was a sponge, and I wanted to soak it all up.

But, there was one thing that no amount of studying and no amount of education would ever prepare me for. Something that I had never considered; something that no one at the university or at the clinics had ever mentioned.

What was going on with some of the parents?

Chapter 2

Meet the Parents

If someone wrote a book about sports parenting
they should call it *Temporary Insanity.*
—Dr. Rob Gilbert
Sports Psychologist
Montclair State University

WHILE I WOULD WITNESS countless acts of egregious behavior on behalf of disgruntled parents over the years, perhaps there is one that stands out the most.

As my assistant coach, Ray Renshaw, and I walked across the outfield grass, our feet quickly became sopping wet.

"Scott, with the puddles in the outfield alone there's no way we're playing today," said Renshaw.

It was early on a Saturday morning, and after heavy rains throughout Friday evening, we wanted to check on the condition of our field before making an official decision as to whether or not to cancel our game scheduled for that afternoon.

Renshaw had starred for West Essex as a catcher under Mike Christadore when I was an assistant. He later went on to become an All-American at William Paterson University. Ray was my friend and someone whose heart I admired. He had a presence about him: brown hair, blue eyes, athletic build, and a bright expression. What I admired most was that he was as intense a competitor as you could find, and he wore his heart on his sleeve.

Ray was known as "R. C." throughout the community. He and I connected instantly when I first met him as a junior in high school. We stayed in touch and grew closer over time. He was scouted by a variety of area scouts, but at five foot ten and 180 pounds, he was probably just a tad shy of meeting the typical height and weight requirements for major league catchers. When he finished playing, he gladly joined me as my assistant in 2000.

"I know, R. C. If the outfield is this bad, imagine how soft the infield must be," I responded.

As we neared the infield dirt, we noticed several puddles. Then we headed toward home plate.

"Jesus!" Renshaw exclaimed. There was a shocked expression on his face.

Walking over, I looked down where he was staring. There I saw one of the largest pieces of human excrement that I have ever seen, roughly ten to twelve inches in length, strategically placed on top of home plate.

"What the hell is wrong with these people?" Renshaw asked.

"It wasn't meant for *us*, R.C. It was meant for me. I'm the guy who makes out the lineup card," I explained.

"Scott, I'm gonna kill somebody! I know who it is, and so do you. I'm goin' after him!" Renshaw fumed.

"R.C., look at me. You're not going to do anything! Listen to me. This stays between us. The kids can't know, all right?" I said.

Renshaw didn't respond.

"Okay?" I asked.

Renshaw reluctantly nodded. "This is the last straw. You work too hard; you give too much for this," he added.

Renshaw wasn't far off. I gave a significant portion of my life to coaching my teams. I spent endless hours at the field working with players. It was not uncommon for me to sit down and eat dinner at nine thirty at night. By the time I finished planning the next day's practice and typing up a practice schedule right down to the most finite details, it would be twelve thirty or one in the morning. Former NFL coach John Gruden said the life of a coach becomes one of "coffee breath and bloodshot eyes." He was right.

Covering all the bases during a team huddle in 1998.

During the season, I traded in my social life too. Friday nights were over and done with, given the time that I would arrive home and the time I'd be required to be at the field on Saturday mornings. Sundays became designated as "Put Your Life Back Together Day," as they would be reserved for laundry, housecleaning, groceries, paying bills, grading papers, and possibly a visit to see Mom and Dad. I had relationships fail, as not every girl I dated viewed high school baseball with the same importance that I did.

I also made sacrifices in the summer, running as many as three teams to help our younger players develop. I organized the West Essex Knights Summer Baseball Camp to develop future Little League players. If I had calculated my salary based upon the amount of time that I devoted to coaching it would have worked out to about thirty-five cents an hour. Yet, I did it without reservation and without complaint. Why? Because that's what coaches do.

Something happened inside me as I taught and worked and saw the light in my players' eyes. Something happened when the game was on the line and runners were on base in the bottom of the fifth inning. I did it because of the feeling I had when a senior told me he remembered something I had taught him when he was a freshman. I might not have remembered it, but I knew that I helped him. And most of all, I did it because at the end of each season a senior would walk over, place his jersey in the box, offer his hand, and say, "Thanks, Coach!"

But not everyone would say thank you.

The moment I became a coach, I automatically won both false friends and true enemies. Consider this: if a baseball team has fifteen players on the roster, and nine of those players are in the lineup, by definition there can be six unhappy people. That could equate to twelve unhappy parents. Then consider the likelihood of fifteen players with fifteen sets of parents agreeing on every coaching decision.

When I began coaching at West Essex, I was only five years removed from high school, but I already noticed that things had changed. On my first day, they gave me team sweatpants, a sweatshirt, and a short-sleeved T-shirt.

"Wow. Where do you guys get all this stuff?" I asked.

"The Booster Club," answered Mike Christadore.

I had never heard of a Booster Club. "What's that?" I asked.

I would learn that this Booster Club was a parent-run fundraising organization that provided supplemental funding for the benefit of the baseball program.

My first reaction to the parents in the baseball program was that they were much closer in proximity than what I was accustomed to. They were too close to the bench area, often hovering around during pregame and waiting right outside the locker room after games.

In my world, parents were always supportive and attended the games, but they also kept their distance. They had boundaries.

Initially, I had polite and innocent dealings with the parents I met. But why wouldn't I? I was only the assistant coach. I didn't mind them as long as I didn't have to wait on the tables where they were seated. And they didn't mind me either, because from their standpoint, I didn't make out the lineup card. There were times when parents would try to use me as a sounding board if they wanted to get a message to the head coach or needed to just blow off steam. That notion, by the way—that the assistant coach has no input on the lineup and will agree with a disgruntled parent's point of view—is completely irrational, yet remarkably, remains quite prevalent. Nevertheless, the assistant coach is usually the most popular guy in the park, especially when the assistant is young and well intended.

It's amazing how you ask God for certain things and pray that they happen for you, and then, when you get promoted or achieve what you want, it inevitably brings new enemies into your life. Motivational speaker Joyce Meyer calls it: "New level, new devil!"

I wanted more than anything to be a head baseball coach. When I had played baseball, parents didn't dare complain to the coach about who got cut or who sat on the bench. They would seldom even consider themselves smart enough to question the coach's strategy or decisions. Then again, I believe it was former Saint Louis Cardinals Hall of Fame manager Whitey Herzog who is credited with saying: there are three things that every man thinks that he can do better than any other man: build a fire, manage a baseball team, get laid.

Where I grew up, the parents of the kids who sat on the bench not only knew that their kids didn't belong on the field, they would even jokingly mock their kids about it. I had heard more than one father ask his son if he got any splinters from "riding the pine." And yes, those parents loved their children just the same.

I was naïve when I first got hired, and I thought that the parents of the kids who belonged on the bench would agree that their children belonged there. I soon learned that they didn't necessarily see it that way. I would later hear terms to describe such parents as wearing "rose-colored glasses" or looking through a "fun-house mirror." Yet, in my naïveté, I just wasn't prepared for certain things, nor could I ever imagine that they would happen.

"Thank you all for coming, and thank you for such a wonderful season," I said to the crowd of just under two hundred people at our annual team banquet held at the Hanover Manor. It was June 2000 or, as they referred to it back then, Y2K. Several smiling players approached, and we exchanged handshakes. A few parents did too.

"Thank you, Coach. The kids had such a great time this year," Mrs. Nicholas said.

"Oh, you're welcome. I'm going to miss 'em. You've got a great kid here," I said as I patted him on the back. The boy smiled.

Another parent approached. "Hi, you don't know me. I'm Brian's mother." She was staring right through me. She grabbed my forearm and dug her nails into me, squeezing as hard as she could.

"You ruined his life!" she snarled.

"Take your hands off me," I answered as I attempted to avoid a scene.

She managed to squeeze even harder.

"Get your hands off of me!" I repeated.

Mrs. Nicholas, her husband, and their son stood in shock as they witnessed the exchange. The boy was no longer smiling. I twisted and turned my arm out of Brian's mother's grasp.

"You ruined his life," she repeated.

"No, I didn't. I forced your son to face himself. You should thank me for that," I responded.

My arm felt scratched, so I removed my suit jacket and noticed blood from my forearm seeping through my white shirt. She had broken my skin with her nails, right through my suit jacket.

What was I supposed to do? I had no recourse. I would never hit a woman, even in self-defense, and I didn't want to cause even more of scene at a school function, so I just stood there and took it. The following day, Athletic Director Tom Pengitore suggested that I go to the Hanover Police Department and file a complaint. I didn't think that was the manly thing to do, so I opted not to. Did it hurt? A little. Was it assault? You decide. What I do know for sure is that I didn't deserve it.

My only intent with any child I have ever worked with has been to make him a better person and a better player. In all of my dealings with players, I have always been both honest and respectful. I have a few principles that govern my communication with children who are teenagers. The first is: "Praise in public and criticize in private." If I have a problem with a kid, I call him aside and take it up with him away from his peers. I never want to create a victim by demeaning him in front of the group. The second principle is one I learned from Bill Parcells, which is known as "the sandwich technique." If I have constructive criticism to make toward someone, I sandwich that criticism around at least two compliments. I make them feel good about something even if I have to critique them in some way.

I have always told my players what their roles were before our season even started, and I never hid behind any list. I always felt that if a young man gave enough of himself to try out for the team, then he deserved a face-to-face explanation from me to hear what factors led to my decisions. I know I didn't always tell players what they wanted to hear, but they always got eye contact from me, always got sincerity, and always got the truth. I believe that those principles allowed me to command respect from nearly every one of my players and foster an atmosphere of trust within our program. There is a famous line in the movie *A Few Good Men* where Jack Nicholson screams out: "You can't handle the truth!" I believe that any conflict that I have had with any player or parent has been due to the fact that they simply couldn't handle the truth.

But I was not alone. I quickly learned that disgruntled parents were not unique to West Essex. On our first day back to school one year, I recognized a familiar face. I knew Jacques because he was a highly successful hockey coach at a neighboring school. He informed me that he had left his former school and quit coaching in order to become our new vice-principal. I wished him luck with his new position and asked what led him to leave his former school and enter into school administration. He shared with me a sad and unfortunate incident, which in spite of making several newspapers, I hadn't heard about. Just moments before a state tournament hockey game, he was physically attacked by an angry parent because the man's son was not going to "suit-up" in uniform that night—even though the tournament rule only permitted a maximum of twenty players on each bench. Jacques was one fine coach. He was young, very knowledgeable, and dynamic. He would later go on to become a principal at a top-flight New Jersey school. Jacques never said this to me directly, but I always wondered if that incident—and its accompanying legal battle—hadn't happened to him if he would have remained in coaching for a longer period of time. I had a strong sense that this situation in which he was so terribly victimized had forced him to enter the field of school administration a lot sooner than he originally intended. He had a real passion and talent for coaching, but after that night, he had had it. That was enough.

Parental interference, violence, and instability were fast becoming a national epidemic, with the worst example that I was aware of occurring in January 2002. Parent Thomas Junta was sentenced to up to ten years in prison for beating his six-year-old son's youth hockey coach to death. The victim's son, also six years old, witnessed his father's fatal beating as he stood there helplessly. As I contemplate what the coach could have possibly done with a group of six-year-old hockey players that set Junta off in that manner, my heart bleeds for that poor boy who will never rid himself of that image. As for Junta, I'm sure he has asked himself, "For what?"

More recently, I received headlines that have spread across our country's newspapers, courtesy of an e-mail from Coach Kenny Buford of the American Coaches Academy (ACA):

"Boy's Father, Uncle, and Brother Assault Coach over Benching," *Newsday,* November 3, 2007.

"Parent Attacks Coach after Daughter Cut from Team" *NewsNet 5,* November 5, 2006.

"Dad Pulls Gun on Coach over Son's Playing Time" *ESPN,* October 23, 2006.

"Kirkland Mom Arrested for Assault on Little League Player" *Fox News,* May 4, 2009.

"Warren County Dad Arrested for Alleged Attack on Parsippany Wrestling Coach during Match" *Star-Ledger,* February 2, 2010.

The leading spokesperson to advocate against this type of behavior may be my all-time favorite baseball player and childhood idol, Cal Ripken Jr. In fact, it was the topic of disgruntled sports parents that afforded me the chance to meet him personally.

Just prior to the release of Ripken's book, *Parenting Young Athletes the Ripken Way,* I received a call from the president of the North Caldwell Little League. He informed me that Cal had a business associate who lived in North Caldwell, and he would be speaking to a small group at the Municipal Building prior to making some public appearances in New York City. He offered me the opportunity to attend. I was practically jumping out of my shoes and hopped at the chance to go and meet my hero. While there, I asked Cal about his philosophy on defensive positioning and his multiple batting stances, and I even received a free autographed copy of his book.

As soon as I got to my car, I opened the inside flap of the book and read:

Since he retired from baseball in 2001, Cal Ripken Jr. has devoted his time to coaching kids, including his own son and daughter, who play baseball and basketball, among other sports. With a baseball league of nearly seven hundred thousand kids ages five to twelve named for him, he has had a chance to meet and work with countless young athletes. Cal Ripken's simple yet effective philosophy for helping kids get the most out of playing sports is to keep it simple, explain the "why," celebrate the individual, and make it fun! But Ripken is troubled by what he sees in youth sports: a competitive intensity that removes the element of fun from playing. Now, drawing on his experiences as a father, a player, and a coach to his charges at his youth baseball-based organization, Ripken Baseball, the legend offers his insights and advice on how to approach organized sports with your kids to ensure they have the best experience possible, stay fit, and enjoy themselves.

As I put the book down, it seemed a little surreal that I had really just met and spoken to Cal Ripken. There he was, a Hall of Famer, coming across in such a genuine way while taking the time to answer all of our questions. I pondered how awkward it can be to meet such a famous celebrity. You almost don't know how to act or speak at first.

Then, a key point dawned on me. While most people would have that same kind of timid feeling that I had in Cal's presence, a disgruntled sports parent would probably not think twice before getting out of control and acting like a maniac at a youth league baseball game—even in front of a legend like Cal Ripken Jr. Clearly, when disgruntled parents get emotional, there is very little that they won't do and very little consideration for the repercussions of their actions.

In the fall of 2005, our football team was scheduled to play Parsippany High School. I pulled into our school parking lot around 12:45 p.m. for a 1:00 p.m. start. To my surprise, no one was there.

Is our team on the road? I wondered.

No, I had read our schedule correctly. The game was cancelled by the police. A parent had threatened to kill the Parsippany coach for disciplining his son by benching him when the player violated a team policy. It was a big story; I even read about it the next day in a New York paper, *The Daily News*.

That situation reminded me of one of my own.

When I took over the baseball program, I automatically inherited the West Essex Baseball Booster Club. I soon found that there was a gross misconception on behalf of many parents. They seemed to think that if they served as an officer or contributed to fund-raising, their son would earn playing time. They were mistaken. When they found that their sons were not playing, or were not playing in the roles that they wanted them to, they would often fly off the handle and request a meeting with me and the school administration. I can't even tell you how often during these discussions parents would cite how much they had done for the program as a reason why their children should not be sitting on the bench. I would routinely explain that their fund-raising efforts were benevolent on their behalf, but that I picked my starting lineup based upon the attitude, effort, and ability of each individual player. At that point, some of them would quit the Booster Club. As a matter of fact, my very first Booster Club president actually quit the club midseason, without any formal notification, leaving all of the kids in our program, as well as all of the other Booster Club members, hanging.

It was amazing to me to see the things that parents would do or not do based upon their beliefs about their child's playing time. When I was an assistant hockey coach, we had a set of parents who would regularly bring a large bag of sliced oranges to our games. They would come down near the locker room and give all of the boys on the team fresh oranges to eat while they were recharging in between periods. But this was contingent upon whether or not they felt their son had played as much as they wanted him to. If their son did not play as much as they liked, they would not give oranges to anyone. Instead, they would keep the oranges to themselves in the stands. I once witnessed the mother and father exiting the arena in a huff, a full bag of oranges in hand. Their son had only played sparingly that evening. From that day on, my friend and head hockey coach, Mike Giampapa, and I would refer to those parents—the ones who only seemed to care about their own child's playing time but not the team—as "oranges."

I sensed that parental involvement within the baseball Booster Club was getting to a point where parents were jockeying over who would be president, vice-president, and treasurer based upon their false perceptions that it would equate to playing time for their child. Therefore, I eliminated those positions, made myself the chairperson, and appointed committee heads for specific fund-raisers and our team banquet. Since I never wanted to handle money, I also appointed a financial officer. The incumbent club officers were outraged at my decision.

Two days later, I received an anonymous letter that read, "You take over the Booster Club? What a joke. That's the end of WE [West Essex] baseball!" A week later, a second anonymous letter arrived. It had no return address and was postmarked from Newark, New Jersey. This one was much more direct and to the point. It read: "Illiano, you will die!"

I didn't know what to do with it. I probably should've reported it to the authorities, but I didn't. I just crumpled it up and threw it out. Did I think that I was in imminent danger? No. Did it make me look twice when I went out to my car at night? Yes, it did.

Part of my reasoning for not reporting the death threat was that there was no name attached to it. Joe Torre was once asked about anonymous comments that members of the New York Mets made toward his Yankees. He asked, "Anonymous Mets? Didn't their parents name them?"

My philosophy was that if they didn't attach a name to what they'd written, I would not dignify it. While I may have made the wrong choice, I felt that reporting it would give the sender of the letter the attention that he or she was looking for. So I took my chances and bet my own safety on it. However, surviving this would not shield me from further anonymous attacks.

I'm not completely sure exactly when online chat forums became available, but sometime around 1999 they became extremely popular. NJ.com was the one with the most traffic in New Jersey. Any players who got cut or any disgruntled parents could log on with pseudo screen names and under the auspices of free speech say anything that they wanted to about anyone. These posts were completely anonymous so it was impossible for the victim of the attack to trace the identity of the person or people behind the posts. The things that were written about me over time were dishonest and intended to do one thing—destroy me! Any nameless, faceless person could log on at any time and post whatever he or she wanted. Someone could write a post that "Illiano has sex with unicorns!" and undoubtedly people would believe it. It was amazing to me to see the lengths that some people would go to tear down an entire program just to boost their own son's self-esteem.

Oddly enough, the presumption of truth, rather than doubt, often permeates the online forum culture. No matter how false or dishonest a post may be, people tend to believe that it is true merely because it is written there.

It seemed to me that the dirtier and more vicious these online posts became, the more clicks NJ.com would receive, and therefore, the more advertising money they would rake in. They knew exactly what the forum site entailed, and I imagine that they loved the traffic that it provided. They could have put an end to those cowardly smear attacks instantly by eliminating the anonymity to the posts—only permitting users to submit posts who had registered valid e-mail addresses with the user's personal information. But that would cost too much money!

For me, it got to a point where I just stopped going online and reading, as the cowardice behind the posts was sickening. People had a lot to say, but no one wanted to identify him or herself. Then again, that was consistent. Their death threats were anonymous, their disparaging posts in an online chat room were anonymous, and no one had bothered to leave a name tag on the large piece of excrement that was left for me on top of our home plate either.

In May of 2007, the anonymous attacks on New Jersey coaches on NJ.com became so unfair and so vicious that my all-time favorite sportswriter, Bob Behre of the Newark *Star-Ledger,* wrote a blog about it. Bob is a skilled and witty writer—a member of the media whom I deeply respect and trust enough to know where his interests lie.

You don't even have to read his blog to know what he wrote in defense of area coaches. All you have to know is the title: "Who Babysits the Parents?"

CHAPTER 3

Daddyball

Each one of 'em has two agents, Mom and Dad.
—Tom Pengitore
Former West Essex Athletic Director

INTERESTINGLY, WHILE MANY OF my parental references have been negative, that is not to say that I haven't had any positive dealings with parents. I have.

There have been quite a few clear-thinking, rational, fair-minded parents who have appreciated what my staff and I have done in our tenure as coaches. There are two families in particular, the Skopaks and Cardinales, whose sons Matt and Joe played for me; to this day they remain near and dear to my heart and are people whom I consider friends.

However, the reality in coaching is that you rarely hear from the satisfied parents. Parents usually don't send e-mails, write to the administration, or give you that "evil eye" stare in the parking lot because they are happy. Part of doing their job as supportive parents is staying out of your way and allowing you to do your job as a coach without interference from them. A coach's relationship with the satisfied parent is typically a "no news is good news" type of proposition. Consequently, parental encounters end up being more of the negative sort.

What is it then that causes one parent to quietly remain behind the scenes, while another parent literally foams at the mouth?

I have often wondered about this and to this day remain baffled. The student athletes who I work with are first and foremost healthy. I have worked in the classroom with a student in a wheelchair and with a blind student. I have seen Down syndrome, varying levels of learning disabilities, autism, and even fragile X. But the student athletes I work with are not handicapped. They are popular, good-looking, and, in almost every case, preparing to go off to college. They aren't suffering from any serious addictions, and they have all the creature comforts at home and beyond. I would think that their participation in baseball or any other high school sport should merely be scenery along the way—but it isn't.

So what is really going on here? What would make a parent actually defecate on home plate? Or attempt to rip my arm out of its socket at a formal team banquet? What issue would cause a parent to send me a death threat? How come as an academic teacher from September until March my phone seldom rings, but as soon as we begin tryouts I receive twenty voice mails? What causes such disgruntlement on behalf of parents when their children don't athletically achieve the levels that they expect? Are they facing their own demons? Is something lacking in their marriage? Are they trying to live out experiences through their own children that they didn't have themselves? Maybe it's the mere fact that they love their children so much, and when they see their own flesh and blood upset, they simply cannot handle the situation.

Penn State football coach Joe Paterno said, "Every player we have, someone poured their life and soul into that young man. They are giving us their treasure, and it's our job to give them back that young man intact."

However, when a child does not earn a position that he may have wanted on an athletic team, is it at all possible for any good to come from the situation? It could be a real teachable moment for parents that could strengthen the bond that they have with their child. I would venture to say that 99 percent of the conflicts that I've had with parents have been related to playing time. I would also say that I've yet to meet a parent complaining about playing time who was an accomplished ballplayer in his or her own right.

During the time that I also served as an assistant hockey coach in the winter of 1999, the New Jersey Devils head coach Robbie Ftorek's son enrolled at West Essex as a freshman. Robbie had played in the National Hockey League with the Quebec Nordiques and New York Rangers, and now he was coaching an elite team in the NHL. If anyone was ever qualified to question our coaching decisions it was Robbie. He never did. As a matter of fact, one night while I was home flipping the channels, I saw Robbie on ESPN's *SportsCenter* go into a tirade over an official's call and throw a bench onto the ice at Joe Louis Arena. A day or so later, he was in the top row of the bleachers at our game, keeping his distance away from the crowd. After the games, he would typically walk near our locker area, shake our hands, and talk about how much he enjoyed watching the kids. When his son exited the room he routinely gave him a pat and a kiss on the top of his head and said, "Hey, did you have fun?" That was all he would say to his son. Other than "Thank you," he never said anything to us about hockey unless we asked him. Then and only then would he would share his infinite wisdom. I contend that Robbie's supportive attitude and demeanor were due to the fact that he had already done it himself. He didn't need to live it through his son. He had reached the pinnacle of hockey both as a player and as a coach. He himself was a professional, so he didn't feel that he needed to make his son one. He just wanted his son to have fun. Robbie never provided us with his coaching résumé either. But, I can't tell you how many disgruntled parents—who after requesting a meeting with me and/or the school administration—would volunteer their Little League résumé and express to me what an accomplished baseball coach they were.

As a matter of fact, for a while it seemed as if these "meetings" were becoming a trend, probably because disgruntled parents would form alliances similar to those seen on the reality television game show, *Survivor*, with their common bond being hatred and bitterness toward me. When one parent would come in for a meeting, it would entice another parent to do so as well. If there were five kids on the bench, I might end up having six meetings. One for each reserve player and one more for the player who served as the designated hitter but didn't get to play defense in the field. These meetings began to get to me. So much that they led me to do something I never thought I could do—something that to this day I am ashamed of. I actually made a coaching decision that had more to do with my fear of parental backlash than it had to do with making the right decision on behalf of our team.

Mr. Cartwright was a very active Booster Club member who had coached some of the boys all through Little League. Mrs. Cartwright was politically active in the community. She also knew one of the central office administrators and a board of education member on a personal level. Although most of the administrators were supportive of staff and our needs, some seemed willing to go beyond the ordinary parameters of their position. Two of these in particular—who have since left the school—I thought of as Suit Number One and Suit Number Two.

Clint Hurdle of the Texas Rangers once said, "Sometimes, if you could buy a player for what you think he is worth athletically, and then sell him for what he thinks he is worth, you would be a very rich man." While our coaching staff was fond of Mr. and Mrs. Cartwright's children and considered them to be very good boys, this was very much the case in terms of how our coaching staff viewed their athletic abilities as compared to how their parents viewed them. Then again, it has been said that when a coach, a parent, and the player himself make an evaluation during tryouts, you often end up with three different versions of the same story.

One of my top priorities when I became head coach was to begin a summer baseball team so that our players could play and develop further each summer. Previously, they had to go to surrounding towns in order to play. I believed that the creation of such a team would be a critically important factor for the future success of our program.

I should have run the team by myself and charged the players a fee to participate. I didn't. Instead, I asked the parents of the Booster Club to help raise the funds to get this new summer team off the ground. Since Mr. Cartwright was such an active Booster member, he took it upon himself to do all the necessary paperwork within the league. He single-handedly obtained corporate sponsorship and raised more than enough funds to begin the summer team. Then he purchased equipment for the team.

He essentially gained control of the team. I mistakenly let it happen because I did not know any better. At that time, I gave very little thought to the possibility of any conflict of interest with regard to having one of the player's parents run a team at the high school level.

Prior to the time and date on which his son would be eligible to participate, Mr. Cartwright generously continued fund-raising and performed all of the administrative duties for the team. I gladly coached the team at first. Later on, my varsity assistant coach, Charlie Giachetti, wanted some additional experience, so he became the head coach. The program was a huge success. Our players were getting further development and being taught by an outstanding up-and-coming coach. Charlie was gaining head-coaching experience. Everyone seemed happy.

Coach Charlie Giachetti (#10) and I were initially considered to be harsh for asking our players to condition by running postgame sprints. Today, it is almost unheard of for teams in our area not to run them.

During the following spring, Mr. Cartwright's son tried out for our varsity team as a position player. After we determine a player's attitude and conditioning level, there are five specific criteria that our staff utilize as part of the evaluation process. Most players do not score high on all five criteria, so we look for the best combination of all of the specific baseball skills that we assess. Our staff evaluation showed that the boy did not meet certain criteria we look for in our varsity players as compared to the other candidates. It was within our rights not to select the boy as a member of our team. However, our staff took a liking to the boy, and I, for one, sensed that he really liked baseball. I wanted to keep him involved in some capacity as long as he could accept what we projected his role on the team to be. Our numbers indicated that we could afford to suit up at least one more player if he was willing to accept my offer.

Immediately after our tryouts, I sat down with the boy and had a chat with him. Those conversations are never easy. In fact, they are one of the more difficult aspects of the profession. Since I would be delivering news that ordinarily no player ever wants to hear, I was always sympathetic. I have never forgotten how I felt when the Florida Marlins coach delivered that message to me. At the same time, I could not lie to the boy, nor did I want him to be surprised. After complimenting the Cartwright boy for his efforts throughout the tryout, I informed him up front that I could not guarantee him even one inning of playing time, but if he thought that he could stick it out, I would look to find him some innings and at bats whenever I could. I explained that realistically I could not make any promises for playing time, and those opportunities would be contingent on circumstances that were unknown at that time. I asked him to sleep on our conversation and get back to me because not everyone can accept that type of role. The boy came back. As the regular season got underway, his parents became increasingly angrier with his role. A little more than halfway through the season, Mr. Cartwright could no longer hide his frustration.

We were on the road at Summit High School in the third inning. They had runners on base, and I was honed in. Suddenly, I felt a tap on my shoulder. There was Mr. Cartwright standing in our dugout. He handed me an envelope and told me that the money from our recent Booster Club fund-raiser was in there. Then he said something to the effect that he couldn't bear to stay here any longer while his son was not playing. I was shocked that he was in our dugout area during a game. But I was much more concerned about our pitcher trying to work out of a jam than whether he was going to watch or not watch the game. I hurled the envelope somewhere around our bat rack and the stack of helmets near the backstop.

The next day, Athletic Director Tom Pengitore said that Mrs. Cartwright had called Suit Number One and that I was required to attend a meeting with Mr. and Mrs. Cartwright.

Seldom would anything productive result from such meetings, but the parents would get to have their forum with me. Most of these meetings were very similar in nature. They would attack me, bash other children on the team, and tell me how good a player their son was. In the process, they would imply that somehow my ignorance was preventing me from seeing what they were seeing. I was required to sit there and take the bullets like a sitting duck. It was open season for them!

During the meeting, Mrs. Cartwright was relentless. There is a term "Daddyball" used to describe overbearing and interfering baseball fathers. This was now "Mommyball!"

As we neared the end of the season that year, an incident occurred that caused me great conflict. Our team suffered a rash of injuries. With our starter out, I inserted Mr. and Mrs. Cartwright's son into our lineup. While in the lineup, the boy hustled, and I appreciated how hard he was trying to help the team. In one game, we were trailing by one run in the bottom of the seventh and last inning, with two outs and runners on second and third bases. An error would tie the game, and we would play on. A hit could surely win it. As young Cartwright stepped up to bat with the outcome hanging in the balance, I thought to go to my bench and insert a pinch hitter as I had another experienced player available who I believed may have been perfectly suited for that specific situation. I should have put my shoulders back, made eye contact with our bench, and made the move. I didn't. Instead, my shoulders slumped as I bowed down and cowered at the thought of more phone calls to Suit Number One and having to attend another meeting if I were to remove the Cartwright's son from the game in front of the entire crowd. So, I opted not to make the move that my gut told me may have been an ideal matchup for our team. Young Cartwright tried his best but unfortunately stranded the tying and go-ahead runs and made the final out of the game.

While there was no guarantee of a different result had I inserted another player in order to create the matchup that I was looking for, I was numb. With the game on the line, I was more concerned about the possibility of parental backlash than I was with trusting what my gut told me may have been best for our team during that isolated situation. I was ashamed of myself. His parents thought that I was a terrible coach for not playing their son more often. I thought that I was a terrible coach for allowing parental pressure to influence me. I felt that, by making a decision that had anything at all to do with anyone sitting in the stands, I had reneged on my professional obligation as a coach and also compromised myself as a person. I was ashamed, not so much for the end result, but based upon the factors that I actually gave consideration to in coming to my decision. I would have been equally disappointed in myself had Cartwright gotten a hit, driven in both runs, and led us to victory simply because of the fact that I had allowed parental pressure rather than my gut instinct to lead me toward an in-game coaching decision. I vowed never to do that again. I made a promise to myself that no matter who a parent was, no matter what they ever said or did, that I would never again make a coaching decision for any reason other than what I believed was absolutely the best for our team.

A week or so later, Mr. Cartwright called me to discuss the possibility of more playing time for his son. To his credit, he was polite and gentlemanly in conveying his displeasure about his son's role. I sympathized with him and offered some suggestions for how I believed his son could improve upon his game. Before we hung up, he asked me who was going to be the starting pitcher in the upcoming first round of the state tournament. I didn't realize at the time where my answer to his question would end up. Our number-one and number-two pitchers had been battling injuries. As much as I wanted one of them to pitch, I really didn't have a choice. As I tried to hurry off the phone, I quickly told Cartwright that our number-three pitcher was going to be the starter in the state tournament. Apparently, he didn't know that our other two pitchers were hurt. That evening I received a phone call from a sportswriter named Al Williams. He said that he was doing a story on the state tournament. He also said that an area coach had informed him that I was making a controversial pitching decision because I was bypassing our number one and number-two pitchers in favor of our number-three pitcher.

"Controversial?" I asked. I told Williams that both our number-one and number-two pitchers were unavailable because of injuries. This was hardly a controversy!

Since Williams was questioning me about some supposed controversy regarding our starting pitcher for the state tournament, and because I had just informed Mr. Cartwright of our starting pitcher only hours earlier, I called him on the fact that I believed that he must have gotten his information from Mr. Cartwright. He denied that his source was Cartwright and maintained that his source of the information was an area coach. I then told him that unless he could produce a name of this supposed area coach, we would just end the discussion with the understanding that the source of his inaccurate information had been Mr. Cartwright. I gave him a moment to come clean. He remained silent on the other end.

While this conversation might seem somewhat mundane, it would factor in largely later on, as I had just learned something that I had not previously known—that the Cartwright family was also connected to Al Williams, a very powerful sportswriter.

A couple of days later, Charlie Giachetti and I were in the coaches' office talking about our scouting report for the upcoming state tournament. We heard a knock on the door. It was Mr. Cartwright. He walked in and told us that he was "putting his son on the field this summer" in reference to the summer baseball season. Then he provided us with an ultimatum. If his son played every inning of every game, Charlie could continue to serve as the coach of the team as he had in past summers. If his son did not play in every inning of every game, Charlie would no longer be permitted to coach the team. Within seconds, I asked Charlie to resign; he was in full agreement to remove himself from the situation. The summer team was something that I considered to be vital for the success of our program.

Charlie would later go on to win numerous North Jersey Parochial B State Championships as the head coach at Saint Mary's in Rutherford. He remains as good as any coach that I know, but he was forbidden by Mr. Cartwright to work with and develop our returning players—all because he had refused to play Mr. Cartwright's son in every inning. When we asked Cartwright who would be replacing Charlie as the head coach, he informed us that he would be taking over the team. It was time for Daddyball! He later hired another coach to help him.

During tryouts the following spring, one of my assistants raised a very delicate and serious question that coaches ought to consider when assembling a team: if you do not project that a player will play very much at all, would it be better to not select him as a member of the team? This member of my staff reminded me of instances of parental interference during the previous season. Then he made an analogy to ripping off a Band-Aid: "Scott, if you cut a player, you have to meet with the parents once. If you keep him on the roster, it could be a season-long tug-of-war with phone calls, meetings, dirty looks, and negativity with his parents. It's not right, and it's not fair." He then urged me to cut any player that our staff did not project would at least play occasionally.

While my assistant's thoughts had some merit, I felt that every decision that any teacher makes in education should always come from a student-centered approach and never be made from a parent-centered approach. I couldn't bring myself to levy a final decision that might adversely affect a kid based upon the criteria of avoiding his meddling parents. Just as I was adamant that the people sitting in the stands should not factor into my in-game decisions, they should also not factor into whether or not a player is selected as a member of my team.

As we organized our final rosters that season, I hoped that the Cartwright boy would once again remain with us. I liked the boy and felt that playing on our team could benefit him in many ways even if he did not play as often as he may have wanted to. Like any team member, I thought that keeping him with us would benefit his overall growth. I thought it would give the boy a sense of enhanced camaraderie that comes from being a member of a varsity team. I also thought it could teach him life skills and provide him with a chance to earn a varsity letter. Therefore, I met with the boy again and explained that based upon our tryout I projected a similar role for him this season. I encouraged him to be with us and was honest about what he could expect. I explained that my coaching decisions are not personal and I would never intend to hurt him or any other player. I also explained that the downside to my job is that I am forced to make decisions when selecting our starting lineup that can't make every team member happy.

I did try to play him as often as I could, whenever I could. In one game, our team jumped out to a sizeable lead early in a game. I made sure to get him in the game right away and also went out of my way to make sure that he got his name in the Star-Ledger newspaper so that he could feel good about himself after he had driven in a run with a double as a pinch hitter. However, the boy's demeanor was noticeably different this time around. He was a senior now. He was not happy with the innings that I could realistically offer to him. Neither were his parents. In fact, they were thoroughly convinced that I was giving their son a raw deal—withholding a starting position they believed he deserved. As the season progressed, his attendance became more sporadic; he did not attend one of our games, choosing instead to attend a summer job interview.

Prior to the last game of the season, I read our starting lineup to our team. When young Cartwright learned that he would not be starting, he immediately walked off the field, got into his car, and drove away. With one game to go, he had just quit the team.

Just prior to the start of our game, Suit Number Two walked into our dugout. He informed me that Mr. Cartwright had just gone into Suit Number One's office. He then told me that Suit Number One had ordered me to put young Cartwright into the game.

"I would never do that just because you told me, but I couldn't put him in right now if I wanted to because the boy left," I said.

"What do you mean?" asked Suit Number Two.

"After I read the lineup, he walked straight to his car and drove off without saying a word to anyone. He just quit," I explained.

Suit Number Two was baffled by what I explained and stared a blank stare. What really blew me away was that Suit Number Two was actually in my dugout relaying a message that Suit Number One was now making my lineup decisions for me. I had never heard of anything like this.

I thought long and hard that evening. What would have happened to me if the boy had remained at the field? The promise that I had made to myself to only play my best regardless of a boy's parents took precedence over Suit Number One's directive. I would not have put the boy into play at his urging. I would have defied his directive. As a matter of fact, I would have walked into Suit Number One's office and handed him the lineup card before I would ever compromise myself in such a disgraceful manner. Would I have been fired for insubordination right then and there had the boy not walked off our team? I guess we'll never know. They never said anything about this during those senior seminar or practicum in teaching courses that I had taken.

I share information about this true occurrence, not for the purpose of revealing how I was treated or what anyone had done to me. There is a much more relevant and poignant question to consider: why did they feel the pressure to do it?

Over time, I have reflected on this unfortunate happening. Again, my only intent was to do something positive for the young boy. I worked with him as a player, giving him just as many reps in practice as everyone else. I taught him skills that can be helpful in his adult life and awarded him two varsity letters for his efforts. What humbled me as a coach is that although I would never intend to hurt a player with any of my decisions, the reality is that players can perceive them to be hurtful regardless of what my intent may be. During times like this I am envious of lower-level coaches whose responsibility is often to focus more on development rather than winning. That is something that I experienced first-hand as a JV hockey coach. There were times that I would walk through the lobby at Floyd Hall Arena after a game and be greeted by parents in a similar manner to the way New Yorkers must have greeted former New York mayor Rudy Giuliani during the recovery effort at Ground Zero. Why would I receive such a warm and kind reception? Because we only had twelve skaters on our team and everyone had to play. In the spring, as a head coach, I am the same exact person, but my responsibility is very different. In fact, my popularity has the potential to really plummet as not everyone does get to play. By the time summer comes around it can get even worse.

That August, while enjoying summer vacation, I received a call from Suit Number One's secretary, who informed me that that he wanted to see me. On what should have been a day of my vacation, I met with him. He informed me that Mrs. Cartwright had written a letter to him and to all nine board of education members, mailing it to their home addresses. He provided me with a copy of the letter and scheduled a meeting for me to meet with the board of education and address the charges that she made against me in her letter.

According to our Athletic Code of Conduct, playing time was supposedly "nonnegotiable" and not an appropriate point of discussion with a coach.

Every point that she made in her letter was a point about playing time (but bottled and packaged as if I had no morals, values, or ethics) or about how I essentially destroyed her son's self-worth. Actually, those who read her letter may have concluded that I was akin to Darth Vader or perhaps the ruthless dictator of Iraq. Suit Number One provided me with a date, roughly three weeks from that day, when I was mandated to appear in front of the board of education in order to convince them as to why I should remain in my position.

My job as head baseball coach was now officially on the line!

CHAPTER 4

Let Me Tell You a Story

Stories unlock a player's imagination.

—Skip Bertman
LSU Baseball Coach

DR. ROB GILBERT DEFINES a story as something that happened in the past, that you tell in the present, and will remember in the future.

"Stories are without a doubt the most powerful thing in the world," said Gilbert. "If you want to motivate somebody, tell them a story. If you want to teach somebody, tell them a story. *Gone With the Wind* is a story. The Bible is a story. You're living out a story. I'm living out a story. If you are majoring in history, you are majoring in those last five letters—you are studying stories!"

I had met Skip Bertman, the legendary LSU baseball coach, at a clinic in 1997. Bertman shared with me that he believed that the "most coachable moments" in baseball were those few moments just before a game when one of your players might be questioning himself and thinking, *What if I strike out three times today?* At that time, Bertman would assemble his team in front of the dugout, review their signs, and then tell his kids a story. Normally it was a true story about a person or a team that accomplished something or overcame great odds or adversities. Bertman recommended to me that I do this with my team. He strongly emphasized being accurate with my facts when telling these types of stories and said to make sure that the story always made a point.

As I was aspiring to be a teacher, it was interesting that these two individuals, Bertman and Gilbert, who were the best in their particular fields, both shared a similar belief in the importance and power of a story. They both felt that the best way to motivate and inspire others was through storytelling.

From that moment on, I began to seek out and compile stories wherever I could find them. I attended seminars given by Dr. Gilbert and learned how to properly tell a story. One of Gilbert's teachings about stories was that they give us *hope*, which is also an acronym for "Hold On, Possibilities Exist." He explained that when people hear about someone else's experiences, they may think: "If that person got out of that situation, then we can get out of ours. If someone found their strength and energy, then we can find ours." To this day I tell stories to my teams, especially during those few moments prior to a game.

I entered the board of education conference room and sat down. It was now October of the following school year.

"Thank you all for—"

"Shhhhhhhh," Suit Number Two interrupted.

"We didn't do the Pledge of Allegiance!" he said.

I stopped talking and waited to be called upon.

As I sat awaiting, many thoughts and questions filled my mind. Even today, so many years later, they are still fresh. After all, as stated earlier, I thought, giving this young man a uniform would benefit him. I was fully aware of the difficulty a senior faces when he is not playing. I truly understood that, but I believed that being part of a team and being inserted into the lineup, albeit infrequently, can enhance a student's overall growth and maturation, socially and otherwise. Further what he learns about the game will serve him in good stead should he ever desire to teach baseball. As a head coach it was incumbent upon me to play the best players I had for each game or particular situation. Why, I asked, did his parents not understand my motives? Why did they attack me in such a harsh verbal manner even writing that I was "ethically impaired?" I had indicated to the youngster that my decisions were not personal. I bore them no animosity. I also understood the love that parents bear their children, and how often conflicts can arise when comparing a coach's objective lineup decision with a parent's subjective belief about their own child. I had no wish to disparage a player of mine or his parents. Thus I asked myself how could I best respond to the board?

Our official team statistics proved that some of the statements in Mrs. Cartwright's letter were false. The overall amount of playing time that she cited her son had received was different from his actual amount of playing time that was documented by our official team statistics. Therefore, I began by giving each member of the Board of Education a copy of our statistics in order to discredit her statements about me. Then I explained a core belief of mine—discipline is the greatest form of love that you can show to a child. If you really love a child then you teach him discipline, because it will give him guidance and stability in his life.

Mrs. Cartwright wrote that I was "a baseball technician who cannot motivate, inspire, or teach." I wanted to show the board that I really wasn't the person she depicted in her letter. How could I show them that I really was capable of motivating, inspiring, and teaching? The only way I knew how, of course. I had learned from two of the best in the world: Bertman and Gilbert.

I would inspire the board the same way that I attempted to inspire my players. I would tell them a story.

"Jack Nicklaus's golf coach never knew that Jack would end up being the great PGA champion that he was," I said. "But he knew that he was going to reach his potential, because Jack was the only golf student he ever had who showed up for lessons on rainy days."

Then I told another story.

"In 1968, in Mexico City, the Olympic Marathon had been over for hours. As one of the photographers was packing his camera away, he noticed a man hobbling through the entrance of the stadium. He appeared to be injured and slowly continued hobbling toward the finish line. As he crossed the finish line, one of the reporters asked him who he was.

"'My name is John Stephen Akhwari. I'm from Tanzania.'

"'The marathon ended over two hours ago,' said the reporter.

"Akhwari looked up. He was breathing heavy. 'My country didn't send me ten thousand miles to start a race. They sent me ten thousand miles to finish a race!'"

I added a third story.

"It was a hot August day in Albuquerque, New Mexico. At around noon, several rail workers were busy with their pickaxes when a limousine pulled inside the rail yard. The president of the company, Bill McClanahan, rolled down his window. 'Charlie? Is that you, Charlie? Come over here!'

"Charlie walked over to the car, greeted Mr. McClanahan, and the two drove off. About an hour later they returned.

"One of the workers greeted Charlie, 'Hey, how do you know Mr. McClanahan?'

"Charlie explained, 'Twenty-seven years ago, Bill McClanahan and I started with this same company, on the same day, for the same pay.'

"One of the workers sarcastically asked Charlie, 'Well, how did he get to be president, while you're still slaving here with us?'

"'Because,' said Charlie, 'twenty-seven years ago, I was looking for a job, but Bill was looking for a career. I guess I was looking for something to do, but he was looking to do something. I wanted to make a little money. He wanted to make a difference.'"

I looked at each board member. "I'm sure that all of you know and work with Bills and Charlies every day in your own lives—people whose work ethic and level of commitment vary. I always say that there is a difference between a baseball player and a kid playing baseball. A kid playing baseball is just in it. A baseball player is totally into it. The kid playing baseball is on the team. The baseball player is totally involved with the team. This is not recreation. This is competitive athletics, and as your coach, I have the responsibility to play the best candidate at each position, because this great school deserves championships! A lot of my players show up early before practice, and they leave late. They strength-train in the off -season, work out indoors in the winter, and do all of the extras. Our staff uses an extensive evaluation process that allows us to identify the players who are the most talented, as well as the most committed to our program. I ask all of you to consider for a moment what would John Stephen Akwhari have done in the event that he did not like his role within the team?

As I walked to my car that night, I didn't know if I had coached my last game at West Essex. I imagined that I felt the same way that a defendant feels while the jury is out deliberating his or her fate. I also felt extremely sad that my relationship with one of my players and his family had deteriorated to such an extent. This certainly was not my intention. On the way down the path, I heard my assistant's voice, "If you cut him, you fight the battle once. If you keep him, it will be a three-month tug-of-war."

It was eight months since we had had that conversation. It was out of my heartfelt concern for the boy's well being that I decided to keep him on the team. I felt it was the right thing to do.

"This is what you get for being the nice guy," I said to myself.

I had just practically crawled on my hands and knees and begged the board of education to save my job. As I drove home, one of my hands started to shake. Everything that I had worked so hard for and prided myself on could be taken from me. I didn't sleep much that night, wondering what kind of verdict the jury would return.

The following morning Suit Number One came into my classroom. I wasn't sure if it was a good sign that he came to see me rather than calling me down to his office. I looked up from my desk. He informed me that my contract as head baseball coach would be renewed for the upcoming season.

I could breathe a sigh of relief. I was safe for now.

The entire experience shook me up. For a time, it also changed how I viewed seniors who might never play an inning.

Trust me, nowadays it is a rare, and I mean rare, senior who predominantly sits the bench for twenty-five games and then says "thank you" at the end of the season. While it may seem hunky-dory to them in March, before the grass even turns green, by mid-June, they do not feel the quite the same. However, those types of players still could exist. "Throwbacks" if you will, who would be willing to stick it out like they did in the old days, when both they and their parents knew that they belonged on the bench, yet they were still thrilled to go along for the ride.

During the following season, I cut a senior during tryouts. A week or so later, a girl he was friends with rudely greeted me in the hallway.

"What did you have to cut him for? He just wanted to be on the team!"

This was an introspective moment for me. The girl had a point, a valid one. Maybe the boy really did just want to be on the team. Did I blow the call? Had I become jaded from my experience with Cartwright's parents? Or perhaps even paranoid that other people could be like them?

If I hurt that boy, Lord knows, I did not mean it. Trying to determine what would hurt a boy more—cutting him or keeping him on the bench for the entire season—remains one of the most delicate and difficult questions a modern-day coach will ever have to answer.

CHAPTER 5

Cancers

What would happen to a bottle of spring water if you
poured just a single drop of Clorox bleach into it?
—Coach Mike Tully
Head Volleyball Coach
Motivational Speaker/Author

IN THE *BASEBALL COACHING Bible*, Coach John Scolinos wrote, "As the family loses its influence in its children's upbringing, so does our nation lose control of its destiny. The teacher and the coach are part of the family!" But, what happens when the intentions, beliefs, and viewpoints of a coach contrast with those of a player's parents?

"I tell our parents that it's a fragile relationship that I have with their son," Seton Hall Prep coach Mike Sheppard Jr. once shared with me during an Iron Hills Conference Sportsmanship Summit. The importance of family resonates loudly to Sheppard Jr., and the bond that his family has shared in baseball is incredible. His father, Mike, won 998 games at Seton Hall University while molding several major league players, such as Rick Cerone, Craig Biggio, Maurice Vaughn, John Valentin, and Matt Morris. When Mike Sr. retired, his brother Rob succeeded him as head coach at Seton Hall University and currently serves in that role. Another brother, John, is also a successful baseball coach at Morristown-Beard, a prep school in New Jersey.

Seton Hall Prep is the best baseball program in the state of New Jersey, primarily due to Sheppard Jr.'s tutelage. He had been an All-State shortstop there in 1977 and became the New Jersey College Player of the Year in 1980 while playing for his father at Seton Hall University. After a stint in the Houston Astros organization, he returned to his alma mater and became the head coach in 1986. Since that time, he has won more than five hundred games, seen more than forty of his players go on to play at the Division I level, while fourteen of his players have been drafted to play professionally. His teams have won the Greater Newark Tournament (GNT) twelve times, been ranked number one in New Jersey five times, and been ranked nationally seven times.

One of the things I admire most about Mike is that through his incredible run of success he has remained extremely humble. He also has always been more than willing to generously share coaching points and tips with me in spite of the fact that our teams have played one another. In one instance, we bumped into one another at a county seeding meeting. I complemented him on how well his hitters distracted opposing catchers with a fake bunt while their runners attempted to steal.

"The key," Mike said, "is to get really deep in the batter's box, as deep as you can, and pull the bat back in the catcher's eye path."

I went home that evening and jotted it down on paper.

If you ever attend a game at Seton Hall Prep, you will notice a sign that hangs on the fence in front of the spectators' bleachers placed there by Sheppard. The sign reads, "The greatest opportunities for sportsmanlike conduct arise when there are the greatest opportunities for unsportsmanlike conduct."

Before every season, Sheppard Jr. holds a meeting with the Seton Hall Prep parents. He provides them with a set of guidelines that deals extensively with this all-important relationship that he refers to as the "The Athletic Triangle," which consists of three components: the player, the parent, and the coach. Enclosed in "Shep's" guidelines is an explanation of a parent with a "Little League mentality," which is a circumstance in which the parent is "the coach, the spectator, and the umpire all in one [and] … has seen it all and done it all."

"I explain to the parents," said Sheppard Jr., "I'm the one spending four and five hours a day with your son. If he goes home at night, and you start telling him 'Coach is screwin' you,' when he comes back the next day, he's seeing me differently. He's not looking at me the same way."

I had witnessed this type of divisiveness firsthand in my early years. Disgruntled parents were angry at me for the changes that I made within our Booster Club. They decided to make a statement. Typically, during our games almost all of the parents would sit in the bleachers located in the infield area. As a statement of protest toward me, a faction of parents decided to stand beyond the right-field fence during our games.

I suppose that the nonverbal message they were communicating was that they were there at the game but not in support of me. By doing so, they placed more value in their opposition toward me than they did in their support of their own children. I viewed this behavior as sad more than anything else. After all, there is a reason that tickets in the right-field bleachers at Yankee

Stadium can cost twelve dollars, while premium club seats in and around the home plate area opened at twenty-five hundred dollars per seat in 2009.

I am certain that their actions were intended to hurt me, but my feelings aside, who did they ultimately hurt? Did they possibly hurt themselves? The reality is that parents get one chance in a lifetime to watch their children participate in varsity athletics, and that time seems to pass in the blink of an eye. Regardless of how you feel toward your son's coach, is it worth missing your son's career because your own disgruntlement led you to stand four hundred feet away from home plate?

Equally important, did their actions hurt the team? Abraham Lincoln said, "A house divided against itself cannot stand." By opposing me, the parents were in essence rooting for their kids to win and for me to lose, yet we were all wearing the same uniform. Without a doubt, that behavior created factions and cliques within our program, and divisiveness began to spread like a disease.

In his book *The Winner Within*, basketball coach Pat Riley dedicated an entire chapter to what he referred to as "The Disease of Me." He pointed out the many debilitating effects on a team when agendas develop and when individuals begin to believe that their own importance is greater than that of the team.

Similarly, coach Bobby Knight pointed out how any form of negativity, whether through a player's words, thoughts, or actions, could spread from one team member to the next like a cancer. That type of negativity can create an atmosphere in which a team can develop an expectation of failure. Knight believed that the negativity he experienced on behalf of one of his Indiana teams became so widespread that the team was "on the brink of not winning again" for the remainder of the season. Hence the title for his book, *A Season on the Brink*.

"Let's go now. We got two ducks on the pond!" shouted Mr. Doubleday, a parent of one of our players. It was May 2004. We were playing second-seeded Nutley in the semifinals of the Greater Newark Tournament at Verona High School. The setting at Verona was picturesque for a high school baseball game with its concrete stadium-type bleachers that wrapped around the infield.

The place was packed. We led 2–0 in the top of the third inning and had runners on second and third bases with one out. That's when I made "The Infamous Call."

Our hitter was a young and frail sophomore. He was a very capable bunter. At the time, I felt that at his early age he was somewhat overmatched by a senior All-Essex County pitcher. Our runner on third was lightning quick, and I didn't think it would be too far-fetched for Nutley to be caught off guard and maybe even mishandle a well-placed bunt.

Therefore, I put on a safety squeeze bunt play. A safety squeeze bunt is different from a suicide squeeze bunt because by design it is not nearly as risky. During a suicide squeeze attempt, the runner breaks toward home plate before the ball is pitched and hopes that the batter protects him by successfully bunting the ball on the ground just a second or two before he crosses home plate. The batter must attempt to bunt the ball no matter where the pitch is in order to protect the suicidal runner. A safety squeeze is more conservative, as the play calls for the hitter to first and foremost select a good pitch and then bunt the ball on the infield grass anywhere except hard and right back to the pitcher. The runner on third base does not break toward home plate on the pitch. Instead, he takes a few shuffle steps on the pitch while gaining momentum toward the plate. As soon as he sees that the bunt has been placed down on the ground, he breaks for home plate in an attempt to score. If the hitter doesn't like the pitch and pulls the bunt attempt back, then the runner is supposed to alertly hustle back safely to third base.

Unfortunately, our runner on third base had a momentary lapse in concentration and seemingly forgot about the possibility that our hitter might take the pitch and not bunt the ball. He was so intent on getting a good jump toward the plate that his momentum carried him too far. As he tried to recover and return to third base, he slipped. The Nutley catcher easily threw him out at third. The Nutley crowd erupted on the play, and then erupted even further when the Nutley pitcher induced an inning-ending ground ball to shortstop to escape the jam. The momentum shift toward Nutley was huge!

"What the hell is he doing? How could he call for a bunt there?" screamed Mr. Doubleday. "I swear as long as this guy's the coach we'll never win anything. Jesus! That was a stupid call!"

Doubleday began to hold court with the other parents and spectators. "We've gotta get rid of this guy," he continued.

Nutley tied the game at 2–2 in the bottom of the inning and went on to defeat us 8–3.

"I'm telling you if that guy didn't put that bunt on and take us out of that inning, it would have been a totally different game," Doubleday stated, just after the final out was recorded.

Boston Red Sox coach Terry Francona was once asked to comment about members of the Boston media who questioned his coaching decisions.

"Well, you guys are always right. Absolutely! Because no one ever second-guesses a right decision. The only way it will ever be fair, and this will never happen, would be if each of you were to write down what you would do before each play occurs and explain why. If I'm right you won't second-guess me because it worked, and if I'm wrong you have the advantage of criticizing the move after the play is over."

Obviously the play hadn't worked. However, if the play had been executed properly, we would not have been picked off. Instead, our runner would have safely retreated back to third base while our hitter put himself in a 1–0 advantage count. Doubleday formed his opinion after the play was over. He made no mention of the boy's mistake and never commented on the boy's lapse in concentration that caused our breakdown. He lambasted me up and down for putting the play on. He accused me of costing us the game—and also the Greater Newark Tournament championship. My infamous call served as the foundation for Doubleday's, "We can't win with Illiano" smear campaign. Not only did he think that I was a lousy coach, he also thought I was a jinx.

"This guy's got some kind of cloud over him," he said one day in the stands; it was as if I was in the old TV show, *The Munsters,* which featured a family who would drive around on sunny days with the rain pouring down only on their car. "This guy has a hex on him!" he added.

It was then that I began to notice a mysterious phenomenon that I would witness with more frequency over the years. Strangely, as Doubleday's son matured physically, his athletic performance declined. Barring injury or addiction, this was not supposed to happen. Logic dictates that as a boy grows and physically matures into a young adult, he is supposed to perform better athletically. What was it then? He wasn't hurt. He wasn't hanging out with the wrong crowd. He was an excellent student. I even asked Renshaw to serve as a conduit between our players and myself to find out if Doubleday had a girlfriend who perhaps was distracting him, but that wasn't the problem. What was it? This raised some suspicion in my mind. Was his father placing too much pressure on him?

If a parent places too much pressure on his son, that could turn the game into more of a source of stress, more of a burden, and more of a chore for him rather than a source of fun and enjoyment. I am sure that any parent's actions would stem out of love for their children, and I'm sure that they all of them mean well and are only trying to help. But when a parent lets their emotions get the best of them, that can at times place an unfair burden upon their son, and in some cases create expectations for them to be more than what they are even capable of being.

In my experience, I have noticed a strong correlation between overbearing parents and players whose abilities actually regress rather than progress. In contrast to wine, they actually worsen over time!

Years ago, many parents had what was known as "Mickey Mantle syndrome." They would develop visions of grandeur in which they would dream that their son would one day play shortstop for the New York Yankees, switch hit, bat third in the lineup, and wear number seven. But most of those parents had a grasp on reality, and realizing that there was only one Mickey Mantle, they managed to keep their fantasies in check.

More recently, it is likely that Derek Jeter's number two has replaced Mantle's number seven in the eyes of a parent, but the dream is the same. However, the behavior is far different.

These "New Age" parents serve as agents for their sons and micromanage every facet of their lives. They are willing to invest every dollar—and every minute of their time—to turn the dreams they have for their sons into a reality. Consequently, they are guilty of "professionalizing" their sons way too early, in some instances before they are even teenagers. At twelve years of age they already have them traveling across the country and playing close to eighty games in a season. At fifteen years, a boy has acquired a team of trainers hired at roughly seventy-five dollars an hour. By the time he is seventeen, he has a strength coach, a pitching coach, a hitting coach, a speed coach, and a nutritionist. They pay thousands upon thousands for them to play on AAU (Amateur Athletic Union) travel teams and attend college showcases with the hope of one day earning a scholarship. They fly across the country with these travel teams, but in spite of the hundred or so games that they play over the course of the year, many of them don't even learn how to play the game properly in the process.

Former University of Illinois coach "Itch" Jones shared his thoughts at the Be the Best You Are Baseball Coaches Clinic at Cherry Hill, New Jersey, on what he has observed of the players at travel showcases. "They've learned to exploit and expose themselves, but they haven't learned the game. They have become one dimensional: 'me!' Nobody wants to pay five hundred dollars for an area-code game to bunt and move a runner or to hit a ground ball to the right side. They have different agendas."

In one instance, Jones became turned-off by a player after watching the boy's father walk in like "a gladiator," carrying his son's bag, only to hear the boy reprimand his father for not remembering to bring his Gatorade.

For a select few travel players, the parents' investments work out, and their son earns a scholarship. However, the great majority of club players do not. As a matter of fact, less than 2 percent of all high school players earn a scholarship before graduation. Rather than earning a scholarship, I have seen several of these boys become burned out from playing. I have witnessed their passion and love for the game dissipate. I have noticed them develop uncoachable attitudes, and I've seen their athletic performances decline with age. In some cases, I have also seen some of those boys act resentfully toward their own fathers.

Interestingly, Doubleday's son liked and respected me, but he knew of his father's disdain for me, and it greatly confused him. This is the exact type of fragile player-coach relationship that Mike Sheppard had explained to me. The boy appreciated what I had taught him and how much I worked with him to improve his game. I actually had a wonderful relationship with the boy. We got along great. I believe if I were to see him today we would hit it off just the same. I admired him, still do, and vividly recall how much he gave to our program. In that sense, he was a model athlete. Since my relationship with the Doubleday boy was different from my relationship with his father, one can only surmise that the boy became increasingly conflicted with the tug-of-war that was occurring between us. Having a completely different relationship with a parent than you do with his or her son is not unheard of in coaching and probably more prevalent than most people realize. While he never confronted me directly, Doubleday continued to bash me up and down to anyone who was willing to listen, both in and out of the community.

Apparently, his criticism of me became so extensive that it prompted a supporter of mine to reach out to me and tip me off. "Scott," the parent said to me, "He's talking to a lot of people. As a matter of fact, he's trying to build up a following." Considering what I now knew, I had to decide how I would respond. What should I do? Should I call him out? No. I decided that I would just ignore his subversive behavior. Moving forward, I decided to ignore his comments and just go about my business. I figured that anybody who knew anything about baseball, and most people in general, would probably see his "Little League mentality" for what it was. But just as one might avoid trips to the doctor for a routine checkup, when a form of cancer becomes too widespread, it can no longer be ignored.

Prior to our semifinal game against Nutley I had scouted them. One thing in particular stood out to me. They ran the bases aggressively, particularly during a first and third double-steal play. On that play, the runner on first attempts to steal second base. If the catcher tries to throw the runner out at second, then the runner on third breaks to steal home as soon as he sees that the catcher's throw has gone through to second base. A potential pitfall on the play is that one of the middle infielders or the pitcher may cut the throw off and attempt to throw the third base runner out while he is trying to steal home. The Nutley runners ran this play exceptionally well. If you ever hesitate as a base runner, you lose. There are some risks involved in this play, but the Nutley runners didn't seem too concerned about them. They ran the bases the way I prepared my players, and exactly how I ideally wanted to see my players run them. Instead of hesitating, they showed an outstanding ability to anticipate. They bought into aggressiveness and seemed to want the extra base, and as a result, placed a lot of pressure on an opposing defense. Nutley's aggressiveness on the base paths was something that we spent a lot of time preparing for.

Soon after Nutley, we played Dover. With runners on first and third bases, I put on that same double-steal play that I had watched Nutley execute to perfection. As our first-base runner attempted to steal, the Dover catcher threw the ball through to second base. Our runner on third was supposed to break toward home plate and attempt to score a run. He didn't. Instead, he stood there, too scared to run. Like a deer in headlights, he stood frozen, while he watched our other runner get called out on a tag play at second base. Our opponent was willing to give us a run in exchange for the out at second base, but our runner's lack of aggressiveness prevented us from taking what our opponent was willing to give us. He had been trained to anticipate and think aggressively, but he had become too scared to make a mistake. He was not playing to win. He was playing not to lose! As Doubleday threw a tantrum in the bleachers, I let our runner have it—deservedly so.

A few days later, one of our players came to me and revisited a discussion regarding that play.

"Coach, that's just too hard a read," he said.

"Too hard?" I asked.

"Yeah, we were all talking the other night at Mr. Doubleday's house about how tough it is to see that throw," he explained to me.

"Let me ask you something then," I responded. "How come it isn't too hard for a Nutley player to execute that play? Why are Nutley's base runners crossing home plate and making it look easy to score runs on that same throw, while we are standing on third base complaining that it is too hard to read the play?"

At that moment, it became abundantly clear to me that Mr. Doubleday wasn't merely being critical of me. He was spreading one of the worst forms of cancer that can afflict a team—a defeatist attitude! He was trying to coach the team, and through his attempts, he was trying to remove or negate aggressiveness, the most important part of our offensive philosophy! His negative influence was literally taking the aggressiveness out of my players. His defeatist attitude was influencing them to think like losers and to hold back. Just as Coach Knight had described, negativity was now spreading among the players, from one to the next, as quickly as a deadly disease.

It would be one thing for Doubleday not to like me. But, now that his actions were having a negative effect on how my team played, I could no longer ignore it. The potential ramifications of this and the potential for this kind of negativity to spread any further within our program was something that I took very seriously. To me, it was like an elephant in the living room that could not be ignored. To not address it would be to allow my program to die a slow death. Prior to the next season, I decided to call for a mandatory meeting with the parents in our program.

Doubleday attended the meeting, which was held in our school cafeteria, as did the majority of the parents in the program. I explained my philosophy about baseball and elaborated on why I believed in it so much.

"I'm asking for a commitment from your sons," I said to the parents. "That commitment involves an incredible amount of sacrifice. I spend five hours a day with your kids. The moment you begin to bad-mouth me or spread negativity about our program, you are tearing apart the commitment that I'm asking for and ultimately hurting our team."

I also explained that maybe the best example for young kids about the importance of a positive attitude toward a team could be taken from a story in the news. In spite of the fact that wide receiver Terrel Owens was a healthy, world-class athlete, when he was suspended with pay, Philadelphia Eagles owner Jeffrey Lurie paid him over a million dollars a weekend to stay at home, preferring that he not be around the team or even attend the team's games.

I also shared with them some of the dos and don'ts that I had learned from Mike Sheppard's guidelines for parents: "Don't coach! Don't try to coach at the game when you should be cheering. Don't try to coach at home when you're supposed to be parenting. We want players who are coachable and parents who allow us to coach."

I believed that if I could get enough people to buy in to what I was trying to teach their children, it could potentially stamp out the negativity that was corroding our program and spreading like wildfire. Doubleday sat quietly with a scowl on his face, but many of the other parents were attentive and seemingly very interested in what I had to say.

And, while I had the parents attention, there was another problem facing all of us, teenage drinking.

CHAPTER 6

Prom Night

I never cared about what a player thought of me while he played at Arizona State. I did care what he thought of me ten years later. I believe a coach can be a large influence in character building. When a coach takes time to make a definite contribution to the life of his player off the field, he has every right to feel good about himself.

—Bobby Winkles
Arizona State Baseball Coach

COACH BOBBY HURLEY'S BASKETBALL program at Saint Anthony's High School in Jersey City is nationally known as one of the top programs in the country. A sign located at the entrance to Saint Anthony's reads "The Street Stops Here." The obvious inference is that just because something may be accepted outside in the community does not mean that it will be accepted as a part of their school.

In May of 2005, an article appeared in the West Essex school newspaper *The Wessex Wire*. The article was entitled "Beer Pong With Parental Consent." The article described how many West Essex parents allowed their children to drink alcohol and, in some cases, even played drinking games, like beer pong, with them. One West Essex parent spoke anonymously, to no one's surprise, about why she thought permitting her underage child to drink was actually very beneficial for her daughter. "They're just going to do it anyway," said the nameless parent. "Doing it now is preparing them for what they will be doing next year at college."

The article exposed something that I already knew—that the culture throughout the West Essex community was in many cases, a permissive one. Underage teenage students often spoke freely in front of teachers about how "wasted" they intended to be at the next party or how "wasted" they had gotten at the last one. They would openly pass photos taken at parties in front of staff members. The pictures would show stacks of beer cans and bottles strewn about a room, empty liquor bottles, and students with their cocktails of choice in hand. I was mindful of the fact that teenage drinking was not something new to society, but there was a distinct difference between the culture that I had grown up in and the one in which these students currently lived. We knew it was illegal. I pictured Michael J. Fox taking a trip in Doc Brown's DeLorean with its "flux capacitor" and imagined what his reaction would be upon seeing how much society had changed. If he were to hear how kids were speaking to adults and staff members, he would probably fall out of his chair.

While it would be erroneous to indict the entire community or entire student population for contributing to this problem, what shocked me as a teacher was that a significant number of students within our school had made no attempt whatsoever to hide their alcohol and drug consumption from adults. They had seemingly become so accustomed to an environment where alcohol was permitted that they actually lost sight of the fact that underage drinking is illegal. The same went for smoking marijuana; they would routinely publicize it, without hesitation, in front of anyone.

I once overheard a conversation between two teenage students in our cafeteria. Our football team had advanced to the upcoming state tournament finals to be played at Giants Stadium. One girl said to the next, "Someone said that you're not allowed to drink inside Giants Stadium for the game. Are they like kidding me? I'm just going to have my mom write a note in case anybody says anything to me. They can't do anything if I have a note from my mom!"

In 2003, I was only in my early thirties, so chronologically I was not that far removed from their generation. But in actuality, we were worlds apart. I recalled that most of what went on when I was a high school student was behind a parent's back. No one would ever dare breathe a word about a weekend party in front of a teacher, and parents never joined in any drinking games. Picturing one of my high school buddies fathers doing a "keg stand" is not something that I can visualize, nor could I see my high school sweetheart's mother playing beer pong, but this was the world in which we lived.

Perhaps one of the most glaring examples of the permissiveness that I witnessed was the West Essex Junior Prom. The students who attend prom are just seventeen years old and not yet seniors. Their tradition called for them to be driven in limousines down the shore to a particular hotel in Seaside Heights, New Jersey, after the prom was held on a Friday evening. What would happen next at the hotel would be an approximate forty-eight-hour drinking binge, not much different from what I have seen both movies and television depict during spring break. How did I know such serious allegations to be true? Because not only did many students throughout the school make no attempt to hide it, they actually bragged about it. I have seen pictures and heard all the stories from the students themselves, without any provocation. While the legality, hazards, and potential pitfalls of underage consumption of alcohol could be widely debated, perhaps the best rationale for trying to discourage teen use of alcohol and drugs came from Fox news analyst Bill O'Reilly, who once said on his radio program: "Once a child becomes intoxicated his childhood is over. The moment that happens, he has just ended his childhood. But, the problem is they are not yet ready for adulthood, so they end up in this no-man's-land world of their own."

O'Reilly also added, "Children evolve when they are supervised, but they devolve when they are unsupervised. We saw that in *Lord of the Flies.*"

Something must be said here. Administrators, both central office and building, along with class advisors, staff and even to some extent parents, have strong control on the events leading up to the prom as well as the actual prom itself. The post prom activities, however, are another matter. In many instances parents are able to supervise and chaperone. Some may have a home at the Jersey shore or relatives nearby. Indeed this work by no means asserts that every junior boy and girl will evolve into a roaring drunk following the prom. Nor does it contend that most parents are so totally permissive that they give license to such behavior. But to a large extent, many youngsters are on their own and are expected by all of those mentioned above to act responsibly. Sometimes the joy of the event, newly discovered freedom, or overwhelming peer pressure counter a youngster's proper upbringing or what a school is trying to teach. What I was hearing and seeing caused me great concern.

West Essex High School had two policies to help protect teenage athletes from the dangers of underage use of alcohol and drugs. The first policy was the West Essex Regional School District Athletic Code of Conduct, which read: "Substance Abuse: Any student involved in athletics and also involved in the sale, consumption, or distribution of drugs or alcohol will be suspended from participation in the program for the period mandated by the school district policy governing substance abuse." The second policy was the West Essex Regional School District Regulation R2431: Interscholastic Athletics and Substance Abuse Policy, first issued in September 2000. This policy was even more strict than the Code of Conduct as it stated: "This rule includes student athletes in proximity of alcohol and controlled substances. That means if the police break up a party and athletes are in attendance, they are in violation of their training rules, even if they were not taking part in the consumption." R2431 also stated: "Simply, if police report to us that they broke up a party and give us a list of names, those students athletes may be in violation."

Each player and parent was required to sign both the Code of Conduct and the R2431 policy as part of their eligibility requirement.

The more I thought about prom weekend, the more it reminded me of a speech that I had heard by New Jersey Devils general manager, Lou Lamoriello, during a New Jersey State Interscholastic Athletic Association luncheon for the 2004 NJSIAA State Ice Hockey Tournament Finals. Lamoriello mentioned that the Devils organization takes all precautions to minimize risks; they put their players up in hotels, even for home games during the playoffs. He said that he wants his players to "eat well, rest well, and take care of their bodies."

Over the years, I had always taken precautions, demanding certain sacrifices when I felt my athletes might have been at an unnecessary risk. I forbade them from participating in student-faculty volleyball games, jello wrestling, or intramural dodge ball. I warned them not to play basketball, as I had seen many baseball players injure themselves playing pickup basketball during the baseball season. I couldn't forgive myself if any of my players ever injured themselves unnecessarily during the season.

Over the years, I had dealt with complaints over my demands and confronted them head on, but when it came to some of my players attending what I knew to be a weekend drinking binge, I just sat there on the sidelines with my head down on the bench. The scuttlebutt surrounding the prom was so much in my face that I feared that some of my athletes would be covertly violating both the Athletic Code of Conduct and the Interscholastic Athletics and Substance Abuse Policy. I also knew that the prom would coincide with the weekend of the Greater Newark Tournament semifinals, and if we were to ever get there, we needed to be at our best if we were to have a shred of hope of winning.

I had always been taught that great leaders were people who choose the difficult right over the easy wrong. I didn't. I should have stood up. Instead, I sat down. I chose the easy wrong because of just that, it was easier. The truth is that I was afraid to put my foot down because of the noise that it would make and the inevitable backlash that I knew it would cause.

One of my players could have gotten hurt, arrested, or God forbid, even killed, but my fear of rocking the boat was greater than standing up for what I knew was right. Instead of trying to do something to prevent it, I sat my players down and attempted to appeal to their maturity. I told them that I was not naïve to what went on and that they needed to be careful and make good decisions. I expressed my concern about the environment that they would be putting themselves in. I told them that they needed to pick their spots better, because they would have the rest of their lives to go out and party but only one chance to accomplish their goals as a high school athlete. Worse than that, I conveniently provided them with an ideal schedule made for weekend partying. On Friday, the day of the prom, we held an optional workout for the select members of the team not attending the prom. As a team, we took

Saturday off and then came in for practice at 6:00 p.m. on Sunday evening to get ready for Monday's game.

At that Sunday's practice, players who had never previously arrived late were uncharacteristically not on time. They blamed traffic on the Parkway from the shore. They were absolutely lethargic at practice. When we traveled to Parsippany on Monday afternoon, I turned around on the bus and saw that several players were sound asleep. They looked like corpses as they laid comatose with their heads plastered against the windows during our short drive. Our team was lifeless during our pregame and played like zombies during the game.

"My God!" I said to Renshaw. "It's three days after the prom, and they're utterly useless."

After each game, I had a ritual in the evenings. I would sit outside on my patio. It was quiet there. There was no crowd noise. It was a peaceful and tranquil environment, and I would sit alone, by myself with the exception of a few deer that would occasionally wander by. It was during these quiet moments that I would review my score card and make a self-evaluation of all of my game decisions, both good and bad. Then I would jot down some notes, so I could learn from the experience. What went right? What went wrong? What would I do differently? Why? It was on one of these evenings that it all hit me. If anyone was to blame for the fact that my team was rundown and ineffective, it was me! I had allowed it.

By admitting to them that I knew what went on over prom weekend down the shore and asking them to just be careful down there, I had essentially told them that it was okay to break our code and to abuse their bodies. By not speaking out against it, I had knowingly given them my permission to renege on the commitment that I was asking of them. I was complicit with the fact that some members of my team had violated our policies and showed up on the field with less than their best. In the process, I had reneged on my own commitment as their coach and compromised who I was as a person and everything that I believed in. It was eating me alive, and I could hardly let it go.

The Bible says "the spirit is willing but the flesh is weak." I interpret that to mean that deep down, children really want to be disciplined. They just need someone to give it to them and to show them the right way. In *Sports Illustrated* (October 2009), Penn State football coach Joe Paterno said, "I think kids today, they are confused. They long for some kind of discipline. They want something bigger than themselves, something bigger to be a part of. We can still offer that here."

Between the seasons of 2003 and 2004, I vowed to give my players a greater sense of discipline and a greater sense of belonging. What I had done or hadn't done in regard to the prom was not something that I could accept from myself. John Wooden wrote in his book, *Wooden,* "If we can't be true to ourselves, we cannot be true to others. As Polonius said to his son, Laertes, in Shakespeare's Hamlet, 'This above all: to thine own self be true, and it must follow, as the night the day, thou canst not then be false to any man.' You must know who you are and be true to who you are if you are going to be who you can and should become. You must have the courage to be true to yourself."

Prior to the 2004 season, I held a team meeting in February. I pointed out that our goal was to win the Greater Newark Tournament and that the semifinals would be held on the same weekend as the prom. Then, I made an analogy and explained that just as it could take years to build a building but only seconds to knock it down, a team could be exactly the same way with just one destructive decision. Then, I provided each candidate with a copy of the Athletic Code of Conduct, The Interscholastic Athletics and Substance Abuse policy, and also a typed letter from me entitled: Notice Regarding Junior Prom.

I reminded players and parents that they were agreeing to our code as part of their participation. I expressed my concern about underage alcohol and drug abuse. I also informed both players and parents that we would have a curfew one hour after the prom ended, and although we hoped to be playing, if we weren't, we would have early morning practices on both Saturday and Sunday during prom weekend. Each player and parent were to sign off on a statement from me indicating that they read and understood my notice regarding the upcoming prom weekend. These signed forms and the signed policies had to be turned in several weeks before our season began, more than two and a half months before the prom would be held, so that there would be no surprises. All was quiet for a while. Then, by mid-spring, all hell broke loose.

As the weather warmed up, prom tickets went on sale, and students who planned to attend had to make arrangements for their hotel rooms. As I walked down the hallway between classes, two female students approached me. One of them greeted me in a manner that had become quite fashionable within the school, but I still considered it to be disrespectful. She said, "Hey, Illiano, what's this about you ruinin' prom?"

I stopped and responded, "That's 'Mr. Illiano,' or are you too rude to know how to properly address an adult?"

"Uhh, yeah, sorry. Mr. Illiano, what's up with you not allowing the baseball players to go to prom?"

"I don't discuss my team policies with anyone not on my team. If you know of any player of mine who has any questions about my policies, then have him see me," I said.

By the following morning I had eight messages on my voice mail left from parents of female students accusing me of ruining their daughter's prom because I was forbidding her date to go down the shore. One asked, "Who the hell do you think you are?"

I did not return any of the calls from parents whose children were not students enrolled in my classes or players on my team. Later, I received a message from a baseball parent, Mr. Spicolli. I called him back.

"Scott, my wife and I were talking and basically came to the conclusion that we're his parents, and you don't have any right to tell our son what to do. He has our permission to go down the shore, and you can't tell him that he can't go," he scolded me.

"I'm not telling anyone what they can or can't do, Mr. Spicolli. And, yes, you are right. I have no right to tell your son where he can or can't go. But, I am his coach, and as his coach I have every right to implement a team curfew and conduct a team practice as I see fit. Curfew will be one hour after the conclusion of Friday night's prom. Practices will be held at 7:00 a.m. on both Saturday and Sunday mornings. Your son can choose to go where he wants to during that time, but all team policies are in effect."

"By the way, Mr. Spicolli," I added. "I'm trying to keep your son sober and off drugs so he can perform at his best. I'm really surprised that you're fighting me on this one."

As I hung up the phone, I was floored. I would later share this exchange with Athletic Director Tom Pengitore.

He then recited to me perhaps his most famous saying, "Scott, remember this: a parent is a parent is a parent!"

My next encounter was with a student whose words proved quite prophetic. She barged right into my classroom.

"I can't believe you're ruining prom. You're not going to get away with this," she threatened.

I reiterated my position that I did not discuss team issues with non-team members, but she was absolutely correct. An outpouring of venomous parental anger and hostility so permeated the environment that I had no choice but to abandon my plans for a curfew and subsequent Saturday and Sunday morning practices.

While I was totally disheartened at such a response, since my only intention was to protect the vulnerable teenagers in my charge, I emerged from this incident as a stronger person and coach. I became satisfied that I had given it my all in an arduous attempt to ensure that my players were safe. More importantly, parents became aware, advertently or otherwise, that I truly cared about the welfare of their youngsters. I had also raised the consciousness of the entire West Essex community as to what many of their children were either involved in or subjected to during prom season.

Our athletic substance abuse policy stated that "participation in athletics at West Essex is a privilege that requires dedication and discipline by its participants," and "the primary purpose of these regulations and procedures is to promote the health and safety of each individual athlete and the team as a whole." Therefore, while the street would stop at the front door at Saint Anthony's, I felt that I was justified, if not obligated, to hand these policies out at the door and to expect our student athletes to follow them while they were on the street. But I remained a voice in the wilderness and was considered by many to be an outcast. To some, I was the Grinch who almost ruined prom, but at least I was true to myself and had the courage of my convictions to show it.

"This is your school, your community," I would eventually shout at a future mandatory parents meeting, holding up a copy of the "Beer Pong With Parental Consent" article.

"Alcohol and drugs are a cancer that can destroy a team," I continued. "I suppose that, although it's against the law, if somebody on our team showed up at one of your homes on a Saturday night with a thirty-pack, and each kid on the team had two beers apiece, my guess is that nobody would get hurt. But, that's not what's going on here. I'm talking about binge drinking, and Lord knows what else. I don't even want to think about the other stuff. I'm asking your sons to stay sober and off drugs, and I'm asking you as their parents to support me in my efforts." My voice beckoned through the room.

Most parents just stared a blank stare, a few nodded in agreement, while Doubleday still scowled. But there was one parent who actually appreciated it.

"Coach," she said. "You have no idea how much this means to me. I was afraid I couldn't forbid him to go down to the shore on my own because none of the other parents would. I can't believe what goes on with these kids. Now that you're saying it, he'll listen to you. You just made my job easier. Thank you." This message was not lost on parents of my future players.

Incredibly, it was the greatest irony that three years later, a number of parents approached my own father at a game just prior to the junior prom. They told him that many of the parents of team members were discussing their concerns about post-prom activities, and they were hoping that I would impose a curfew and a Sunday morning practice to lessen or even prevent what they felt were the particular dangers their sons faced. My father reminded them of these events from three years earlier and that although I had fought the good fight, I had been so overwhelmed by the tidal wave of misdirected parental disapproval that I would not go there again. These parents expressed their sorrow that this happened and vowed greater diligence in monitoring their children's behavior. Indeed, the tide eventually turned, but three years earlier I could not foresee the change.

As the 2004 season wore down, I became increasingly bitter. But it taught me an incredibly important lesson and one in which I had to experience a great deal of pain in order to learn. I realized that although my efforts were courageous, they had led me down a dead-end road and made a lot of people very angry with me in the process. Initially, I wasn't able to see the reality of the situation, but by the end I had realized a crucial point: until the players' desire to win became equivalent to their desire to find a way down to the shore to party, we would never be able to obtain greatness beyond our capabilities. I have since adjusted my approach to this situation. I explain to the players that if they show up and they are not prepared to give their best, then they simply do not play! The burden is now on the player.

On the final day of that 2004 season, we were eliminated by Harrison in the first round of the state tournament. We hit into tough luck all afternoon, stranding countless runners on base. With two outs in the top of the third inning, a Harrison batter reached first base on an error. The next Harrison hitter deposited a home run that landed on our softball field beyond the left-field wall. We lost 2–1.

I sat miserably in the coaches' office for over an hour. On my way out, something struck me. A brand new blue New Balance sneaker was just sitting there in the middle of the locker room. It had no partner. There was only one.

"Any school that has kids who leave hundred-dollar sneakers on the floor and don't even miss them, can never win in this game," I uttered to myself.

That was it. I was finished. I quit!

CHAPTER 7

A New Balance

Courage isn't always a loud roar. Sometimes it's a quiet resolve
at the end of the day that says I'll try again tomorrow.
—Source Unknown
Quoted by Coach Ed Agresta
On Ed Agresta's *Power Thoughts*

Boom! WAS THE SOUND the sneaker made as it crashed into the wall inside my garage. I picked it up and threw it again.

Boom! I picked it up and stared at it. I was sick! I was sick of losing. I had built up a competitive program and had won many more games than I had lost, but after just losing to Harrison, it was now nine years of never having won a championship. Beyond that, thanks to Doubleday and his disciples, the perception that I was a jinx was gaining some traction. I was sick of kids who didn't want to sacrifice the same way that I had when I was a player. I was sick over the prom. I was sick of interfering parents with unrealistic expectations for their kids. I was sick of what I perceived to be an entitled culture in the community too.

The next morning, I wrote my letter of resignation. I nearly put it in the mail, but I wanted to be sure that I wasn't overreacting out of pure emotion. I figured I'd take some time away. Summer vacation was around the corner. For the first time in my career, I avoided the summer baseball team's games. I avoided baseball altogether. I watched far less baseball on television, did not go to one Yankee or Mets game, and did not go to one New Jersey Jackals game, even though my JV coach, Jim Whalen, worked there as a public relations promoter and had offered me free tickets. I seldom even tuned into ESPN's *Baseball Tonight*, which was normally a nightly occurrence for me.

It was unclear whether I was going to resign at West Essex and look to go elsewhere, take a break from coaching, or quit permanently. I just needed some time. Nearby Caldwell High School's head coach had just resigned, and

I considered applying for that job if it had not already been filled. They had won two state section championships in recent years, and I had this belief that their kids might be less entitled and probably wouldn't leave an expensive sneaker behind on the locker room floor without a thought as to where the other one might be.

Obviously, I had picked up that sneaker off the floor and taken it home with me.

If anyone asks why I quit, I'll just show them the new sneaker and explain how and where I found it, I thought.

The sneaker immediately became a symbol to me of everything that I felt was wrong with West Essex and why I had to quit. After finishing my tirade after the Harrison game, I tossed it on top of a few boxes in my garage where it remained for most of the summer.

Dr. Gilbert once told me that the one thing that he knew about every problem was that you should never try to deal with it alone. Taking his advice into consideration, I called on several friends—one of them was a guy by the name of Thomas Gargiulo.

Thomas was an outstanding baseball coach who had an incredible run of success at Nutley High School, where he led his teams to several championships. In 2001, he was the Essex County Coach of the Year in the *Star-Ledger* and yet, within months, was brought in by their board of education due to complaints made by disgruntled parents.

The field of coaching, in many ways, is a "lose-lose" proposition. You will get crucified if you do not win, but if you win and don't play everyone on the team, inevitably someone's parent will be up in arms. You often have to take the heat either way. Thomas had to make some tough decisions in the spring of 2001, and he replaced some seniors with some more talented younger sophomores. His team won big, but the parents of the boys who didn't play as much went on the attack.

It seemed that the political game always played out the same way in these situations. First, the parents would go to the administration and/or the board of education and complain about the lack of playing time for their son. The administration would explain to the parents that the coach reserves the right to play whomever he feels is the best candidate. The parents do not give in. Instead, they "restrategize" and continue to attack the coach in any way, shape, or form that the system will permit—call it "systematic abuse." Rest assured, they will get more creative and come up with a new and different type of complaint, and go back to the board of education or superintendent at a later date. In the meantime, they typically get other disgruntled people to join them in the process and often hover around the players while attempting to make their presence known.

Years ago, parents acknowledged and understood that the dugout served as a boundary between themselves and their children during a game. Nowadays, parents are often brazen enough to cross that line without batting an eye. Sometimes they look for loopholes to get their kids' attention and communicate with them while they are in the dugout before, during, and after a game. Some parents would bring a Gatorade for their sons, while others brought sunflower seeds. Often times, they wouldn't bring drinks or sunflower seeds for the entire team. Instead, they would bring just a small supply for their own child. Typically, they would hand off the Gatorade or sunflower seeds and remain standing at the side of the dugout, talking to their sons. In many instances, their close proximity would lead to meddling with the coaching staff.

"Cut the umbilical cord!" I would eventually say to my team, after having had my fill of meddling parents trying to interfere and talk to their kids in the dugout before a game.

"Tell your parents that I think it's great that they are here to watch you and support you in your career. Then tell them that you will talk to them after the game."

I added, "And tell your parents to go buy your Gatorade and sunflower seeds the night before a game, so you can bring them with you!"

When it came to discipline, I had a simple philosophy: never make a rule that you can't enforce, and never make a threat that you won't keep. But at one point, this type of interference forced me to come up with a solution, and I had to think long and hard if I was really willing to uphold what I was about to threaten.

These visits became such a distraction that I finally decided to put any player who talked to a parent during a game in the stands with the parent, no questions asked. I meant it, and they knew it too. Once I put it on them, and they saw that they were a fraction away from being removed from our dugout and sent into the bleachers to sit with Mom and Dad during a game, it all stopped.

But the disgruntled parent seldom, if ever, stops. While trying to restrategize, they will try to dig up any form of dirt on a coach that they possibly can. And if a "witch hunt" is well orchestrated, you can probably find something on even the most honorable and ethical coach if you try hard enough and put your own spin on it. For example, every coach in the country at some point has made his players run. The parent who is in the process of restrategizing their attack on a coach will twist what would normally be considered to be ordinary conditioning into an allegation that the coach unmercifully "corporally punished" his players. There is usually no end to this type of systematic abuse toward coaches, as it often goes on and on.

I had seen it happen in countless communities and always knew to never corporally punish a player or to ever utter a curse word. If I had to literally bite my lip or say "dang it," I would. I never wanted to give parents any ammunition whatsoever outside of their playing-time complaints, but that was never easy to do when people were trying to put all of a coach's actions under a microscope with the intent of twisting who he really was or what he really did.

In fact, one former coach who is one of the most well-respected coaches that I know was a victim of this exact kind of systematic abuse. One of his players had played very sparingly and failed to meet the minimum number of innings played in order to earn a varsity letter. Therefore, he followed the criteria outlined by the school athletic department as he always had and did not grant him one. The player's mother was the school superintendent's secretary. The administration overruled the coach's decision and awarded the player a varsity letter. The coach was fired soon after for what the superintendent claimed was insubordination for conducting a practice on Good Friday. No pun intended, he had practiced religiously on Good Friday during each season in his lengthy and highly successful career. He had also always excused any player in the event of a religious conflict. In all those other seasons he had always received high praises for coming in to work with his players on that morning and giving them extra reps. What had always been seen as a testament to his work ethic and dedication was now considered to be a form of insubordination and the reason that his supporters were told why he was fired. What had started out as a complaint about a varsity letter eventually turned into an attack about a virtuous man's religious beliefs and personal integrity. This entire travesty was like systematic abuse on steroids! Sadly, in the end, it was systematic removal.

Thomas was also systematically abused and a victim of similar political nonsense as evidenced by having to appear in front of the Nutley board of education just months after being honored as the *Star-Ledger* Essex County "Coach of the Year."

He was not fired. But, inevitably, he felt underappreciated and grew tired of having to defend himself after giving so much to his players and to his community, so he resigned from his position. Since then, he has coached at Montclair State University, Paramus Catholic, and Caldwell High School. He also runs an annual winter coaches clinic as well. Nutley didn't just lose out on a great baseball coach in Thomas, they lost out on one of the most quality human beings I've ever been associated with. I knew no one would understand what I was going through better than Thomas, so before I handed in my resignation, I reached out to him.

The night we met, Thomas said something to me that not only changed my life, but without question it saved my coaching career. I told him about all the frustration and bitterness that I was experiencing, from beginning to end. He looked at me and said, "Adversity is like a gallon of gas. You can either put it in your gas tank and use it as fuel, or you could pour it all over yourself, light a match, and burn yourself up. There are two ways that you can look at it. It's up to you!"

Thomas also gave me another important piece of advice: "Never leave a place unless you've got someplace better to go." I made a mental note of that. If I had resigned and didn't have a better place to go to in my back pocket, was it worth the risk?

A few days later I went out to get my newspaper, and mysteriously, the New Balance sneaker had fallen off the boxes onto my garage floor. I picked it up and heard Thomas's words: "Adversity is like a gallon of gas. You can use it for fuel … or let it burn you up. There are two ways to look at it!" An incredible feeling came over me.

I was seeing it all wrong. The sneaker wasn't a symbol of why I needed to quit. It was a symbol of why I had to stay. I could use that sneaker to fuel me rather than to burn me up.

Maybe if I hung on just a little longer, a championship awaited. Maybe my kids needed me in order to learn the meaning of sacrifice. Maybe they needed me to teach them how valuable it is in life to earn something that can last you a lifetime, especially when it isn't being offered for sale or purchase. Maybe the parents there needed me so that they could hear the truth about their children. Maybe a possible move to nearby Caldwell would equate to nothing more than a disappointing "grass-is-greener syndrome" sucker bet. Rather than symbolize why I should quit, that sneaker would now serve as a symbol that would remind me to never give up. That day, I ripped up my letter of resignation.

I asked myself, *Have I accomplished everything that I wanted to accomplish the day I first walked through the front door?*

No, I had yet to accomplish what I had originally set out to do. I recalled the day that I first walked down the path to the main entrance and looked up at those white letters on the front of the building: West Essex Senior High School. I had vowed to bring a Greater Newark Tournament championship to West Essex.

I was either going to do so or die trying.

From the moment I looked up and first saw those white letters, I felt like it was my calling to help bring a Greater Newark Tournament championship to West Essex.

CHAPTER 8

The Road to Heaven Goes through Seton Hall

The consensus among North Jersey public high school athletic directors is to support Joe Piro's plan that would eliminate schedules that place powerhouse private schools with recruited players against teams whose members, by law, must be residents of the local community. Piro, now in his second year as Nutley's athletic director, has gradually built a consensus among the nearby public high schools to take corrective action. During the past week, Piro's team has sent the entire statewide scholastic sports community into a revolt that has been page-one headlines in nearly all of New Jersey's daily newspapers.

—newjerseyhometown.com, December 7, 2007

IF WE WERE EVER to obtain the Greater Newark Tournament championship, we would have to go through Seton Hall Prep. When we would have to play them would depend upon what seed we would earn in the tournament. But I knew that they would be standing in our way, and in order to get the championship, we would have to beat them.

Actually, that was another reason why I felt that it was paramount for the players on our team to stay sober and off drugs. I felt that even when we were healthy, at full strength and at our very best, we were still athletically outmanned against several teams within our county. When it came to Seton Hall, we were simply in way over our heads. They had made a record twelve consecutive appearances in the GNT finals from 1996 to 2008 and had won the tournament eight times in that span and twelve times in their storied history.

Some argued that Seton Hall, a private school, should not be allowed to play against public schools like ours because they had a competitive advantage by recruiting top athletes from different towns. I never agreed with this. My father pitched against them in 1959 and they were a power then; they have a long history of being an outstanding team. I personally believed that many of North Jersey's top players voluntarily chose Seton Hall because of its traditional commitment to academic excellence as well as its excellent baseball program, the success of which, characterized by outstanding coaching from Mike Sheppard Jr., affords players an opportunity to gain more exposure to college and professional scouts.

Seton Hall Prep has one of the best scholastic baseball programs in the United States. The reason for that success, in my opinion, is Coach Mike Sheppard Jr. Photo by Richard Morris

Nonetheless, New Jersey has been the scene of a great debate, which eventually stopped just short of snowballing into a court hearing. After citing that private schools had an "unfair competitive advantage" over public schools, Nutley and Bloomfield High Schools seceded from their conferences at the expense of being ineligible for the state tournament. The New Jersey State Interscholastic Athletic Association (NJSIAA) had its four-hundred-plus member schools vote on whether or not to separate private and public schools, eliminating them from being placed in the same conference. If the election to separate these schools passed, it would force private schools to be placed in all-private school conferences and mandate them to compete only against each other. Since the southern half of New Jersey was relatively unaffected by the dilemma, most southern schools opted to vote against separating the schools and chose to keep the conferences together in their current form. However, in spite of the apathy on behalf of nearly all southern schools, the vote was just eight votes shy of passing and nearly separated public and private schools from competing in the same conferences together. Since the vote had such a narrow margin, the NJSIAA realized that they had to do something to create more of a competitive balance throughout the state. While they did not separate private and public schools within the same conferences, they did realign more than two hundred northern New Jersey schools in Essex, Morris, Bergen, Hudson, Somerset, Union, Sussex, and Warren Counties into six brand new conferences, which they believed would be better geographically and promote a more favorable balance of competition. The debate is still ongoing, as some schools in the newly placed conferences now have to compete against top private school programs, whereas under the old format, they did not. I predict that eventually the outcome of this debate will be determined in a courtroom.

In 2006, Seton Hall was not just a top private school baseball team in New Jersey, it was one of the best teams in the entire country. Trying to figure out a way to beat them was becoming my life's work, but the question remained, how much time did I actually have left to do it?

My critics argued that I had already had more than enough chances to prove myself as a coach and had failed to come through. Some felt that I needed to be replaced. After nine seasons, my overall record was a respectable 123–101. We had winning seasons in six of those nine years and finished second in our conference twice. But I had never won a championship of any sort. The critics felt that failing to deliver a championship was my fault. My supporters felt that I had gotten the most out of the talent that I had and that we always played up to our competition.

The most compelling part of the private versus public school debate was that the level of talent that you have to work with within a public school is contingent upon who happens to walk through the front door. That premise served as the entire basis for the debate and resulted in the statewide realignment of conferences.

Just as professional teams can draft players, and colleges can recruit and offer scholarships to attract more talent, private schools have the ability to accept students from a variety of different towns. Public schools, in many respects, are stuck with whomever they get for their athletic programs. Public schools like West Essex do not accept tuition students from outside the sending district and therefore are limited only to the amount of talent that happens to live within the community. Without the benefit of tuition students, public school talent can fluctuate greatly from one year to the next, and in some seasons, the cupboard can and will go completely bare.

Tom Pengitore would often say that you always want to see where your program is every three to four years, as you should keep a freshman class together, groom them, and look to win something when they are upper classmen. Then after that group graduates, you look to rebuild again. However, there was never a guarantee of a promising freshman class. As a result, there could be some years where you might be strong in one area but lacking in another. Some years you could be pretty good but maybe just a player or two short and lacking that necessary depth. It all depended upon who happened to stroll through the front door.

Could we honestly ever beat a national powerhouse like Seton Hall Prep? Would we ever have enough talent to pull it off? Had I quit back in 2004, I would have deprived myself of any more opportunities to try to do so. But, how many more opportunities would I get?

As I stood in the hallway one day in between classes, Suit Number Two approached me. He told me that he had scheduled a game between us and his son's high school varsity team. His son attended a high school in North Jersey located outside of our county. Like any player in that program, his son was trying to make a name for himself within their lower-level programs.

Suit number two was now acting like a dangerous baseball parent himself, who was now meddling his way through his son's program. Using the "Booster" mentality, he probably figured if he helped the varsity coach in his son's school with his schedule, then it could in some way benefit his son and perhaps give him an in with their varsity coach.

I did not want to play his son's school for a few reasons. For one, our 2005 schedule was already done. Secondly, most of the schools in our league were from outside our own county and located in Morris County. Therefore, I tried to schedule independent games with schools that were located within our own county, Essex County, in order to help us gain further exposure in regard to local team rankings and postseason All-County recognition for our players. When I explained this to Suit Number Two, he told me to cancel my scheduled game with a colleague's team and tell him to just suck it up.

Chris Benecquista was an excellent coach in both football at West Essex and baseball at Glen Ridge High School. He also taught history at West Essex. Most of all, he was a good man. Suit Number Two figured that since he had authority over Chris as a teacher, it didn't matter if I bailed out on the game contract that we had with Glen Ridge and left Chris high and dry in order to play his son's school. I had too much respect for Chris to do that, aside from the fact that it would have been unethical and not beneficial to our own students.

When I told Suit Number Two that I just couldn't fit his son's school on our schedule, he said, "All right, you'll see!" and stormed away from me. I did not know what "You'll see!" meant, but I took it to be a threat of some sort. Would I be fired? Would it affect me as a teacher? As a coach? Both? Would it hurt my program?

The university had not prepared me for this either. And I share this true occurrence not for the purpose of revealing what had been asked of me, but more so for one to ponder- why did he feel compelled to ask?

Suit Number One had attempted to make out my lineup for me. Now, Suit Number Two was attempting to make my schedule by booking games with other coaches behind my back. Didn't they have a school district to run? That was the last conversation that Suit Number Two and I would have.

Shortly after my arrival at West Essex, I had met Ronnie Anello, a highly successful football coach who had resurrected the West Essex football program. When Ronnie took over as head football coach the program had so few players that they nearly cancelled the program and eliminated football as a varsity sport. Within a few years, he had brought the program to be one of the best in Essex County. It just so happened that Ronnie had his own falling out with Suit Number Two over the management of his football program, and whenever I asked him how he was doing, he would jokingly respond, "You can't kill me. I'm already dead!"

After Suit Number Two's threatening "You'll see!" remark to me, I felt exactly the same way. I felt I was a dead man walking.

I was tenured as a school teacher, but there was no tenure in coaching. They could fire me in an instant. All they needed was the right angle in order to do so. It didn't take long for them to get exactly what they needed.

History had shown that Mr. and Mrs. Cartwright had made an effort to have me removed as head coach. The circumstances surrounding the aforementioned conversation with Al Williams led me to conclude that they were familiar with one another. There was at least one more avenue for them to pursue, perhaps just beyond the school administration and the board of education, and could potentially lead to my removal as head coach if it were to be exploited enough. The Cartwrights may have had just the right ally to do it in journalist Al Williams.

It remains unclear to me whether they actually sought out Williams and asked him to join their effort to oppose me, or whether Williams had his own reasons for putting my job in jeopardy. Either way, this would be the strongest effort yet as it would advance into the open an effort to remove me as coach. This would not be an attack on me that occurred behind closed doors. It was an attack on me that happened publicly for the entire community to see. My not having won a championship was now a focus of attention that Williams would exploit in his column.

In March of 2005, long after Mr. and Mrs. Cartwright's son had graduated, their confidant Al Williams called me and conducted an interview for over thirty minutes for the purpose of doing a "preseason preview story" on our team. I spoke at length about each player and went around the field position by position, elaborating on each individual boy on our team. When the article came out in the paper, it was not at all a season preview about our team. Instead, it was a nine-year chronology about my tenure as head coach. More than half of the article focused on the fact that we had not won a championship while I had been at the helm. As a matter of fact, the article actually listed my exact won/loss records for seven of my seasons. It made no mention of the many statistics that I had provided to him about our returning starters, nor did it include any noteworthy comments that I made about all of the kids currently playing on the team. In regard to our winning records that we achieved in previous seasons, Williams wrote, "The reason why few have noticed? No titles."

You didn't exactly have to be Sherlock Holmes to figure this one out. I knew immediately where this stemmed from and what Williams was trying to do. This was so obvious that even Chief Inspector Jacques Clouseau or Inspector Gadget could see through it. Williams was going out of his way to expose to the community the fact that I had never won a championship with what I felt was an intent to embarrass me, to discredit my competency as a coach, and to help garner support against me. I didn't like it, especially after giving him over a half an hour of my time in the midst of planning my next day's practice schedule. Although I was insulted by his article, I never complained or took it up with him, because what he had reported was based upon fact.

We finished 14–10–1 that season, 13–5 in our conference, which was good enough for third place. Our record was respectable, but after being eliminated in the first round of the state tournament by Ramsey High School, we had just finished another season without having won a championship.

And Williams did not stop there. He was a man on a crusade. Prior to the 2006 season, he called me and again interviewed me for another "preseason preview" story.

Just as he had done the season before, the preview was not really a preview at all. This time it was a ten-year chronology of my tenure as head coach, specifically listing eight of my won/loss records. As part of his 2006 baseball season preview, Williams wrote, "The one thing missing, however, has been a championship, a title of any kind. The closest the Knights have come to that goal recently has been a runner-up finish in their conference, while they have reached the GNT final-four just once in recent years and always have trouble getting beyond the first round or quarterfinals of the state tournament. The baseball team, in fact, seems to be the West Essex program with the best record, but no titles, over the past ten years."

Clearly, Williams had written another chronology of my tenure as head coach, just as he did in 2005, under the guise of a preseason preview of our team. I wondered why he had even pretended to interview me for this story. He could have just written an editorial without me entitled "Fire Illiano!" or as disgruntled New York Jets fans once harshly chanted, "Joe must go!" while calling for head coach Joe Walton's removal; perhaps "Scott must go!" would have been a more fitting title for his article about our team.

What made me even more certain of his blatant agenda was the fact that there was another boy's athletic program at West Essex that had also been enduring a long dry spell without any championships and had done significantly worse than we had in terms of putting together consistent winning seasons. Williams had given their head coach and that program a pass for their failures in his coverage of them as he did another coach and athletic program at Caldwell High School who he also covered as well. They did not receive the same scrutiny that I had. I was not as fortunate as those other coaches.

I did choose to respond to his article, because this time he had crossed a line by doing something that he did not do the season before. The first time he had only reported facts. This time, he went as far as to predict that we also would not win a title during this upcoming season. As Williams wrote, "Unfortunately, it is unlikely that their dearth of titles will come to an end this year."

This was now becoming my legacy. The players read it, the parents read it, and the community at large read it. Williams had gotten the word out: the West Essex baseball team can't win a title. In fact, one of his headlines stated, "West Essex Baseball Quiet Contender," which implied that we just could not get over the hump. This was the exact type of headline that the Suits and any detractors that I may have had anywhere in the community could be looking for. Williams had now provided them with the ammunition that they needed to remove me.

At one point Suit Number One had called me into his office and informed me that he was receiving more complaints about me than any other coach in the district. Then he asked me why I thought that was.

"Because," I said, "In many instances, I'm the first person in their life who has ever told them no. Very often, if a kid wants a stereo, he gets a stereo. If he wants a truck at age seventeen, he gets a new truck. If he needs forty dollars to go to Hooters at night, he gets forty dollars. But what if the kid wants to be the catcher or the first baseman and has someone in front of him? Then what? They aren't sure exactly who to call when they want to buy a position on the team, so instead, they call you and complain about me."

With Williams declaring me to be the coach who couldn't win the big one and widely publicizing to the community the fact that I had never won a championship, I felt that I was now on borrowed time.

This was a reality that I could no longer escape. Clean record or not, the Suits could easily get rid of me for not winning a championship, especially if that word was circulating as Williams had planned.

I normally placed a lot of pressure on myself, but this was something entirely different. I needed to win in order to save my job. It was win now or else!

PART II

CHAPTER 9

Impossible Is Nothing!

Motivation is like food or bathing. It is something
that you have to do every day!
—Skip Bertman
LSU Baseball Coach

"YOU NEVER KNOW WHAT effect a quote might have on a kid. Sometimes they'll bring it up to you years later," said LSU baseball coach Skip Bertman during one of his sessions at a clinic in Cherry Hill.

Bertman kept volumes upon volumes of quotes and anecdotes. Before each practice he would post one in the locker room and have a senior or captain on the team personally hand a copy to each player. It was Bertman's belief that if parity existed between two teams, and they were athletically equal, the difference between those teams would be "motivation." Bertman explained that it was the coaches' responsibility to constantly find ways to motivate their teams, and he urged us to become both resourceful and creative in our attempts to do so.

Just as some people take a daily vitamin, I religiously called my motivational hotlines. To my benefit, they were free and updated daily. These hotlines provided me with opportunities to compile stories, anecdotes, and also quotes that I could save in my binder to use later on. I would take notes each day while listening to these messages and place an asterisk next to anything I believed would be valuable for my team.

It was late in January 2006. I called Mike Tully's *Pep Talk*. His message for the day was a quote that he had recently seen on a Nike poster sometime after the twenty-fifth anniversary of "Miracle on Ice," Team USA's men's ice hockey triumph in the 1980 Winter Olympics at Lake Placid, New York.

In the picture, Team USA celebrated wildly. The quote below the picture read:

Impossible is just a big word thrown around by small people who find it easier to live in the world they've been given than to explore the power they have to change it.

Impossible is not a fact. It's an opinion.

Impossible is not a declaration. It is a dare.

Impossible is potential.

Impossible is temporary.

Impossible is nothing!

I called Mike's hotline three or four times in a row to make sure that I copied each word exactly as he recited it from the poster. Then I typed it up and placed it in my binder.

Basketball coach Bobby Knight said that enthusiasm is the most important trait for an athlete, because players could have all the ability in the world, but if they'd rather be sitting in the fifth row somewhere, they would never help you.

I sat at my desk grading papers prior to the beginning of school. I looked out at the snow across the courtyard. It was February 2006. Two of my players, junior catcher John Baab and senior pitcher Mike Bustamante, came in.

"Coach, we got something for ya!" said Baab.

Bustamante reached into a brown shopping bag, pulled out a new baseball, and handed it to me. In our red and black school colors, the ball had my number twenty-one on one side and the phrase "one week" on the opposite side.

"One week away, Coach. We got one for every guy on the team," said Bustamante.

"Thanks, guys. This is going to blend in outside, you know," I said, while pointing to the snow-covered grass outside my window.

"That's all right," Baab said, smiling.

Baab was a returning player. He was a very bright boy and talented. He had outstanding work habits that I'm sure were passed onto him from his parents. His mother was from Brazil and came to America when she was just nineteen. His father had played Division I college hockey at Yale. They taught him the meaning of commitment too, perhaps to a fault. A year earlier, John had come out for our team as a sophomore. He had just finished the wrestling season, where he had lost an exorbitant amount of weight in order to be eligible to wrestle at 130 pounds. As a result of the weight loss, not only did he look sickly, but he had no strength. His throws were weak, and his reactions were slow, which rendered him as our backup catcher. Toward the end of that spring, he gained a considerable amount of weight back and slowly regained his strength. He then became our starting catcher. Standing in my room that morning, he looked like a different athlete than the season before. He had given up wrestling, and he had strength-trained in the off-season. Perhaps undersized for a catcher, he stood five foot eight and weighed 170 pounds, but he was solidly built. John was a leader and a field general behind the plate. He was a student of the game, understood it quite well, and most importantly, he had immeasurable heart.

John Baab, an excellent catcher, but more importantly, a true leader.

His counterpart, Mike Bustamante, came from a very nice and generous Italian family. On more than one occasion his parents hosted pasta dinners for our team, complete with everything you would find in an Italian restaurant: sausage and peppers, meatballs, chicken francaise, and more. Mike happened to be hysterically funny too. He had an uncanny ability to imitate almost anyone in Rich Little fashion. He could do voices, mannerisms, and also a litany of different major league pitchers' deliveries. Mike loved pitching, as much as any player I've had. He would study deliveries, partially for imitation and partially to develop good mechanics. The interesting thing about Mike was that he had an unhittable knuckleball when he could find a way to control it. However, a knuckleball is by far the most difficult pitch to control. Since he would have his knuckleball on some days but not others, he became a bit of a long-term project with our pitching staff. Interestingly, late in his career, something that our staff had suspected for a long time finally dawned on him. We always felt that Mike didn't need a gimmick pitch like a knuckleball to be a productive pitcher. He just needed to trust his abilities. He had already developed excellent mechanics, and when that reality set in for him, he began to utilize them to his advantage. He soon developed an effective repertoire of a fastball, curveball, and changeup. Consequently, he started to believe in himself and gained more confidence with each outing.

Mike and John could also set up our pitching machine faster than anyone and took great pride in doing so. As they left my classroom that morning, I smiled. *Any significant accomplishment is a triumph of enthusiasm*, I thought to myself.

Their gesture was small in one way. It was only a ball. It was large in others. It would breed camaraderie within the team. It was also filled with enthusiasm!

But within an instant my smile would turn to a frown.

"Casey!" yelled Pengitore as he entered my classroom. Casey was short for Casey Stengel and what Tom called me.

He walked over to the window and looked outside at the snow covered grounds.

"Take two and hit to right, Casey. You're a week away."

"Hey, Peng."

"It's going to be a while before you get on a field," he said.

Then, he broke the news. The Suits had informed him that they needed half of our gym, which served as our indoor practice facility, for additional storage until a construction project in the school was finished. They asked him to relay that message to me.

"You'll see!" I said to Pengitore.

"What?" he asked.

"That's what Suit Number Two said to me. 'You'll see!'"

One of the challenges of playing baseball in the northeast was that our spring season began on the first Friday in March. Far too often the weather was either rain, snow, or bitter cold, especially at the beginning of the season. During times that the weather was inclement, the boys and girls lacrosse teams and volleyball team used our larger-sized gym, which was where our basketball games were played. That gym was spacious and had bleacher seating that could house a large crowd.

Our baseball team wasn't as fortunate. We had a small-size gym known as the "West Gym" that was equivalent to most elementary school gyms. Now the gym would be divided by a half wall that extended the full length across the center of the gym, thus dividing the gym in two separate halves and only giving us about a a forty- by seventy-five-foot area area with low ceilings for practice space. Our middle school team, freshman team, JV team, and varsity team would all have to somehow share this half of a gym. The other side of the wall would now be "storage."

Oddly enough, the construction project in our school had begun in June 2004. For close to two years they did not need to use the gym for storage. Now, in March 2006, the Suits mysteriously needed to find more storage space and decided the only place that they had available was where they knew we had to practice.

We were not expected to win. But, by the way I was now being treated—by having our practice facility reduced–I feared that this may increase the chances that we didn't win. When parents called and complained that we were not provided with the proper practice facilities, the Suits said there was nothing that they could do about it and they needed our practice facility for storage until the completion of the construction project.

We would have to make do, and we would have to get creative.

"Peng," I yelled as he was about to leave. "If that's all the room that we have to practice in, I'm going to need a hundred Wiffle balls."

Wiffle balls were safe. They also didn't travel very far, and you didn't need a batting cage with netting to hit them. We could have several hitters simultaneously taking batting practice if we had enough Wiffle balls.

"I'll see what I can do," he answered.

"C'mon, Peng. If I have nowhere else to practice, find the money and get 'em."

"Okay."

Having our practices restricted to a half of a gym wasn't the only reason things looked grim for us as we neared the beginning of the 2006 season. We didn't have Will! Gone to graduation was first-team, All-State, first baseman Will Courter. Will would later go on to star as an All-NJAC Conference first baseman at William Paterson University. However, the season he had at West Essex in 2005 was unlike any I've witnessed on behalf of one of our players. He batted close to .600 with twenty-seven extra base hits—becoming the first first-team All-State player I've coached. There were many times that Will would hit at least two doubles per game. Now, many people both in and outside of our program wondered how we would possibly manage to score runs with the void that his departure left in our lineup.

There were also questions about the condition of ace pitcher Domenick Raimondo's right elbow. Dom had moved to the town of Fairfield in 2003 as an eighth grader and was called up to our varsity team about midway through his freshman season. He was small in stature, standing five foot eight and weighing 170 pounds. Like major leaguer Pedro Martinez, he was somewhat frail, but he threw hard for his size—I would say consistently about eighty miles an hour, and occasionally, he might pop a little harder than that. He also had excellent movement on his pitches. While he seemed in some ways to be an ordinary pitcher, a few things stood out about him. He always wore a red-colored Rawlings glove that had faded into more of a pinkish hue by his junior year. And more importantly, he was hungry. He was a competitor. Dom wasn't originally from the West Essex area. He grew up in Belleville, New Jersey. His father was a maintenance man at a Belleville elementary school. His mother was a teacher's aide. It was a bit of a struggle for his family to move to Fairfield, but his father wanted more for his family, and somehow he made it happen. As a result, Dom had developed a strong work ethic by watching his father work tirelessly to provide for his family. Thus, a hunger to work and earn things in one's life was instilled in him very early.

As a sophomore in 2005, Dom had ascended to the top of our rotation but then suffered a severe case of tendonitis in his elbow. After sitting out for three weeks, he came back and later pitched in the first round of the state tournament against Ramsey. He did not regain his form. He seemed tentative, was erratic, and got hit very hard. We lost 7–0, and that game marked the end of our season. At the start of the 2006 season we didn't really know how his arm might respond. He claimed to feel better, but based upon the extent of injury, he decided to rest his arm for the duration of the off-season. Would he be healthy enough to return as a starter? How much stamina would he have?

I believe that Dom Raimondo's heart and
competitiveness were what made him special.

March 3, 2006, was the first day we were allowed to begin practice. I had
taped up the "Impossible Is Nothing" quote on our locker room door. As I
exited my office and headed for the gym, I saw Kevin Picardo pointing at the
quote and talking to his teammates about it.

Kevin had come from an athletic family. His father, Carmine, had served
as athletic director at Wayne Valley High School, and I had previously coached

his brother Mark, a very good right fielder who graduated in 2004. Mark batted and threw left-handed. Kevin was the opposite. He batted and threw right-handed and was our returning shortstop. He had become our shortstop as a sophomore in 2004 and would now be a three-year veteran at his position. He had always had good arm strength and had built himself up a little thicker coming into his senior year. Kevin was rather quiet by nature but also very intense. No matter the situation, I always knew Kevin would compete to the best of his ability. Now, with some added strength, our expectations for him were very high.

I often tell current players of Kevin Picardo's intensity seen here in his expression. Kevin was always a study in concentration.

CHAPTER 10

It's in Our Covenant

The one-minute manager's symbol: a one-minute readout from the face of a modern digital watch is intended to remind each of us to take a minute out of our day to look into the faces of the people we manage. And to realize that they are our most important resources.

—Ken Blanchard
Author of *The One Minute Manager*

"IN ONE WORD!" I exclaimed as I passed out pencils and index cards to each player who reported to practice that afternoon. "What does this program stand for?" I asked.

Dr. Rob Gilbert once told a fable about a fisherman at sea. The fisherman was sipping from a flask of vodka and working his line when he heard a knock on the side of the boat. He peered over the side and saw a snake with a frog in its mouth. The fisherman felt sorry for the frog and carefully took it out of the snake's mouth. To make amends, the fisherman unscrewed the cap of his flask, leaned over, and gave the snake some vodka. Sometime later, the fisherman heard another knock on the side of the boat. He leaned over and again saw the snake—but this time the snake had *two* frogs in his mouth. The moral: Whatever is rewarded, gets repeated!

"A covenant is a binding agreement," said LSU coach Skip Bertman at a clinic back in 1997. "At LSU, I write up a team covenant that outlines all the things that our coaches pledge to do and exactly what is expected of our players. Everything that goes into our program is in our covenant." Bertman has each player sign the covenant prior to the season.

Some of the answers on the index cards that I collected were good, such as *hustle* and *commitment*. Then, someone nailed it.

"*Excellence!*" I said as I held up the card for the team to see. "Excellence both on and off the field" was our team mission statement that I borrowed straight from the LSU team covenant. Actually, our covenant was a potpourri of team principles that I would borrow over time from some of the best coaches in the world.

Bertman once told me, "Teamwork isn't just how you act. It's how you think." It was important to me to define our program as one of class and integrity and to teach our players to think unselfishly. I would first introduce the principles in our covenant at our winter meeting and then build on them throughout the season.

I stood in front of our team as I continued flipping through the index cards. Then I recited our "Unifying Principles," which I borrowed from University of Florida coach Pat McMahon:

1) We will do everything in a first-class manner with high principles.

2) We will commit to an excellent performance in everything we do.

3) Do little things right. They become big things.

4) Be good to the little guy. Treat everyone with respect, especially the guy who takes out the trash.

I also shared perhaps the most powerful quote I have ever heard from Bertman; it was a quote from Paul J. Meyer (the founder of Success Motivation International) and was in the form of the acronym VASE: Whatever you *vividly* imagine, *ardently* desire, *sincerely* believe, and *enthusiastically* act upon must inevitably come to pass. Most of my players already knew it, as it hung on a sign in our locker room, but I repeated it anyway. Then I gave them an example.

"Walt Disney saw what wasn't there. He had a vision. Central Florida used to be nothing but swamps and orchards, but he saw the world's greatest amusement park. He saw the fireworks exploding above the Magic Castle on Main Street. He saw the bright lights during the electrical parade. He could literally smell the popcorn and hear the laughter of children. Unfortunately, before it ever opened, Walt passed away.

"In 1971, Walt's wife was asked to cut the ribbon at the opening ceremony. A reporter said to Mrs. Disney, 'It's a shame that Walt didn't get to see this.'

"She looked at the reporter and said, 'Of course he saw it! How do you think it got here?'"

I paced in front of the players. "Walt Disney had a dream. What's yours?"

"To win the GNT, Coach," answered Mark Ruggiero intently.

Mark, a blonde-haired, blue-eyed boy, stood about five foot nine. He had been our starting second baseman since his sophomore year, and he was now geared up for a strong senior season. It has been said that a key to a great team may be when your best players are also your hardest workers. Mark had ability, but when it came to work ethic, he was second to none. He was also a coach's dream as far as his attitude was concerned. Mark was the type of boy that a father hopes that his daughter will bring home someday. It was clear that his mom, a secretary for an accountant, and his father, a security systems owner, had instilled strong values in him. Having Mark was in some ways like having another assistant coach.

Mark was extremely disappointed with how we had finished the last season, bowing 7–0 in the first round of the state tournament to Ramsey and losing to Cedar Grove in the first round of the GNT. He was also disappointed with how he performed as an individual and was now determined to finish differently as a senior. Although he was small in stature, about 160 pounds on a good day, he had actually added about ten quality pounds to his frame since his junior season as the result of a dedicated off-season effort in the weight room.

Mark said to me, "Coach, I would literally convince myself that if I didn't finish one more rep in the gym, then that one rep would be the difference between us winning the GNT or not. That's how consumed I was in the off-season."

Mark Ruggiero is the epitome of a West Essex baseball player.

"Your dream has to be vivid! It must be clear," I said.

The players sat silently.

"C'mon, boys. Dream big! Willie Jolley once said that if people aren't laughing at your dreams, then your dreams aren't big enough."

"To beat Seton Hall Prep, to win the GNT, Coach," said senior Nick Santomauro.

Nick, an excellent student, had recently committed as an early-decision applicant to continue his career at Dartmouth College. He stood six foot one at 180 pounds. He threw right-handed and batted left-handed and hit with more power than any player I've ever coached. There was an instance during his sophomore year when Coach Renshaw and I were watching him take batting practice for the first time outside in early March. The way he was driving balls into the opposite field gaps had the two of us staring at each other.

"What do you think?" asked Renshaw.

"If I consider that he has outstanding arm strength to go with his power, I think he's going to be a draftable player," I answered.

There was one day on our varsity field when a slight wind was blowing out and he hit balls unlike any I have ever seen hit on our field. At one point, our entire team just stopped their station work and stared awestruck at what they were seeing as he launched balls into the junior high school parking lot well beyond our fence.

I saw professional potential in Nick Santomauro as early as during his sophomore season.

There was quite a cast of personalities on our team, with the ringleader usually being Bustamante. I always thought there was perhaps a tinge of jealousy toward Nick, because the kids on our team knew that he would take baseball well beyond our program at West Essex. Every once in a while, Nick would get out on his front foot, pop a ball up, and exclaim, *"Ahh!"*

However, the characters on our team embellished that into something much different. They would pretend to get under a ball and go, *"Whoooooooaaaaaaaahhhhhh."*

I always defended Nick from their light-hearted razzing, which at times could get annoying as *"Whoooooaaaaaahhhhhh"* would ring out when he walked to the plate in practice.

"I've never heard you do that, Nick," I would say as I shook my head.

Nick worked extremely hard at his game, but he was also naturally blessed with talent and God-given strength.

Rob Gilbert believes one key to sport psychology is to perform with as little thought as possible. He once pointed out to me how often successful athletes use the phrase "I just" during a postgame interview. There were times when people would ask Nick for an explanation as to how the ball would explode off of his bat.

He would smile and simply say, "I just hit it."

There was an instance during a game against Weequahic in 2005 when Nick nearly injured Will Courter severely with a low-sinking line drive while Will was running at first base. We've all heard of pitchers not having enough reaction time to line drives hit off aluminum bats. Well, Will was ninety feet away, and if he hadn't turned, his shin would have shattered. Fortunately, he took the ball off of his calf, and while he did have a severe welt, he lived to tell about it.

John Wilson, a scout for the Minnesota Twins, had taken a real liking to Nick, and after Nick's sophomore year, several Division I schools also contacted me to express their interest. I knew he had professional potential, but I also thought he should go to school first so he could grow into his body a little more and develop further while getting an education. His mother, an attorney, and his father, a highly successful fitness center owner, valued education highly and wanted him to attend Dartmouth. I also felt that Dartmouth would be a perfect fit for Nick, as he could play right away and receive an Ivy League education. When he was accepted there as an early-decision applicant, I was happy for him; I also knew that it would be easier for him to play his senior year without the distraction of having to decide which college to attend. Now that he would attend Dartmouth, he could just relax and play.

Both Mark and Nick had made it clear: Our goal was to beat Seton

Hall Prep for the GNT title. To us, winning the GNT would actually be more significant than winning the state tournament. There were thirty-seven schools in Essex County. The schools ranged from tiny Group I schools to very large Group IV schools, as well as Seton Hall Prep, which was a large Parochial A program and a nationally ranked power. Since West Essex was a small Group II school, winning a title with the magnitude of the GNT against such larger opponents was arguably more of a worthy accomplishment than the state tournament in which our opponents would be limited to Group II schools of equivalent size.

"Do you know that you can never accomplish your dream unless he accomplishes his and he accomplishes his?" I asked as I pointed to several different players. "The only way we can ever do it is together, by thinking as one, as a team!"

That had always been a struggle for me. West Essex was a regional school comprised of four different towns: North Caldwell, Fairfield, Roseland, and Essex Fells. Between the four towns they had three different Little Leagues, so it was difficult to establish any continuity in regard to a feeder system. It was a challenge to bring players together from separate towns, especially when they had not previously played with one another, but as Ken Blanchard said, "The best minute I spend is the one I invest in people." Therefore teamwork would be an integral part of our team covenant, as would the most crucial part of teamwork—trust.

A lack of trust can destroy a family, a team, or an organization.

I shared an anecdote with the team about Fire, Water, and Trust hiking in the woods. They were discussing a plan for what to do if they were to get separated.

Fire said, "If you lose me, look for the smoke, that's where you'll find me."

Water said, "If you lose me, look for the green grass and flowers, that's where I'll be."

Trust said, "You'd better not lose me, because if you lose me, you'll never find me again."

That was a core belief of Bertman, who used the example of a Jewish wedding tradition to make his point. After the rabbi has pronounced the bride and groom as husband and wife, the groom steps on a wine glass wrapped in a napkin. In this time-honored ritual, the glass serves as a symbol of both fragility and strength.

I wanted to make the same point to my players about our team. Rather than use a wine glass, I used a prop in the form of a crystal baseball that I had purchased. It was really made of acrylic, so that I didn't go broke, but it was hard for one to distinguish it from real glass with the naked eye. I held it up in front of the team.

"If I took this ball and dropped it on the ground, could I ever put it back together again?"

The players shook their heads no.

"Well, trust is the same way," I said, while sharing Bertman's wisdom. "It's digital, like a clock. It's either 3:05 or it isn't. You can't be half-trusting. You are either trustworthy or you are not."

This was especially true when bringing kids from separate towns together. Cliques could easily form. One of my peeves was when players would bad-mouth their teammates behind one another's backs. It was a cardinal sin in coaching for any coach to talk negatively about a student to another student. Inevitably, the student being bad-mouthed would hear about it. When that happened, and in many programs it did, the coach created a victim out of his own player and sabotaged trust within the team. That type of damage can be irreparable. How teammates and coaches treat one another, particularly when they are in the presence of other people, is critically important when it comes to trust within a team.

"When you genuinely care about each other and commit to a cause larger than yourself, it transcends out onto the field," I added. "If we establish trust in each other, then we can be one. That's when we can be a team. However, if in a selfish moment you drop the ball—"

At that instant, I dropped the crystal ball. It made a thunderous sound and shattered all over the gym floor.

"Then the core of the team seeps out. We can never put it back together again. Maybe next year we can get a new team, but we can never regain that feeling of trust."

Then I took a new crystal baseball out of my pocket.

"But if we guard it and protect it, it can last us a lifetime. Outside of your families, the trust that you have in each other can be the strongest thing you'll ever have in your lives," I said.

Being trustworthy requires a great deal of loyalty on behalf of each player, especially when frustration sets in and things don't go your way. For that reason, I patterned the last line of our team covenant to be just like LSU's.

"You have to reach deep down in your soul where character is born with all its attributes of courage, self-sacrifice, loyalty, and selflessness. Have fun and play like the champions that you are!"

CHAPTER 11

Two Slings and a Neck Brace

Turn your wounds into wisdom.

—Oprah Winfrey
TV Talk Show Host and Producer

"GET STRETCHED!" I SAID, after setting the tone through our covenant. Three boys stood off to the side. Two of them were in slings, the other in a neck brace. The boy in the neck brace was junior pitcher and centerfielder, Mike Cordasco.

Tragically, Mike had fractured both his fourth and fifth vertebrae back in November in a state tournament football game. At the time he was taken off the field on a stretcher, it was not known if he would ever walk again. According to his doctor, Mike was actually very fortunate. One of the fractures was just millimeters away from causing him to be paralyzed and relegated to a wheelchair for life. Eventually, he would regain his strength and mobility. However, it would be a long road back, and Mike was far from ready. He had remained out of school in a halo brace for over three months and had just returned to school in a neck brace. While at home he had received at least six hours of home instruction per week in an effort to keep him up-to-date with his courses.

"You're lucky to be walking, Mike. When I watched them carry you off on the stretcher, you weren't moving," I said as I walked toward the boys standing against the wall that divided our gym in half.

"I know, Coach. I am lucky. It's been since November. The fracture on the fourth vertebrae is completely healed. But, I still have to have one more test on the fifth one. If the X-ray comes out okay, I can begin physical therapy," he said.

It was March 3, and he was still in a neck brace. How long it would be for him to get out of the neck brace, be given clearance by his doctor, and complete the physical therapy process was anybody's guess. Personally, I questioned whether he could make it back at all during that spring, and if he did, whether or not he would have enough strength to perform the way he had before. Would it be too risky a decision?

"We want you back as soon as possible, Mike, but we'd never do a thing to hurt you. I'm happy that you're even walking, but do you honestly think it's realistic for you to return this spring? I mean what if you dove for a ball in center field?" I asked.

"I'll be back, Coach. I'll be back!" Mike assured me.

Mike was extremely valuable to our team. He was a crafty left-handed pitcher, whom we were heavily counting on, and he also was an exceptional center fielder. He was gritty at the plate and could bunt too, which automatically made him attractive to me in our lineup. Without Mike, we were stuck without a center fielder and with a void in our batting order. I had no idea who could possibly replace him, if anyone.

I turned my attention to the other two boys, junior pitcher Anthony Tundo and senior pitcher Anthony Cerza.

"How 'bout you guys? How long?" I asked.

"Just a muscle pull in my chest from lifting, Coach. It'll be all right," said Tundo. He was a big strong kid who had excelled as a lineman on the football team. A lineman/pitcher was a combination not frequently seen in our program, but Anthony could do it. He threw a heavy fastball and had pitched extremely well for our JV squad the season before. Now, given his added physical maturity, we were optimistic that he was ready to contribute to our varsity staff.

"And you? What happened?" I asked Cerza.

"I strained my shoulder in a fight. It's getting better. I'll be able to start throwin' soon. Coach, all I want is a chance to tryout," said Cerza.

"Well, what are you getting into fights for in the first place? Tryouts just started. Where are you?" I asked rhetorically.

I walked away before he could answer. I was aggravated that he had put himself in that position, but I admired Anthony.

Anthony was the younger brother of Frank Cerza, our ace pitcher from our 2004 team that reached the GNT semifinals. In 2003, Anthony had tried out for our freshman team and was cut from the squad. The following season he came back and tried out again. The fact that he even returned for another tryout put Anthony in 1 percent of the players in our program. After he was cut, I never heard from his parents, nor did he complain. Instead, he worked hard to improve his game and came back out as a sophomore. He made the team and pitched well for the next two seasons on our JV team. After his junior year, he worked hard in the weight room and hit a bit of a growth spurt in the off-season. Physically, he looked good, about five foot ten and 170 pounds. It remained to be seen if he could now make the jump and perform on the varsity level. We wouldn't be able to evaluate him until he got out of his sling, and we had no idea when that might be.

At our first practice of the season, I always got together with the pitchers and catchers before our full squad. On that first Friday, March 3, our pitching staff shaped up like this: We returned three varsity pitchers who combined for only five wins in 2005. Junior Dom Raimondo had earned four of those five wins, as he finished 4–2 with a 3.57 ERA and would now begin his battle back from a significant elbow injury. Junior Mike Cordasco had earned the other win. He had finished 1–2 with a 5.37 ERA and was now helplessly in a neck brace. Senior Mike Bustamante did not earn a win in 2005, going 0–2 with a 5.25 ERA. Anthony Tundo and Anthony Cerza were newcomers and just stood there in slings. We also had another newcomer, senior Steve Zurawiecki.

Steve was an interesting prospect. He was very athletic and had done an excellent job as a field-goal kicker for our football team in the fall. He ran exceptionally well, had some pop in his bat, and had arguably the liveliest arm of any pitcher in our program. He could really rear back and fire a baseball. However, as a senior now, he had yet to pitch an inning for our varsity team. The problem was that in spite of the fact that he threw incredibly hard, he had some difficulty consistently throwing strikes. There is a lot of emphasis placed on velocity in pitching. Clearly control is more important because it does not matter how hard one throws if one cannot throw strikes consistently. As Tulane coach Rick Jones once instructed, "I can't defend ball four!" Steve's arsenal was electric, but there were times that he could lose his command. We had done extensive analysis on his mechanics and provided him with a drill series that would keep his delivery sound while maintaining rhythm, but to date, nothing seemed to work. Control problems were prevalent in baseball even in the major leagues. We wondered if his control problem was perhaps a mental one, similar to that experienced by major league pitcher-turned-outfielder Rick Ankiel of the Saint Louis Cardinals. Other players, such as the Dodgers' Steve Sax and the Mets' Mackey Sasser, had experienced those challenges as well. I felt that if Steve could sort this out, there would be no telling how successful he could be and how much he could really help our team.

In spite of some of his past struggles, I was rather optimistic that he was destined to come through for us. My reasoning was not based on any drill work, instruction, or mental imagery. It was based upon an e-mail that Steve had sent to me the day after his football season had ended. In the e-mail he explained to me just how excited he was to begin the season, how hard he was willing to work, and how determined he was to have a good senior year. His e-mail was something Coach Bobby Knight would have loved, as it was beaming with enthusiasm. I knew right then that Steve was going to find his control and be a real winner for us. Eventually, he would prove to be invaluable to our team as both a pitcher and also as a hitter.

Our plan was simple: throw strikes, play catch, and pressure the defense any way we could. The detail that went into our plan was intricate. My players would have to heighten their awareness.

The *Washington Post* had conducted an experiment with musician Josh Bell, and I explained that story to my players in order to emphasize both heightened awareness and attention to detail.

During the experiment, Bell, one of the world's greatest musicians, was placed incognito in a Washington subway station during the morning rush hour. He wore a pair of jeans and pulled a Nationals' baseball cap down over his face, more or less posing as a street bum. During Bell's forty-five-minute performance, 1,097 people passed by him. Only seven stopped, while twenty-seven people donated money to his cause. He collected a total of $32.17. Just a few days earlier, Bell had sold out Boston's Symphony Hall with very few tickets available for less than a hundred dollars. His violin he used in the subway that morning was a Stradivarius valued at over a million dollars.

"What is happening that you are not aware of?" I would ask my players at the conclusion of that story. "If people could walk right by one of the world's most famous musicians, playing some of the world's greatest music, what else could they be missing?"

Later, I would tell my teams about the tiny O-rings on the space shuttle *Challenger* that exploded just seventy-three seconds into takeoff in 1986. The O-rings measured roughly 2.5 inches in length and were .005 inch thick. They were supposed to seal a joint that would prevent 5,800-degree gases from leaking out of the solid rocket booster. Due to erosion and cold temperatures, which loosened the O-rings, sparks turned to flame, and the flame mixed with oxygen and hydrogen and caused the shuttle to explode, killing seven crew members—among them school teacher Christa McAuliffe. The O-rings appeared to be small, insignificant, and even inconsequential. They were not. They were largely responsible for the explosion.

I wanted our team to focus on the countless minute details that were involved in the game of baseball. Each time we overlooked a minute detail, it could have an O-ring type of effect and, in essence, blow up our team. We would break the game down to the finest details and then build from there. On our first day, I literally began our instruction by holding up a baseball and stating, "This is a baseball!"

Pat McMahon had said "Little things mean a lot in baseball. They become big things." We would try to find any way imaginable to get our players to focus on the details.

McMahon would paint the front third of first base black to emphasize to his players where their foot should make contact with the base in order for them to cut down their running times. We would paint the front third of our first base black too.

The New York Yankees had hired tennis pro Sean Brawley to help them improve their drill work. Some of his findings were incredible. First, he asked the Yankee brass to identify the single most important element to being an extraordinary hitter. Nearly every member of the Yankees brass agreed that element was tracking or seeing the baseball. Miraculously, the then twenty-six-time world champions had no drills at all to enhance a hitter's ability to see the baseball. Brawley used his expertise to set one up for them. The split second the hitter would see the ball released from the pitcher's hand he would yell "pitch." The split second the ball would make contact with the bat he would yell "hit." It is impossible to do this "pitch-hit" drill without practicing how to track the ball. We did this every day. While we were stuck in a half of a gym, only one hitter at a time could be in our batting cage using baseballs, but ten other guys could do this drill all at once using Wiffle balls.

Our core belief for our pitchers came from Leo Mazzone, longtime pitching coach of the Atlanta Braves. Leo strongly emphasized to me to teach my pitchers to "own the fastball down and away."

Rick Peterson of the New York Mets once explained, "Hitters have a .180 average on balls located at the knee."

I would take those points to heart. At my request, freshman coach Steve Trongone built two steel posts that could disassemble when necessary so we could take them on the road with us. We placed those posts in our bullpen and tied a yellow string across home plate at knee height.

"Pitch to the string," said Cal State Fullerton coach Dave Serrano. Coaches tell pitchers to keep the ball down. The yellow string gave them a visual guide to what *down* really was. This was critically important to our success, because none of our proven pitchers threw overly hard.

As Pat McMahon said, "A located fastball wins at any level at any time."

We would require our pitchers to use a drill technique defined by Peterson as "active visualization," where they would perform all of their skills with their eyes closed to develop a kinesthetic feel for their mechanics. If we were to ever be successful, it would be because our pitchers could consistently command their pitches—beginning with their fastball. However, that was contingent upon whether or not we would ever get healthy. If two slings and a neck brace weren't enough, we would now have a labrum too.

After our second practice, we were changing in the coach's locker room and heard a knock on the door. It was our shortstop Kevin Picardo.

"Coach, my shoulder's really hurting. I felt something pop while long-tossing today," said Kevin. We had been out on the field turf on our football field, one of the limited time slots that we were permitted to use it, and he strained his shoulder while we stretched out our arms.

I advised Kevin to immediately see our trainer, John Mascola. As he closed the door, Renshaw and I just stared at one another.

"Two slings, a neck brace, and now him," said Renshaw. "You've got to be kidding me!"

CHAPTER 12

Who's on First?

An army of deer led by a lion, is more to be feared
than an army of lions led by a deer.

—Unknown

CHING! THE BALL RANG off of Nick Santomauro's bat inside the batting cage.

"Scott, this kid is a beast," said Renshaw. "He's all set to go to Dartmouth?"

"Yeah. I spoke to Coach Enriques over there, and they love him. They're excited to get him," I answered.

We were one week into our training camp. On a good note, Raimondo had thrown three bullpen sessions without experiencing pain. Both Cerza and Tundo had gotten rid of their slings and began to toss lightly but had yet to pitch from a mound. Cordasco was still in a neck brace. Picardo had not picked up a ball in six days.

We were scheduled to travel to Warinanco Park in Union County on March 11 to play our first exhibition game against Roselle Catholic. Our field was still snow covered. Miraculously, theirs was ready. At that point, we had been out on the football field turf twice, but we were required to share it with our girls' softball team, which limited our use to roughly fifty yards of practice area for both varsity and JV candidates.

During the Roselle Catholic game, I played a sophomore at shortstop in place of the injured Picardo. I had questions at that time as to whether or not the young man was ready to play shortstop at the varsity level. I also pondered who exactly would play center field in Cordasco's absence.

Anthony Dalonges stood five foot seven and weighed 145 pounds. He was a cousin of pitcher Mike Bustamante. He was a clean-cut Italian boy who had struggled the season before as a shortstop on our JV team. His struggles were so significant that we did not even select him as a member of our team over the previous summer in preparation for this season. In reality, Anthony was nowhere on our radar screen. I believe that he knew that too, because he expressed to me a desire to try out for the outfield rather than the infield this time around. Aside from the two instances that we got outside on our field turf, we did not get much of a look at his defensive ability as it was difficult to really stretch out our outfielders while having only fifty yards of turf to work with. From what I saw in that brief and limited evaluation period, he looked good enough relative to our other candidates to give him a try in center field at Roselle Catholic, so I gave him a shot. Then, he caught my eye.

A Roselle Catholic player hit a long drive into the gap. Off the bat, I thought it would be an inside-the-park home run at the fenceless Warinanco Park field. Out of nowhere, Anthony ran back and to his left to make an over-the-shoulder catch with his glove fully outstretched. The play was worthy of an ESPY award had ESPN filmed the game.

"Wow!" I said to Renshaw. "We just found a center fielder!"

Raimondo threw pretty well, as did Zurawiecki. Bustamante was not happy with his outing, but it wasn't bad either. I was thrilled to find a player who appeared reliable as a defensive center fielder.

Now all we need is Kevin back at shortstop, I thought to myself on the long bus ride home. It's one thing to not have a center fielder; it's another thing to be without a shortstop.

"You guys suck!" said Gary Gloom to a group of our players seated at the table inside our cafeteria. It was Monday, March 13. Our players all ate lunch together, and, naturally, they talked about what all boys talked about—girls and sports, not necessarily in that order. The Roselle Catholic scrimmage was the topic of the day, prompting Gloom's comment.

"You never win anything," Gloom continued.

"Hey, we're working hard. I think we're gonna be pretty good this year," answered Mark Ruggiero.

"You'll be lucky to finish fourth in the conference. Hanover Park, Morris Hills, Mendham, forgettaboutit!" Gloom rebutted.

"You watch. We're gonna step up this season," said junior third baseman Vin Valerian.

Vin was a good-sized athletic player with a lot of raw talent. He was six foot, 180 pounds, brown hair, blue eyes, and he was very strong. During training camp as a sophomore the season before, he had shown glimpses of what I hoped he could be. My concern about Vin at that time was that he was prone to mental lapses. I actually sent him down to play for our JV team after he forgot his pants for our team picture.

"How in the world do you show up for pictures without your uniform pants, Vinny?" I asked.

At that time, I felt that he needed some added maturity in order to be able to play for me. To his credit, he accepted the demotion, worked hard, performed well, and then got called back up to the varsity at my request. Once he came back, he was outstanding and also had his head together. In one instance, he hit a game-tying home run against Morris Hills deep to left center field. His home run spurred us to a dramatic come-from-behind win against an outstanding team. He was competing at a higher level than I had previously seen and finished out the season as our third baseman. Now as a junior, I expected him to be a year more mature, both mentally and physically. I expected him to really put it together after getting his feet wet a year ago.

I'll always remember Vin Valerian for playing his best when our team needed him the most.

Donnie Doom, another student seated at the table, chimed in, "You guys might end up around .500 and qualify for the states, but then you'll get crushed. And there's no way you could ever win the GNT. You guys can't beat Nutley in our county, let alone Seton Hall. They're the best team in the state, and they're *loaded* this year!"

"Dude, you can't play with Seton Hall. They got guys like goin' to the Yankees and stuff," Gloom added.

"Yeah, Eric Duncan," said John Babb. "That kid hit the farthest home run I've ever seen off Frank Herman from Montclair Kimberly a few years ago in the GNT. It was a bomb! It rolled under the scoreboard like five hundred feet from home."

"Yeah, Duncan!" said Doom. "I saw him on the *Yes* network the other day. He played in a big league game in spring training and had a couple of hits. They showed him sitting in the dugout with Joe Torre. Brian Cashman said the Yanks drafted him out of Seton Hall Prep in the first round and signed him for over a million dollars. Imagine that kinda money, man? That's sick!"

"I hear they got another first rounder this year, only he's a pitcher," said Doom. "A kid named Porcello. You guys are joking, right? I mean if you think you can beat this team when they're sending guys to the Yankees, keep dreaming! I mean, talk about a pipe dream. West Essex beats Seton Hall. Sure, and then your alarm clock goes off, and it's time to go to school!" Gloom and Doom laughed hysterically as they high-fived one another.

"Remember, guys, if people aren't laughing at our dreams, then our dreams aren't big enough," said Picardo.

"The GNT, boys. What's bigger than that? That's big! It's the oldest tournament in the state. Some of the greatest players to ever come out of New Jersey have played in it," added Baab.

"Guys, Lawrence and me were talking about it the other day. We're seniors. This is our last chance to do something big," said Ruggiero.

Lawrence was senior right fielder Lawrence Caprio. Lawrence stood five foot ten and 185 pounds. He was a physical specimen, built like an Adonis. He was also a National Honor Society student who was very intelligent. By nature, he was quiet but commanded a great deal of respect when he spoke. The girls all loved Lawrence too. At least that's what they said in my classroom. As a junior, Lawrence had hit .380 with four home runs and twenty-five RBIs, and he had played stellar defense. We expected the same from him this season. However, baseball was not his primary sport, football was.

Tragically, in the first quarter of his opening football game during his senior year, he suffered a season-ending knee injury. Lawrence was so distraught over missing essentially his entire senior year of football that he decided to wrestle in the winter time just to expose himself to some competition that he was desperately missing. The knee injury would linger and require him to wear a brace during our spring season. Fortunately for Lawrence, football recruiters were interested enough from what he had shown during his junior year, and he had decided that he would continue his career as a recruited walk-on at the University of Richmond.

"I pretty much missed my whole senior year of football. How long have we all been playing together? A year from now we'll all be at different schools. I don't wanna have any more regrets. This is our last chance to play together, so let's go out in style and win something together," said Caprio.

Caprio was trying to follow in his father Larry's footsteps. Larry Caprio had been a stand-out player who had won the Greater Newark Tournament in 1975 while playing for Essex Catholic High School. He later went on to star at Upsala College and play in the Cape Cod League. Athletic ability was obviously in Lawrence's genes.

Lawrence Caprio (third from the left between Baab, Santomauro, Picardo, and Valerian) was a warrior with tremendous drive and determination.

"I don't know about you guys, but I'm sick of watching the GNT after we get knocked out," said Ruggiero. "We've gotta win it this year. We can't let four years of high school go by and not win something. I'm sick of being that team. You know, that team that's pretty good but never wins anything? We've worked too hard to let that happen. We've just got to come out, act like brothers, have each other's backs, and get after it. You know what else? My grandfather passed away last December. He loved baseball more than anybody! This will be the first time he won't be at our games, so I'm dedicating this season to him. I want to make him proud!"

"You got it, Mark. We'll do it for him, man," said Valerian.

Prior to practice that afternoon, I wanted to remind our players where their focus needed to be. We had won the scrimmage at Roselle Catholic by a narrow margin, largely because one of their lower-tier pitchers blew up late in the game. I never put much stock in the scores of scrimmages and knew that if we were to see them during the regular season we would not have benefited from seeing a weak pitcher with the game on the line. The kids tended to place their entire focus on either wins or losses in any games. This was in contrast to one of John Wooden's core beliefs, which was that players and teams should only focus on the things they can control. Wooden believed strongly that winning was something that was beyond your control.

"We can't control what people say, think, or write about us," I stated. "We can't control the weather here. We *can* control how we respond to it. We can control how well we prepare indoors, even if we only get to use half a gym. You are 100 percent responsible for how you choose to respond to whatever happens in your life. Winning is beyond our control. The one thing we have the most control over, no matter who we play, no matter where we are, is our effort!"

Then, I invited Anthony Dalonges to volunteer in front of the team.

"Anthony, jump up as high as you can and touch the wall," I commanded.

Dalonges jumped up and touched the wall. I used a step ladder to mark the spot that he touched with a black marker. Then, I took a five-dollar bill out of my pocket and taped it two inches higher above the spot.

"Can you jump higher, Anthony?" I asked. "If you can reach the money you just made yourself five bucks!"

Dalonges jumped up and missed on his first try.

"Ohhhh!" the team groaned.

On his second attempt, he jumped higher and grabbed the money as the team roared. He held the money high in the air as the team applauded.

"Why didn't you jump that high the first time, Anthony?" I scolded. "I asked you to jump as high as you could, and instead you held back. Why didn't you give me your best effort? Winning is beyond our control. Your best effort, boys. We can control that!"

I scanned each player looking for eye contact. "Who wants to be great?" I asked, and several hands went up. "Great players choose to give their best effort, their best focus on every single pitch. Baseball's a cruel game, boys, far too unforgiving to ever give you a second chance."

After practice, we sat in the coaches' office. It was there that a brotherhood was formed. During my first two seasons, an older gentleman by the name of Jack Burke served as my assistant coach. Jack was a wonderful man, who is now deceased, but he told me something that stayed with me: "Some of the closest friends you will ever have in your life, you will meet through coaching."

The 1997 West Essex baseball staff. Standing from left to right are assistant coaches Jack Burke, Harry Ambrosino, Charlie Giachetti, and me.

As time went on, what Jack had said became more and more clear to me. Our staff would sit in our office for countless hours over the course of each season, discussing everything from our personal lives, to our practices and games, to the quirks and woes of society, to the shortcomings of the public school system.

Most nights would not end until Reshaw and I were done kicking it around with freshman coach Steve Trongone and JV coach Jim Whalen. The two of them were both former pitchers and college teammates where they became Division III National Champions together at Montclair State University in 2000.

Prior to the 2002 season, I had two coaching openings in my program. We had advertised for these positions in the *Star-Ledger*, through the NJSIAA website, and in a variety of other classified publications, only to come up empty. After several months, winter was approaching, and we barely had any applicants—certainly no one qualified for what I was looking for in an assistant coach.

We would all meet in an ironic fashion. Renshaw and I went over to Pub 46 in Clifton, New Jersey, for a bite to eat in November of 2001. There, Renshaw bumped into a former Montclair State player, Marc Hauser, who he once played against while at William Paterson. Renshaw asked him if he knew anyone interested in coaching high school baseball.

"Jimmy Whalen!" said Hauser. "I'm supposed to meet him later over at Just Jakes in Montclair. Come by and meet him."

Renshaw and I decided to take Hauser up on his offer and headed over to Jakes. Upon arriving, I noticed a tall thin guy wearing a blue jersey of my beloved New York Rangers with Adam Graves's number nine on the back. We weren't there five minutes when a scuffle broke out. Suddenly, the guy in the Graves jersey streaked across the bar and forcibly pulled a larger guy away from a friend of his while breaking up the fracas. Moments later, Hauser found us and motioned for the guy in the Graves jersey to come over.

"This is my friend, Jimmy Whalen," said Hauser.

"You looked like the real Adam Graves sticking up for Messier!" were the first words I ever spoke to Whalen.

We talked about the Rangers for at least the next half hour. By the end of the night I had hired him. Then, to my surprise, Whalen explained that he had another guy for us too.

"I'll introduce you to Steve Trongone."

We had literally spent months advertising in every credible publication worth reading and could not come up with even one applicant worthy of interviewing. Then within approximately two hours in two North Jersey bars I had somehow found two prospective coaches that I couldn't wait to work with.

"Maybe it's me," I said to Renshaw as I dropped him off. "If I knew bars were such a haven for qualified coaches, I'd have gone out a lot sooner."

Trongone was a great pitcher himself, who I had watched pitch Roxbury to a Morris County championship in 1997. He contributed greatly to Montclair's national title as a sidearm righty out of their bullpen. He was very intense, very knowledgeable, incredibly passionate about baseball, and very loyal. Some people thought that he had a screw loose because he would do things like get home from a Yankee game at 3:00 a.m. because on the way to the parking garage he would somehow end up in a pickup game of basketball with a bunch of street kids from the Bronx on one of those courts adjacent to the stadium. I felt that was only part of the reason why our kids would come to love him so much.

Whalen had pitched sparingly at Montclair State but never stopped working. In the fall of his senior year, he had a solid outing against Division I Rutgers that earned him more of a role within their staff that spring. Whalen was more reserved than Trongone as far as personality was concerned, but was incredibly detail oriented and extremely professional. The two of them were roommates as well, and what cracked me up was that they both called anyone they spoke to "Moose," including one another.

Evidently, Montclair State coach Norm Shoening had coached under legendary coach Fred Hill at Montclair State before Hill became the head coach at Rutgers University. Hill was affectionately known as "Moose" and supposedly referred to everyone else as "Moose" too. Shoening, a Hill protégée, adopted the same lingo and referred to all of his players as "Moose" and they returned the favor toward him. Within months of Trongone and Whalen's arrival at West Essex, "Moose" had become a term of endearment more common than "Dude" within our program with these two new coaches leading the charge.

"Baseball junkies" from left to right in 2003 are assistant coaches Ray Renshaw, myself, Jim Whalen, and Steve Trongone.

As we sat in the office that evening, the topics of discussion were Anthony Cerza and the lack of a varsity shortstop.

"I'll tell you what, I know we're still indoors, but this Cerza kid has looked good since he started throwing," I said to Renshaw and Whalen.

"He's got this!" answered Renshaw, while twisting his wrist in a curveball motion.

"He was solid with me last year, Moose. I know it's JV, but he did go all nine innings at Parsippany Hills," added Whalen.

"He's filled out a little bit since last season and picked up more than an inch on his fastball. More than anything, I like the kid's attitude. You guys know he got cut as a freshman? How many kids come back and try out after they've been cut?" I asked.

As Renshaw pointed out, the question was: did he have enough talent to pitch at our level?

"I don't know," I answered. "But he's got his head together. In the corporate world, they say hire for attitude and train for skill. How many kids with more talent than Anthony have let us down because of a bad attitude?"

"Too many!" answered Renshaw. "Remember the kid we had way back when? He had more talent than anybody, and yet ended up quitting. Remember all the conversations we had with him trying to get his head straight?"

"Yeah. Do you guys know the four words that can haunt you for the rest of your life?" I asked. They shook their heads no in confusion.

"I thought you'd change!" I exclaimed. "How many times did we take a kid with talent and talk to him, trying to pump him up and hoping that his attitude would change, only to be let down? Well, this kid, Cerza, got cut and came back. That's an attitude I want in my dugout."

"He was by far my hardest worker last year, Moose," said Whalen.

"Enough said. My mind is made up. He's made the team. We'll run him out there in the scrimmage against Wayne Hills tomorrow," I said.

Kevin Picardo knocked on the door and came into the office. He explained that he didn't think he could throw yet and was hoping for a return by Saturday's scrimmage game against Saint Mary's. It was now ten days since he first hurt his arm, and not only could he not throw, he had yet to be even checked out by a doctor.

"I could leave your bat in the lineup by making you the DH, but it's been ten days now, Kevin. Don't you think you ought to get checked by an orthopedic doctor?" I asked.

"Yeah, my father is going to call a guy he knows and get an appointment," he answered.

As Picardo left, Renshaw exploded. "What is with him? At this point, the kid should either be back on the field or have gotten it checked out by now. Scott, what are we going to do? We open in two weeks, and we don't have a shortstop!"

Trongone entered the office and placed two fungo bats in the corner. "Just had a great practice, and we're ready for Wayne Hills tomorrow."

"I just don't see anyone who wants it in Kevin's absence," I said. "If I'm a backup and the starting shortstop goes down, I'd be showing the coach a 'hit-it-to-me' attitude. So far, no one's done that. No one!"

"Joe D'Annunzio, Moose. I'm telling you the kid can come up right now and get it done for you," said Trongone.

Joe D'Annunzio was a little fourteen-year-old boy, fresh out of the eighth grade. He was tiny, standing only five foot four and weighing 135 pounds. He had done an outstanding job as an eighth grader for our junior high team and seemed to be a very promising infielder with good feet and hands. But, could he physically make the jump to varsity baseball? And if that was possible, would he be able to emotionally handle such a transition?

"He is young for his grade, but I think he can do it. He's got balls, Moose!" said Trongone. "I'm telling you, he's got balls. He's not one of those 'poodles' that you talk about."

D'Annunzio had been described by several parents as a "cute little kid," the kind you want to pick up like a teddy bear. I first met him years back when he had attended my summer camp as an elementary student.

When I called him into my office, I noticed that he wasn't just small, D'Annunzio also had a baby face. The boy was a fourteen-year-old freshman but actually looked younger than his age. He seemed petrified as I spoke. I explained to him that because of an injury, I would like to take him with us to our scrimmage tomorrow and look at him. He may have tried to speak, but nothing really came out. He just nodded okay while grunting something that sounded a little like an okay. As he walked out, I called him back.

"Joe," I said, "you wouldn't be here if we weren't already impressed with you. Relax, have some fun, and enjoy yourself out there."

He smiled, tried to speak, and again grunted something that resembled an okay.

Joe D'Annunzio began a four-year stint as our varsity second baseman as only a fourteen-year-old freshman in 2006.

Renshaw and I would stand side-by-side in our dugout in front of a sign that read "Never tell a Knight he can't do something—believe!" In the first inning against Wayne Hills, a ball was hit through our shortstop's legs for an error.

Renshaw tapped me, "What are we waiting for? We're two weeks away. Let's get the kid in there and see what he's got."

I nodded and inserted D'Annunzio at shortstop. Raimondo had worked two scoreless innings. I removed him. He asked me if he could throw one more inning, but given his prior injury and the thirty-eight-degree temperature, I was adamant that he was done for the day.

"Go run ten foul poles," I told him as I inserted Cerza on the mound. Cerza was terrific, pitching two scoreless innings while striking out two and walking none. D'Annunzio made a fantastic play on a ground ball, fully extended to his glove side. Then, he fielded a routine ground ball for one of Cerza's six putouts. He also made a fantastic play to his backhand side on a ball hit into the hole between shortstop and third, but the runner was safe. The next hitter hit a line drive at D'Annunzio, which he caught and threw to Mark Ruggiero, covering second for an inning-ending double play. His teammates mobbed him as they ran off the field.

Renshaw came over to me. "Coach, the kid can play!"

"Yes, he can, R. Finally, someone who wants the ball hit to him," I said.

When we got down into our locker room, I called Cerza into the hallway.

"Anthony, you've looked very good so far. We may have lost a scrimmage today, but we came away as winners by answering some questions, and you're one of them. You've come a long way, and now you've earned an opportunity to pitch for us."

"Thanks, Coach," he answered, beaming from ear to ear.

The next day, Picardo approached me in the hallway between classes.

"Coach, the results came back. My labrum's torn. I need surgery to fix it, but I want to play this season. I'll do some therapy and do the best I can."

"Kevin, you can't be the everyday shortstop with a torn labrum in your shoulder," I responded.

I couldn't afford to lose Kevin's bat in our lineup. I could have asked him to be our everyday designated hitter, but Steve Zurawiecki was showing some pop in his bat, and I needed his excellent speed in our lineup. I had an idea. A few years prior, I had heard Notre Dame coach Paul Manieri say that Notre Dame would at times recruit several shortstops, put the best defensive player at shortstop, and then put the other players who had played shortstop in high school at the other three infield positions. The loss of Will Courter had left a void at first base.

We had two other prospects at first base in senior Santo Barretta and in a promising sophomore prospect named Frank Firavanti. Barretta was a quality player. He was defensively reliable, and as a left-handed hitter, he had a good stroke. But I really felt that we had to have both Kevin's and Steve's bats in our lineup. Like Barretta, Firavanti was also victimized by the fact that Kevin had to move to first base, as that diminished his chances for more playing time. This would be an unfortunate numbers-game break for both players, but more so for Barretta, who was in his final season. Firavanti, had two years remaining, and his time as an everyday player would soon come.

"Have you ever played first base before?" I asked Kevin.

"Umm, no, Coach. I've never played first in my life. Don't they use a different kind of glove or something?" he asked

"Don't worry about that right now. When we get to Verona today, I want you to play there," I said.

On the bus ride over to Verona, I explained the move to Renshaw. He was surprised.

"What, Kevin? First?" he asked.

"Yes, R. C., Paul Manieri theory. Put top athletes at each infield position."

"Okay. What did Kevin say when you told him?" he asked.

"He was stunned, but I told him that's how it's going to be," I responded.

During the game at Verona, Joe D'Annunzio made two errors: under his glove and through his legs. He later came back and made a play on a routine ground ball.

That night, I tossed and turned through a sleepless night. I wondered, could a fourteen-year-old freshman handle the pressure that comes with being a varsity shortstop? Is it fair to even ask it of him? I got up to shower at 5:45 a.m. after barely sleeping a wink. At 6:45 a.m., on my way to school, I called Renshaw from my car.

I informed him that I was up all night, and I had decided that I was moving Mark Ruggiero to shortstop and Joe D'Annunzio to second base. Mark was not a shortstop. After Kevin, no one in our program was, but Mark was an experienced infielder, and he was a fierce competitor. There would be less pressure on D'Annunzio at second base, and I wanted a senior in the more demanding shortstop position. I made up my mind Picardo would move from shortstop to first base, Ruggiero would move from second base to shortstop, and D'Annunzio would earn the second-base job.

Renshaw felt D'Annunzio at short might be the better option, because that would require us to make fewer changes.

"Wait," he said. "Let's give it one more game. One more game, and if we don't like what we see out of Joe, then we'll do it."

"No, I'm doing it today," I answered. "If I do it today, he'll have at least one scrimmage there before the opener."

I tracked Ruggiero down in the hallway by his locker.

"Mark, have you ever played shortstop?" I asked him.

"Umm, no, Coach. I've been a second baseman my whole life," he answered.

"Mark, I'm moving you to shortstop. You're the best infielder I have, and I need you to step up and play there," I explained

"I can do it, Coach. I'll do it!" he responded.

Renshaw opened the door to the coaches' office before practice and asked me how it went with Mark. He wanted to know what Mark had said to me when I informed him of the change.

"It wasn't what he said, R. C.," I explained. "I knew that he would say yes. It was the way that he looked at me. The look in his eyes told me everything I needed to know."

CHAPTER 13

Safe Is Death!

The problem isn't the problem. How you handle
the problem. That's the problem!

—Dr. Rob Gilbert
Sports Psychologist
Montclair State University

ONE WEEK BEFORE OUR opening game against Morris Hills, the team met in my classroom for a lesson on sports psychology and to outline our plan. I held a small black pot in my hand. In the pot there were several small BBs. I slowly dropped the BBs into the pot; they made a loud trickling sound.

"Everyone has a little voice in their mind. That little voice talks to you constantly throughout the day," I said. "When you're faced with a challenge, what does that little voice in your mind tell you?" Again, I dropped the BBs inside the pot.

On the chalkboard I had written the word "problem" with two capital Fs underneath. The Fs were a way of classifying the two ways that one can deal with a problem. You could either get "frustrated" or you could get "fascinated." Fascination beats frustration every single time!

"Sarah's mother has three daughters. One's named Penny, the other's named Nickel. What's the name of the third daughter?" I asked the team.

"Dime," answered Baab.

I shook my head.

"Sarah!" answered Caprio. "If Sarah's mother had three daughters, and the other two are named Penny and Nickel, then Sarah is the third daughter."

Caprio had nailed it. The obvious answer would be the name of another coin, but I wanted my players to understand that in order to solve problems effectively, you must think outside the box!

I also wanted them to think about what their own little voice in their mind told them when they were presented with a challenge.

"Try this one," I said. "What happens once in a minute, twice in a moment, but never in a thousand years?"

"An eclipse," answered Dalonges. The whole team laughed.

"C'mon boys. Think outside the box!" I said.

"The letter *M*," answered Zurawiecki. "*M* is used once in a minute, twice in a moment, but not in a thousand years."

I wanted to know if they had become frustrated or fascinated by the problems.

"Do you get turned on by difficult things?" I asked.

Underneath the word problem on the board, I wrote A + S. The A stood for the word *ability*, and the S stood for the word *strategy*. Underneath A + S I drew a slash with the letters PMA, which stood for *positive mental attitude*. This served as our formula for problem solving: Ability + Strategy, divisible by Positive Mental Attitude.

I told a story to illustrate the point.

"Years ago, our astronauts encountered a problem," I explained. "They couldn't write anything in outer space, because their pens would not write when they were floating upside down. In order to solve the problem, they looked into what strategy the Russians were using. The Russians used pencils. You can solve any problem. All you need is the right strategy. As a baseball team, what's the biggest problem we'll encounter?"

"A really good pitcher," answered Valerian.

He was exactly right. The biggest obstacle we would face was a top-flight scholarship pitcher. We were not a power-hitting team. Instead, most of our hits were singles. Therefore, I asked them, how many hits does it take for us to score a run? The players all agreed that it typically took us three hits to score one run.

"So let's assume on a good day we get nine hits; how many runs do we score?" I asked.

"Only three," answered Ruggiero.

We knew that we could not expect to win too many games if we only scored three runs, and it would be a good day when the hits would come easy. This was the most critical point that I needed my team to understand: Occasionally, there would be games against weaker opponents when we would pound out thirteen hits. When that happened, we would kind of just sit back and allow things to happen for us. However, I wasn't training them to beat a lower-tier team with their right fielder on the mound. I was trying to train them to beat a nationally ranked power with the best pitcher in the country on the mound. If we saw a pitcher of that caliber, we could not expect to rack up thirteen hits. It was more realistic for us to hope for three or maybe four hits against a scholarship pitcher. How then could we score enough runs to win with such a shortage of hits?

"Are we just going to give in and say this guy is too good for us? Say we can't win? Or do we come up with a strategy to beat him?" I asked.

We would have to come up with a strategy. We needed to devise a strategy for us to beat the best when they were at their best. That meant that our strategy had to be so well planned that we could have a chance to beat Nutley with their ace, Rob Gariano, on the mound or beat Seton Hall Prep with their ace, Rick Porcello, on the mound. If we were training to beat the Boston Red Sox, our strategy had to somehow be good enough to beat Josh Beckett. The team sat silently in a focused manner.

"In 1997, there was an award winning ad for Apple Computers," I said. "The theme of the ad was 'Think Differently!' They called the people in the ad the crazy ones, the ones who saw things differently, the round pegs in the square holes. Who were these crazy ones? Only some of the most successful people in the world: Albert Einstein, Bob Dylan, Martin Luther King Jr., Thomas Edison, Muhammad Ali, Ted Turner, Muhatma Gandhi, Picasso. They didn't think conventionally. They thought outside the box. They saw things differently. Conventional baseball wisdom says that teams should only look at their batting averages and how many home runs they hit. We need to think unconventionally and see things differently."

I pointed to the board where I had written the five keys to our offensive strategy:

1) Base on balls (BB)
2) Hit by pitch
3) Bunting
4) Two-strike hitting
5) Aggressive and intelligent base running

"How can we find ways to score if we only get three hits?" I asked.

We would need to draw at least a couple of walks in the game. Therefore, we would practice count hitting in every batting practice session in order to develop discipline during our at bats. If we were to get hit by a pitch we could also put additional runners on base. I had initially taught my players the importance of eliminating the fear of being hit by a pitch and as a safety precaution taught them how to best avoid a serious injury in the event they were ever struck by a ball. We often practiced this using a soft "Incredi-Ball." The key coaching point that aided in our safety was to first get your face and head out of the way by turning toward the umpire, and then we would lock our feet and roll with the pitch. What started out as a safety drill somehow became a bit of a pride issue among our players, as our teams would routinely finish with more hit batsmen than we had games played, with a good percentage of those runners eventually turning into runs scored. This also made opposing pitchers afraid to pitch inside against our hitters.

We would spend hours practicing bunting. I felt that it was easier to bunt a pitch than it was to hit one against a scholarship pitcher, and my experience had taught me that even excellent teams often misplayed bunts. Pitchers often bore down with runners on base, especially on third, so the safety squeeze bunt and suicide squeeze bunt would serve as a huge component of our plan. I believed that, in many cases, it would be easier for our players to bunt a run home than it would be to drive one home.

"How do you practice hitting into an error where the other team boots the ball?" I asked.

Some of that could be luck, but we believed that we could actually practice hitting into an error and increase our chances of doing so by consistently getting the ball in play with two strikes on our hitter. Therefore, we practiced two-strike hitting in every round and drill that our hitters did.

Having speed in our line up was important to us because we knew that it would show up every day, even on those days when we might hit a few line drives right at the defense. We would run the bases intelligently and as aggressively as we possibly could, under the premise that the more pressure that you place on your opponents, the more likely they will be to make a mistake.

"Aggressiveness wins out," I explained to the boys.

Mark Messier once told Hall of Fame defenseman Brian Leetch, who played for the New York Rangers, that some of the greatest plays he would ever make would just miss being his biggest mistakes.

My belief was that it was better to go all out and lose than it was to play it safe and win, because when you played it safe, you were training yourself to always play it safe, and I knew that when it came to facing a great pitcher, "safe" would be our death!

I also knew that if we were to ever beat a scholarship-caliber pitcher, it would only be because we had the guts to take chances and make things happen. If we sat back and waited for thirteen hits, they would never come. We would have to think unconventionally, outside the box, and be as aggressive as possible in order to pressure our opponents into mistakes.

"Safe is death," I told the players. "You have to press the defense."

"Would you rather be a lion for a day or a mouse for life?" I asked the team.

That is why we didn't always play by the book. We would sometimes steal third with two outs, knowing that we could get thrown out. We would run first and third trick plays. We attempted to steal home too.

At the 2010 Winter Olympics, US skier Lindsay Vonn was asked what she was thinking before her gold-medal run.

"Thirteen words," said Vonn. "I've got to just do it. Go for it. Don't hold anything back!"

"There will be times when we will make mistakes and times when we will hear groans in the stands. You can't hold back. You can't be afraid to make a mistake," I pleaded.

The moment players become afraid to make a mistake is when they will, because their fear will cause them to hesitate and play tentatively.

I knew that we could turn those groans in the stands into cheers. Instead of screaming "What the hell is he doing?" If the play were to work then they would all scream, "What a move!"

"Would you rather fight the warrior who wants to conquer or the warrior who is not afraid to die?" I asked the team.

"The warrior who has no fear is far more dangerous!"

CHAPTER 14

Rise Above It

Great spirits are always faced with violent opposition from mediocre minds.
—Einstein

I HIT A BALL to Mark Ruggiero. We had days left to make him a shortstop before our season opened. He threw to Picardo, who was simultaneously attempting to become a first baseman. The transition was easier for Picardo. His problem was that he was stretching his leading foot out too soon before seeing where the ball was thrown. As a result, he could not recover on throws to his left or right. With some drill work, he made rapid progress.

Ruggiero's struggles were different. As a lifetime second baseman, he knew nothing else. He had never played any other position. One of the luxuries of being a second baseman is that you have more time to complete the play than a shortstop does. As a result, Mark had developed the habit of taking an extra shuffle step toward first base prior to making his throw. When he did this at shortstop, it took him too long to make the play. By the time he finished shuffling and made the throw, the runner would already have safely reached first base.

In order to break his habit, I put him on a stopwatch. Mike Bustamante hit a ground ball to Mark, while I timed him with the stopwatch. With his extra shuffle, he registered a time of 4.6. Good runners could reach first base in 4.2 or less. I instructed Mark not to be concerned with where his throw went, but, no matter what, he was not to take the extra shuffle step. On the next play, Mark eliminated the extra shuffle and recorded a time of 3.8. His throw was a little erratic but within Picardo's reach. It would be a work in progress to get Mark to break this habit. It would not come easily and would require countless repetitions, but this was something that Mark wanted very badly.

Hula hoops lay on the ground in our infield. They came straight from Toys"R"Us and served as targets for where we should bunt the ball on each specific bunting play. We would place them toward the third-base line or hard by the pitcher on a base-hit attempt; on the green grass and out of the reach of both the pitcher and the catcher on a sacrifice attempt; and away from the foul line on a suicide to avoid the ball from rolling foul.

I watched a few of our players neglect attention to detail as they tried to sprint out of the batter's box on a safety suicide bunt attempt. They were neglecting their objective, which was to score a run, not to get themselves on base. I couldn't stand all the mistakes I was seeing. I called them in.

"At 211 degrees water is hot. At 212 degrees water boils. With boiling water comes steam, and steam can power a locomotive. One extra degree makes all the difference. Just one!" I screamed.

"Do you guys know the difference between the first-place and second-place finishers in the luge at the Olympics in Italy this past winter?" I asked.

The team was silent

"One point one second! Just one and one-tenth of a second between a champion and all the rest. Our league is outstanding from top to bottom. When we get out there against the teams in our league, the difference is only gonna be one degree, one second, one pitch!" I yelled.

"Rob, have you ever been bitten by an elephant?" I asked.

Rob was Rob Nichols. He was built on the frail side. I had a conversation with Rob after our tryout period. He came out for the team as a second baseman, and at some point I sat down with him and told him how much I appreciated his hustle and love of baseball. However, it was unlikely that Rob would earn the innings that he wanted or any at all. Rob was unique. He didn't seem to mind.

"Coach, I just want to be on the team," he said. Rob was funny, hysterical actually. He would often explain to me what great lengths he would go to in order to do less schoolwork. He had every angle figured out. When I explained that was detrimental to him, he would agree, but he was far too happy to change it.

"Um, no, Coach. I've never been bitten by an elephant," Rob answered.

"How 'bout a mosquito?" I asked.

"Yeah, all the time."

"Right, 'cause it's the little things that get ya. Dammit, don't you guys get that?" I asked. "Little things mean a lot in baseball. If you don't do the little things right, then we will always lose 2–1! Why are you not paying attention to detail? Do you know why it bothers me when you don't do the little things right?"

"Because they're the easiest things to do!" I exploded.

I grabbed my gym bag and took out a sponge and a sieve. Then I opened a bottled water.

Rob Nichols, a great team guy.

"It's amazing how one player absorbs everything that we've taught, while another player in the same place, at the same time, hearing the same information, just lets it pass right through."

I poured the water into the sieve and watched it seep through to the ground. I threw the sieve across the field and took out the sponge. I poured water into the sponge and showed them how it absorbed the water.

"What are you—a sponge or a sieve?" I asked. "Do you soak in the details and finer points of the game? You'd better think about it now, so you don't have to think about it later! Because if you've gotta think about it later, you'll have just been beaten 2–1. Do you guys want to win?"

The team answered yes.

"Well, what kind of half-hearted effort are you giving me? Every team says they want to win, but are you willing to do whatever it takes to win? Morris Hills, Mendham, and Hanover Park wanna win too! If you want something that others want, then you have to do what others aren't willing to do in order to get it. You think Hanover Park is as lazy and unfocused as you are right now?" I asked them.

Ruggiero put his head down, "No, Coach!"

"When I was a kid, my grandfather, rest his soul, bent down and picked up a penny. Then he looked over and said to me, "You know, I can become rich by doing that."

I said, "What do you mean grandpa? You could pick up hundreds and hundreds of pennies and it still won't make you rich."

He looked at me and said, "The pennies won't, but the habit will, because most people will never take the time to stop, bend down, and pick up a penny."

"Ever since that day, when I see a penny, it reminds me that I've got an opportunity to do something that others aren't willing to do," I explained.

"What kind of habits are you building right now in practice? Are you willing to fight through the pain? The physical pain, the emotional pain? 'Cause if you want to get what we've never had, then you must do what we've never done!"

The month of March was crucial and demanding. I was already feeling the stress of training camp. No matter what, you never feel as if you're completely ready for the opener. Even before camp started, I had spent every waking minute in the classroom teaching, in the gym, on the field coaching, or planning for all of the above. Suddenly, it became more stressful.

The ring of my phone almost knocked me out of my bed. It was my girlfriend, Jane.

The season placed strain on relationships. The time constraints could make anyone frustrated—even the most understanding girl. I had pointed out to my staff one evening that I really didn't need to find a girl who knew that 2–1 would be a good count to put on a hit-and-run play. I didn't need that in a relationship at all. I didn't need someone who cared about baseball or even liked baseball. I just needed to be with a person who understood what coaching meant to me and how passionate I was about it. That was it for me. Jane got that. She had brothers who were excellent athletes, and she was one herself. Her family had grown up playing sports. Not only did she understand my passion and commitment to coaching, but she went out of her way to actively follow our team.

I picked up the phone.

"You're not going to be happy," said Jane.

"Why is that?" I asked, perplexed.

"Did you see the paper? Al Williams ripped you apart."

She had just read one of Williams' season previews. She read it to me over the phone. By now I was used to the fact that he would report that I had yet to win a title. I expected that. But, what blew me away was that he actually predicted that we wouldn't win one this season either.

"Hey, Coach, what's with Al Williams dissin' us?" John Baab asked me upon my arrival at practice that day. John's question put in perspective for me that while Williams attempted to take me down, he actually hurt our kids, in spite of the fact that his job description required him to promote them.

I called Williams.

"When you put those little quotation marks around the words, that's an indication that they came out of a person's mouth right?" I asked. "I never said anything about winning a title, Al. You wrote quote, 'I can't tell you, for sure, that we're going to win a championship and I can't tell you, for sure that we're going to finish with a winning record.' I never made that statement. When you asked me about our chances of winning one, I told you that I guarantee three things: we'll be well organized, we'll be well prepared, and we'll work real hard. You can just make up words that I never said and put quotes around them?" "Oh, I just combine things," answered Williams. It seemed to me that he dismissed my complaint. The tone in his voice sounded to me like he was contradicting me.

I had given him over a half-hour interview so he could write a preview about our upcoming season. He ignored almost all of that information.

"When you did this last year you never heard a word from me because you reported fact. But this time you editorialized your own opinion about kids. These are kids, Al. They're not professionals. They're not scholarship athletes. We can't recruit like the private schools either. We're a public school. Why don't you let Mike Lupica tear down the Yankees in the *Daily News,* and you start promoting kids who give the best that they have?"

"What's the matter, Coach, are you or are you not the winningest program in the school that has no titles over the past ten years since you've been the head coach?" he asked. "The football team has won three in the past five years; the field hockey team wins almost every year. Soccer, lacrosse, softball, wrestling, they've all won titles. Everyone can win a title except for you."

For the second time, I called him on his alliance with the Cartwright family. I told him that his agenda to garner support against me was pretty clear when he had written the first article a year ago, but now his most recent negative slant had made it blatantly obvious. I openly accused him of writing those articles because he was in cahoots with the Cartwright family. He did not deny it. If my accusation was false he could have denied it and fired back at me, but he didn't say a word. You could hear the crickets on the other end of the line. I was about to speak again but waited an extra moment just to see if he would even try to rebut what I had alleged; he didn't come back with anything. He just sat silently on the other end, while the two of us experienced an awkward silence.

Realizing that he was not going to deny my accusation, I tried to defend myself from his attack. I felt that baseball could not be compared to those other sports.

"It's the only sport where the defense has the ball, Al."

I also explained that we had played up to the level of our competition.

"But no titles!" he said.

"Al, these kids haven't played one inning yet! Before they have even played a single inning you predict that they can't win a title? I could understand if we were 5–15 and you wrote us off, but we are 0–0 and you don't even give us a chance?" I asked.

"The *Star-Ledger* predicts football games all the time" he said.

"Yeah, Al, they predict games. I wouldn't say anything if you predicted that we might lose a game, but you predicted failure for us for the entire season."

"Everything I wrote was true," he responded.

"You know what, Al, you've never hung in on a curveball. You've never driven to the lane, and you've never had to bear down on a first-and-goal, but you're a real warrior behind that typewriter of yours. You're trying so damn hard to get me, that you didn't even realize that you demoralized kids who you're supposed to be promoting, kids who represent our school and community as well as one could expect. The next time you want to write a story about West Essex baseball, you're going to have to go back to those same parents you are in cahoots with for your information, because I've given you my last interview!" I said, slamming the phone down.

That evening Jane and I were at dinner. One of my flaws is that I carry the games with me away from the field into a relationship. I carry it all: the errors, the mistakes, the near misses, and now, the win-or-else pressure too.

There were times we would be out on a Saturday night and someone would talk to me. I didn't want to put anyone off or ever be rude to anyone, but sometimes I wouldn't hear a word. Instead, my mind would be back in the fourth inning somewhere.

"I can tell you're not yourself tonight," said Jane.

"I'm sure it's not fair, but culturally, we're only judged on whether we win or lose. The scariest part about it is that my success is dependent on sixteen-year-olds, and I don't always know where the mind of a sixteen-year-old is. If he plays well, I'm a genius. If he fails, I get fired for being a moron."

"Wait! Aren't these just high school kids? Aren't you supposed to just teach them how to play and be a good role model and stuff?" Jane asked.

"I've got a job that people care about. There's a lot of doctors, lawyers, and accountants who make mistakes every day, and nobody knows it. Me, if I make a mistake, if I fail, it's all over every newspaper and all over the Internet. How'd you like to read about your mistakes in the morning paper?"

"I don't know how you do it. I could never!" she said.

Then Jane got real quiet.

I asked her what was wrong.

She explained that she was torn between knowing how stressed I was and not wanting to keep anything from me. I told her to come clean with me.

"My brother was on one of those chat forums on the Internet the other night. There were a bunch of posts on there, and someone said that you are jinxed, and as long as you are at West Essex they will never win anything. I didn't want to bring it up or hurt your feelings. I just can't keep anything from you, and I want you to know that I'm here for you, to love and support you, and I don't know what to say other than I'm here," she said.

"I have to act like a hawk," I replied.

"A what? What are you talking about?" she asked.

A while back I had heard a message on Ed Agresta's *Power Thoughts* hotline. His message had made quite an impression on me. It was about hawks. Evidently, hawks have an innate ability to fly higher than other birds. When rival birds fly close to a hawk, the hawk ascends, flying in a circular motion. With each passing circle, the hawk rises higher and higher until it is above the other birds.

"That's what I think of when I get ripped apart," I said, after I explained the story. "Just rise above it!"

Chapter 15

Poodles

Decide that you want it more than you're afraid of it!
—Bill Cosby
Comedian and Actor

Training camp was drawing to a close. With the exception of some typical soreness, Raimondo's arm was healthy. Zurawiecki had shown significant improvement by throwing strikes in his preseason outings. Bustamante had shown to be effective as well. Both Cerza and Tundo's body of work was short after being delayed by injury, but they had pitched admirably when called upon.

Cordasco was still wearing his neck brace, which left a huge opening-day void in two places, center field and on the mound.

During one of the last few practices, I called Dalonges over.

"No one could have ever predicted that Mikey would fracture his vertebrae," I said, "but in his absence you've stepped forward and made the most of your opportunity. Come Saturday, you're the starting center fielder. Congratulations, Anthony. I'm proud of you."

Dalonges was beaming. "Thanks, Coach."

Ruggiero was doing the best that he could to become a shortstop, but that would not come overnight. D'Annunzio was showing that he belonged in our infield as each day passed, but I was uncertain if I should let him bat in our lineup. If I used a designated hitter for him, I could allow our pitchers to hit instead. However, through our training camp he had hung in there and held his own during his turns at bat, which made my decision tougher. I also had reservations about Picardo being at first base, knowing that his shoulder had been rendered useless, and he couldn't throw. How long could we really hide that weakness and get away with it? This dilemma made me consider making Picardo the everyday designated hitter, but I was struggling with the idea of removing Zurawiecki's speed from our lineup. I was more in favor of leaving him at the designated hitter position and leaving Picardo at first base in spite of his injured shoulder. This was a tough call though. What if Picardo had to start a double play at second base or throw a runner out at the plate?

"We are who we are," Renshaw would say. "That's our best team, whether he can throw or not. We'll have to live with it and just ride it out."

Kevin Picardo was a big part of our team too. He was well respected by his peers and had a locker room presence. So much so that he was chosen as the one to carry "the rope" to each game.

Skip Bertman's high school coach once stretched out a long rope in front of his team and held onto one end of it. Then he asked them, "If you were hanging off the edge of a cliff, and holding onto one end of this rope, and there was nothing beneath you other than a one-thousand-foot fall and your certain death, who would you want hanging onto the other end of the rope?"

Most guys on the team would give the customary answers: my brother, my father, my best friend, my cousin. However, as Bertman pointed out, "When you answer, 'any one of my teammates, it doesn't matter which one,' that's when we can become a team. That's when we'll become one and go to a place where only teams can go."

When our team would encounter tense moments, "Hold onto the rope!" would become our motto as an expression of togetherness.

I asked our woodshop teacher, Lee Oberg, to make the rope that our team would bring to each game and keep in our dugout. On one end there was a metal hook that we could attach to either a backstop fence or a hook in a dugout. On the other end of the rope was a baseball that Oberg had drilled a hole through in order for the rope to be looped through and then tied in a knot. The person I made responsible for taking this rope to and from each game was Kevin. This was an important responsibility, and one that could not be taken lightly. Kevin never did. He made it a priority to carry it with him and to always have it in a place where our team could see it during our games.

In addition to our rope, I would also ask one of our seniors to bring a sledgehammer known as "the ant killer." I borrowed this motivational tool from Rick Jones at Tulane University. The sledgehammer was about twelve inches long and very heavy. On one side it read "ant killer" in black ink going from top to bottom. On the other side we would make one slash mark for each victory that we earned. The premise behind the term "ant killer" as described by Jones was: "If you kick over an ant hill you will just incite the ants. But, if you take a sledgehammer to it, it will finish the job!" That sledgehammer went wherever we went and reminded us that no game is ever over until that final out is recorded. It motivated us to finish off teams when we could, and not quit when we were down. Mark Ruggiero took great pride in carrying the "ant killer." He guarded it with his life in his locker. It became a big deal to him, and he welcomed that responsibility.

On April 1, we took "the rope," the "ant killer," and also a plastic "flush-it" toilet bowl and boarded a bus for Morris Hills for our season-opening game. Morris Hills was a perennial twenty-win team. In New Jersey baseball, twenty wins was a barometer for an outstanding season. They had won our conference several times since the mid '90s, and this particular team had at least five players who would continue their careers in college. The most notable one of these was their starting pitcher, Chris McGlynn, who had accepted a scholarship to Seton Hall University.

We spotted them an early 1–0 lead. In the top of the third inning, Mark Ruggiero reached on an error by their second baseman. John Baab singled. Then, Nick Santomauro blasted a towering three-run home run, putting us up 3–1. Our dugout erupted as the ball exploded off Santomauro's bat.

The rope, plastic toilet bowl, crystal baseball, and sledgehammer are motivational tools that I borrowed from coaches Skip Bertman of LSU and Rick Jones of Tulane to help inspire the West Essex baseball team.

Morris Hills answered with two runs to tie it in the bottom of the fourth as Vin Valerian made an error at third base, and Anthony Dalonges misjudged a ball in center field that went for a triple. The runner at third then scored on a groundout to Ruggiero at shortstop.

In the sixth inning, Santomauro hit another towering home run. Kevin Picardo got hit by a pitch, stole second base, and then scored on a single by Steve Zurawiecki, giving us a 5–3 lead.

After four innings, Raimondo's pitch count was up. It was early and cold, so I replaced him with Bustamante. Raimondo allowed three runs on four hits with no walks, a hit batsman, and one strikeout. Bustamante worked a scoreless fifth. In the bottom of the sixth inning, Morris Hills added a run from another error by Valerian at third base with two outs to lessen our lead to 5–4. In the seventh, we added two more runs and led 7–4, needing only three more outs as we headed to the bottom of the seventh.

After getting their number-eight hitter to ground out, Bustamante allowed a double to the number-nine hitter and then walked two straight to load the bases. Then, he walked his third straight hitter to force a run home. I replaced him with Anthony Cerza, who proceeded to walk his first hitter also forcing in a run and now making it a 7–6 game. Then Valerian unraveled. The next hitter hit a tailor-made ground ball to him at third base. He should have thrown to home plate to prevent a run and to record an out, but he seemed confused as to where he should throw. Instead, he hesitated, looked around, and inexplicably threw to second base for a force-out, while allowing the tying run to score, making it a 7–7 game. The next ground ball was also hit to Valerian. He looked like a deer in headlights as he misplayed it off his glove for his second error in the inning and fourth for the game; Morris Hills celebrated wildly at home plate as they walked off with the win.

My heart was in my throat. I fought hard to remain composed in my postgame remarks.

Renshaw couldn't contain himself as he erupted.

Every player's head was down. There were even a few players who did not play that day who were visibly upset.

Wayne McCullough was a senior outfielder and was clearly dismayed by the team's performance. He put forth as much effort in practices as any player I have coached. There were instances when he would dive across the gym floor and make a thundering thud when his body crashed down. I was concerned that his relentless efforts could lead him to injure himself. But Wayne, a very proud young man, knew no other way. Where, in most instances, coaches would seek more effort from players, in Wayne's case I would actually hope for less at times, so that he could remain healthy.

Rich Buonomo was also distraught over the outcome. Rich was a senior and played third base. He was a National Honor Society student who did everything to the best of his ability. He was smart, paid careful attention to detail, and his daily approach to our drill work and team preparation was evidence of just how much of a team player he was.

Players who may not have started regularly were a key part of our team. They, in many ways, were like the oil in a car engine. Without them, the motor could not run. Each and every starter relied on those guys so that they could drill with one another and compete in practices. Just as a football team needed a scout team, a baseball team needed depth on the bench in order to compete with one another in practice. Guys like this made our motor work. They made our starters better, and without them, we would not be the same. They knew that their roles were unsung, but they also knew their value to our team. When we lost, they felt it just as much as any other player.

You could hear a pin drop on the bus ride home. Before we had gotten on the bus, Renshaw had looked at me, completely distraught.

"Scott," he said, "I don't know how you do it. It's the same thing every year. We're good enough to compete, but we'll always make a stupid mistake or an error or just find a way to lose. I don't know if I can do it anymore." RC was such a fierce competitor. He wanted to win more than anyone. I could tell the frustration that he felt from a loss this painful was tearing him apart. I had seen him blow off steam in moments of frustration before, but I had never seen him this upset. We were only one game into the season.

We had needed only two outs with no one on base and a three-run lead in the seventh inning, and we managed to blow it. Morris Hills earned only one hit in that fateful inning, as we handed the game to them, committing five walks and two errors. We had also wasted two home runs off of a Division I pitcher by Santomauro.

As our bus drove along Route 80, Santo Barretta spoke to Nick about his two home runs.

"That kid McGlynn was good." said Barretta. "I think he was throwin' eighty-six."

"That wasn't eighty-six, that was more like eighty-three," replied Santomauro.

This caused Renshaw, who was eavesdropping, to once again erupt. He got up out of his seat, stood in front of them, and screamed, "It's a loss. That's what he was *throwin'!* He threw a *loss*, that's what he threw, and that's what we did. *We lost!*"

I sat on my couch with the New Balance sneaker in my hand. My doorbell rang. It was Jane.

"Hey, I brought your favorite chicken parmesan from Macaroni Grill. Maybe it'll cheer you up," she said.

The problem was that I couldn't eat.

"Did you get new sneakers?" she asked.

"No."

"Then whose are they? Where's the other one?"

"The fact that I don't know, and the fact that the person who owns them doesn't know either, is actually the reason that I have it."

"What are you talking about?" she asked.

I explained to her exactly how I had acquired the New Balance sneaker, and how it was a reminder to me as to why I couldn't quit.

"Maybe it was an accident. Maybe the sneaker fell out of someone's bag or something," Jane said.

"You have to see it, Jane. Polos, Hilfigers, Nautica, Armani, the best name brands that money can buy just lying on the locker room floor," I replied.

It has been said that perhaps the best way to create a handicap in young children is to give them too much money. When I was growing up, I was taught to take care of what I had been provided. Everything had to last and that reality made me hungry to earn things. It was my belief that anything lasting or worthwhile was usually gained through substantial effort.

"If I ever forgot my New Balance sneaker on the floor, I'd have gone home with one bare foot, Jane, because I never had an extra pair," I said.

"So what's your point?" she asked.

"Have you ever seen the Westminster Dog Show at Madison Square Garden? Well, picture one of the dog owners walking his perfectly groomed and manicured white poodle. Somehow it breaks free from its leash and runs down the streets of Manhattan into a dark alley and encounters a pit bull right off the streets. Who wins that fight, the white poodle or the street dog?" I asked.

"Obviously, the street dog," she replies.

That was my point. In order to be successful in baseball, you have to have that tough streak in you—just like the street dog. As a competitor, you need an edge or a chip on your shoulder. My high school coach, Mr. Jack Lynch, whose number twenty-one I would wear on my jersey as a tribute to the influence that he had on me as a young teenager, told us that in order to be a good baseball player you "had to have a set of leather balls."

In many instances, if you were to drive through a high school parking lot you would very often find that many of the cars driven by students are far nicer than those driven by teachers. Is it possible that some of those kids attain rewards too easily at an early age? Is it possible that their culture conditions them to never have to be hungry for something and consequently to never have to face any adversity? If this is true, then how could they handle pressure if they had never been pressed in their lives?

Jane had played basketball when she was younger. "You played basketball," I said. "Who gets the rebounds most often in a basketball game? It's not always the tallest person. It's the one who wants it the most."

"North Caldwell doesn't have a single traffic light in the entire town, Jane. Many of our opponents come from communities which are often described as blue collar. Their kids have that streak of toughness in them. They don't have as much. They have a lot less handed to them. They've got that hunger. I wonder sometimes if we do. Was the meltdown that we had today the result of a lack of talent, or was it the impact of culture? Once we felt the pressure of the late innings, suddenly we couldn't throw a strike or pick up a routine ground ball. If we did, then we didn't even know what to do with it. Today was just a small sample of the past ten years I've been at West Essex," I said.

Jane challenged my thinking.

"How come our football team wins? Those kids are tough," she said, pointing out the incredible run of success by our football program and our outstanding coach, Dave Drozjock.

She was right. Football players are tough—physically. Baseball, however, is a sport that is based solely on a different kind of toughness—mental toughness. What unique factors make baseball a game that has been described by many as "cruel" and "hurtful"? How come it requires such a high level of mental toughness?

For one, the failure rate associated with the skill of hitting is evident, as most players, even those elected to the Hall of Fame in Cooperstown, failed nearly seven out of every ten times that they came to bat. There is also an often-overlooked aspect of the game that creates pressure and places high demands on the individual: baseball is the only sport where the defense has the ball. There is no clock that you can run out and no ball you can kneel on. You can't dump a puck in the corner either. Instead, you have to get on the mound and pitch, and each player has to experience moments where all eyes are on him. Pat McMahon refers to this process of the game as a "series of solo recitals." Lastly, the game demands that each player exercises great patience. A player in the field never knows when and where a ball may be hit at him, but he must always be ready. Most plays occur in roughly six-second intervals in which there is lag time between pitches and balls batted fairly into the field of play. There are also long stretches of the game when a player must wait for his next turn at bat, which in many cases can be time spent dwelling on that last failure. It is for these reasons that I believe baseball places more pressure on the individual than any other sport.

This reality was revealed in a scene from the movie *A League of Their Own*, when catcher Dottie Hinson (Geena Davis) informs manager Jimmy Dugan (Tom Hanks) that she is quitting the team. He asks her why, and she explains that the game just got too hard.

"It's supposed to be hard," says Dugan. "The hard is what makes it great!"

A further testimony to this can be illustrated by Michael Jordan, probably the greatest basketball player who ever lived. Despite his incredible physical prowess, his minor league baseball career was barely mediocre.

While Dugan says, "The hard is what makes it great," not everyone will always feel great about it.

As a matter of fact, one of our former players once committed a base running blunder. When I confronted him about the miscue, the boy could literally not articulate. He tried to speak, but nothing came out of his mouth. After a few attempts, he finally uttered an answer. *"Wahiawa a a,"* was what his response sounded like to me. The pressure that he was feeling had prevented him from articulating his thoughts. Based upon the amount of pressure that baseball places on the individual, it is not surprising that former Major League Baseball (MLB) commissioner Bart Giamatti once said, "The game of baseball is designed to break your heart."

Pat McMahon also said, "In football, you knock someone's head off, but baseball knocks your head off." His statement, more than any other, summed up the difference in the type of toughness required in each sport. One could be tough in football if one were willing to hit somebody and be hit in return. One could only be tough in baseball if one were willing to fail often in front of a lot of people. There could actually be far less pressure for players involved in a football game, because there are instances when a football player could make a mistake and, because of the speed of the game, he could still blend in with the other twenty-two guys on the field. The same can often be said for other sports, such as soccer, lacrosse, and hockey. For example, if a lacrosse player misses a ball, someone else can pick up the ball and run the other way with it. Again, if the pace of the game is fast and there are more players on the field, sometimes the average spectator may not even notice the error. But, if a ball goes through a player's legs in a baseball game, there is nowhere for him to hide. And it's a long and lonely walk back to the dugout after a strikeout.

I have personally seen that little white baseball make some very big strong men cry. I have seen accomplished football and hockey players, who were as tough as nails, be reduced to tears by that little white ball. One former player, who was as tough as any kid I knew, once came into the dugout after making two errors in the same inning. His emotions had gotten the best of him. Tears welled up in his eyes as he asked out of the game.

Perhaps Coach Charlie Giachetti summed up the difference between a sport like football and baseball best when he said, "It's easier to hit a person than it is to hit a curveball."

I recall Jack Lynch once saying, "Baseball is the single most difficult sport to play well. Period!"

It was during my conversation with Jane that I realized something critically important. Actually, it would prove to be a defining moment in my coaching career. While in the process of explaining all of these factors that compared baseball to those other sports, something dawned on me. I was the one who was thinking like a loser! I was giving myself a built-in excuse for failure and buying more and more into it each day. I didn't think that my belief that the West Essex players' culture might not be conducive to instilling a certain kind of "streak" or mental toughness that is required in the sport of baseball was wrong. But my belief that we were helpless and that there was nothing that we could do to try to overcome those cultural influences was wrong. Furthermore, allowing myself to buy into such a self-fulfilling prophecy and resigning to failure was in complete contrast to what I had pledged to do as their coach. I had even claimed that one of the reasons that I felt that I couldn't quit as head coach was that it was my place to bring certain things out of my players that perhaps their culture or parents had yet to bring out in them. I also thought it was my place to point out things to my players and their parents that maybe they had yet to discover. But I wasn't doing that! We needed a culture change, and I was doing little, if anything, to give them one. If their culture hadn't put something in them that they needed, it was my place to do so. If their culture hadn't taken something out of them that didn't belong, it was my place to do that too.

Therefore, it was I who was failing as a coach, not they who were failing as players, because I was the one who was responsible for putting that "streak" and mental toughness inside them, and I had yet to do enough. Instead of trying to find ways to instill those necessary attributes in them, I was too busy complaining that it hadn't already been done in their prior background. The culture that had shaped them was way beyond my control. But, the culture within our team, and more specifically within our practice opportunities, was something that I could control.

I looked inside myself and asked: *Am I designing practice plans that are preparing a team to play at championship level? Are my practice plans designed to groom "poodles" or to breed "street dogs"?*

If a street dog were to play baseball, he would want the ball to be hit to him with runners on base, two outs in the last inning, and the game on the line. A poodle would wish that the ball would be hit to another player. A street dog would want to have the bat in his hands, with runners on base, two outs, and the game on the line. A poodle would hope that the player before him made the final out. A street dog would much rather be standing on the mound, with the ball in his hand and the game on the line, than standing somewhere else out in the field. He would not be scared or defensive and would aggressively go after hitters and challenge them. A poodle would tell his coach that he was tired, even if he wasn't, in the hopes that another pitcher could relieve him from the pressure.

I then asked myself another question. *What would my practices look like if I wanted to turn a poodle into a street dog?*

Our practices changed forever that night! Our practices became the hardest thing that our players ever had to do. I was tougher on them than their opponents were. In fact, our practices became harder than our games, and the games were really hard. These new practices were not always popular, not always fun, but what they did was prepare all of us to cope in the event that we were to compete against scholarship players in front of thousands of people.

How did we accomplish such a drastic change in our practices? We duplicated "game pressure" as realistically as we could in everything that we did. The players would receive penalties or consequences when they failed to execute a particular skill or drill. If they did not come through, there would be sprints assigned, as well as laps, push-ups, and sit-ups. Each portion of the practice had a risk or reward assigned to whether or not we executed it correctly. Situations would be created in which a player had to perform a skill in front of the entire team. If he could not do it, everyone except him ran. The purpose of implementing more consequences was not as a punishment, but more as a means to prepare the players for when they would be pressed. Everything that we did was charted and documented. If we popped a bunt up, we would do ten pushups. If we overthrew a baseball, the player who threw it would have to be the one to run and get it. If we committed an error or overthrew a cut off or relay man, we would have to run a lap around the entire field. And so we stopped overthrowing cut off men. If a player hit a pop-up in batting practice, his round was over. Almost instantly, we stopped popping up. We held intersquad scrimmages more often. If a pitcher fell behind in the count, the entire defense would have to run to the outfield wall. If a player misexecuted a play or a situation, he would have to run and/or pick somebody else to run with him. We would make our practices as "gamelike" as possible by competing as a team in almost every drill that we did, and the losing team would run sprints at the end. Eventually, we put an "easy button" from Staples in our dugout. If they wanted "easy," they could go to Staples; this was something much different from what they were used to. It was really hard!

It was my hope that creating more game pressure in practices and making them more gamelike would help us to improve. I had no guarantee that it would. I just knew that now I had done everything that I could do within my control rather than use something that was well beyond my control as an excuse. Could we duplicate the "exact" pressure that came from the actual games? Probably not, but I knew that we got it as close as we could, and it was better than before. Maybe nothing, no matter how hard they were pressed in practice, could truly duplicate the exact pressure that a player feels when he puts the uniform on, has his parents and girlfriend in the stands, and knows that the final score will go in the newspaper.

I had noticed over time, the difference in several of our players' performances over the summer when their games were played in front of fewer people and the scores did not go in the newspaper. By comparison, something about a varsity environment just intensified everything, and that pressure and intensity made the game speed up in the minds of our players.

Pat McMahon preached, "Great players know how to slow the game down. Poor players play like they are on roller skates."

Perhaps our newfound methods of preparation would allow us to slow the game down when most people allowed the game to speed up. Perhaps it would just be a matter of our own intestinal fortitude. This would be the test of time!

Part III

Chapter 16

Torn Asunder

The person who deals with the most difficulty wins. It's just
a matter of enduring the pain that comes with it.

—Lance Armstrong
Tour de France Champion

WITH OUR SEASON OPENER on the line, we had walked four batters in the seventh inning. We also hit a batter and committed five errors in the game.

"Freebies" was how I typically referred to walks, errors, and hit batsmen.

The ten freebies that we gave to Morris Hills allowed us to hand them the game, and they were more than happy to accept what we had given them. Times like this would make my head feel like it was about to explode. The tendency for any coach is to chew the team out, perhaps right then and there, start throwing equipment, and just lay into them, taking no prisoners. However, something Trey Hillman of the Kansas City Royals once said resonated loudly in my mind and stayed with me. Trey talked about the fact that nearly all coaches blow up and lay into their team after a loss and then praise them after a win.

"No one wants to hear how bad they are after a loss. That's the time that they need you to pick them up," said Hillman. "The time to press them is after a win, because that's when they'll be able to handle the criticism."

I agreed with Hillman and believed that if you wanted a player to bounce back from a poor performance or series of failures, you should not berate him or tear him apart in front of his peers. Edmonton Oilers' left wing, Dustin

Penner, was once quoted in *Sports Illustrated* about how he felt when he was in the coach's doghouse.

"Typically the first sign is decreased playing time, followed by some form of verbal abuse. This is followed by headaches and diarrhea. Merck is working on a pill for it."

On Monday morning after the heartbreak at Morris Hills, Glen Gloom and Donnie Doom approached Raimondo near his locker.

"Hey, Dom, up three runs with one out in the seventh. Couldn't close it out, huh?" asked Gloom sarcastically.

"We'll be all right," answered Raimondo. "We play them again."

"Two home runs by Santomauro, and you still couldn't beat them," Doom said laughingly.

After school, I stood in front of the team at practice, bearing Hillman's words in mind.

"Jet planes don't have rearview mirrors," I said. "You can't look back unless that's where you want to go. Can you move forward in a failure-driven game, or do let your failures drive you down? That's what this game is all about, moving beyond your failures."

I held up the plastic toilet bowl. The team chuckled.

"When you make an error, it's over. When you strike out, or make an out with runners on base, it's over. Don't carry it with you into the field. Make the transition. Focus on the next play. Keep trying! Keep doing your best! Each and every one of you have done something well to get to this point. Each time you fail, it should teach you how you can make adjustments to get better next time. When you fail, you just flush it and move on!"

I flushed the plastic toilet bowl, which duplicated the exact sound of a real toilet bowl. The team erupted in laughter.

"Winners lose more than losers lose, boys," I said to them. "Because winners are able to get over their failures. The greatest player to ever live, Babe Ruth, struck out 1,130 times, but he also hit 714 home runs. English novelist John Creasey received 753 rejection letters and then published 564 books. R. H. Macy failed seven times before his store in New York caught on. The difference between winners and losers is that winners act like winners even when they lose. Losers act like losers even when they win. Act *as if*, boys! Act as if you're the greatest player in the world and carry yourself with a swagger. Michael Jordan was acting like Michael Jordan long before he ever became Michael Jordan, because he knew that when he failed, he was still a winner. Act as if, boys. Act as if!"

Valerian zeroed in as I spoke. He was completely embarrassed by his performance in the Morris Hills game. He was so distraught that he went to see both his Uncle Mike Carter and his cousin Jason Tiseo. Carter had been

Bloomfield High School's varsity baseball coach and still served as their head football coach. Tiseo was a former All-State baseball player at Bloomfield who went on to star at William Paterson University. Valerian called them and asked if they could meet with him as he tried to do some soul searching.

"I struck out twice and made four errors," said Valerian. "I've never been so embarrassed on a field in my life. I was even thinking of asking Coach to move me out of third base and into the outfield or something."

His uncle and cousin had been around baseball and sports their entire lives. They gave him a heart-to-heart and explained that bad days come with the territory, especially in a failure-driven game like baseball. They insisted that he not ask me to change his position and pointed out that even guys in the major leagues have bad days. The key for him was to turn the page, put it behind him, move forward, and let it go. Valerian was very close with both his cousin and uncle. After they talked to him, he perked up. When they told him not to ask out of playing third base, it might have been gospel.

During that week, Raimondo's grandfather passed away. Our team attended the services at the funeral parlor in the evening, after our game against Parsippany was rained out. Afterward, the boys went for a bite to eat together. Ruggiero and Bustamante knew the heartache that stems from the loss of a grandparent all too well. Upon returning home, Bustamante sat with his mother in his kitchen. He spoke about Ruggiero's grandfather, who had just passed in the winter, and how the passing of Raimondo's grandfather reminded him of his own grandfather, who had died when he was only ten.

"I know, Michael," said Mrs. Bustamante. "But fortunately you were able to have ten good years with Grandpa before he passed. He loved you so much."

"I know."

"He used to talk about how much you reminded him of himself when he was your age. You guys were just like each other. He thought you were so funny. He used to go on and on. You know, a few years after he passed, I spoke to a women who was clairvoyant. She said that he's doing great—that he was so happy, and so happy for us. She said if you ever have a tough time, or are facing some kind of challenge, that he'll send you a rainbow."

"A rainbow?"

"Yeah, a rainbow," his mom said, smiling.

Bustamante smiled back as he thought of his grandfather.

On April 4, we beat Weequahic 16–0 for our first victory of the season. Weequahic was struggling to field a team, and we were supposed to beat them as convincingly as we did. On April 5, we traveled to Parsippany Hills for our third game. Again, Raimondo was not sharp on the mound. Through four innings he gave up three runs on ten hits, with no walks and one strikeout.

Anthony Tundo relieved him and allowed one run in two innings. Valerian made yet another error at third base in two chances, but on a good note, he doubled into the gap and scored on a base hit by D'Annunzio, whose bat remained in our lineup for each of our first three games. We lost 4–2, dropping our record to 1–2 on the season.

On the bus ride home, Renshaw informed me that all ten hits allowed by Raimondo were with two strikes on the batter. "He just couldn't finish a hitter," said Renshaw.

Then, he expressed a further concern. "He had four or five strikeouts a game last year. How many has he had so far? One last game, one today?" he asked.

"Yeah, one," I answered, "but I think that's because he only has one pitch right now. We have to get his other pitches going," I replied.

"He's not right, Scott," Renshaw exclaimed

Raimondo approached me outside the equipment room as I was locking up. Dom was a proud person, and he had expected more from himself in his first two outings. His face was flushed; his eyes were moist.

"Coach, I've never thrown this badly. Maybe I should start throwin' a slider, because I don't have a curveball!" he said.

I told him, that on a good note, he had not walked a single hitter in either game, and since he was coming off a significant arm injury, I was encouraged that so far his arm was pain free. I told him to hang in there and not to make any serious changes. We would work together in the bullpen in a couple of days after his arm had some time to rest.

Renshaw's assertion that Raimondo wasn't right was an accurate one. In each of his first two games, he had thrown close to ninety pitches in only four innings. I attributed that to the fact that his fastball was not moving. Hitters were either making contact with two strikes or fouling him off. When Dom was at his best, his fastball would run in and slightly down on a right-handed hitter. As a result, he would induce a lot of groundball outs, which helped to keep his pitch count down. As far as I was concerned, if he could not regain the movement on his fastball, he would not be able to pitch into the later innings of any game.

Two days later, Raimondo and I went into the bullpen as Renshaw took our team through batting practice. He was very fragile, as his confidence had been shaken. He was still reeling from the season before, and now from a poor start as well. In his first two games, I had made some observations about him and wanted him to make some changes in an attempt to regain his effectiveness. However, I knew I had to be careful in how I worded that to him.

John Cohen of Mississippi State once said that when you tell a player that he has to make a change, "you might as well tell him that he has testicular cancer."

Rather than use the word change, I used the word "adjustments."

"I want you to make a few adjustments," I said to Raimondo as he loosened his arm.

It had looked to me in the game against Parsipanny Hills that he was throwing the side of the baseball, when he should be throwing the top of it in order to maximize the backspin on the pitch. The more backspin he could impart on the ball, the more action it would have and the more movement. In an attempt to correct this, I asked him to picture the ball as a cube, and I told him that I wanted him to throw the top of the cube. Then, I had him close his eyes and feel the top of the baseball as he would get to his release point. Then I asked him to throw some pitches with his eyes closed.

"With my eyes closed?" he asked.

"Dom, I don't care where this ball goes, just do it and feel the top of the ball."

After a few tries, he threw a hopping fastball that moved down and in on a right-handed hitter for a strike. Baab, who was catching, was impressed as he yelled out from behind his facemask, "That a boy, Dom. Good hop!"

Then we worked on his curveball. He was trying to throw his curveball too hard, and it was ending up bouncing in the dirt. It seemed like he was trying to force it. I asked him to take just a little off and not choke the ball so much when he gripped it, so he could allow it to happen for him. After one in the dirt, he threw a tight breaking pitch for a strike. Then, I made him throw some more with his eyes closed.

"Feel it, Dom, and don't forget to breathe," I instructed as I watched him go through an awkward delivery with his eyes closed.

Then, we worked on his changeup. When his changeup was effective, it had the same movement pattern as his fastball, only it would actually move more and was about twelve miles an hour slower. He liked to drag his back leg when he threw his changeup. I asked him to stop dragging his back leg, and emphasized that he throw it with the same arm speed that he would his fastball. He made the adjustment and threw a perfect changeup.

"Dom, that's awesome," Baab shouted. "It moved a lot too."

For the first time in more than a year, he looked outstanding. I told him that if we were to go on and win anything, we really may have just won it right then and there in the bullpen with the progress that he made after making those adjustments.

On April 11, we hosted Chatham. Mark Ruggiero had a standout game by hitting three line-drive singles and making two excellent defensive plays at short stop. As Mark jogged in at the end of the third inning, Mike Bustamante threw him a baseball that was colored in black. Ruggiero caught the ball and nodded. The "black ball" was an award that we gave at the end of each season to our defensive player of the year. The whole team had input on it, and anytime a player made a good play, one of the guys in the dugout would throw the "black ball" to him. He would keep it in his glove and use it for the between-innings warm up the following inning.

Kevin Picardo made a fine scoop, sparing us an overthrow at first base. Steve Zuraweicki earned the win, going five innings while allowing three hits, four runs, five walks, and nine strikeouts. Nick Santomauro singled twice and drove in a couple runs as well, and we rolled to a 14–4 victory.

On the morning of April 15, we were preparing to host Parsippany. Raimondo was standing outside our locker room as I walked by. He stopped me and pointed to his black T-shirt.

"Check out my Saint Gerard shirt." Saint Gerard Majella, was the "Patron Saint of Motherhood," born in 1726 in a small town in southern Italy called Muro. To Raimondo, Saint Gerard served as a symbol of his religious faith.

"I got it at the feast of Saint Lucy's down in Newark. I figure this will help me get it goin' a little," he said.

Perhaps he was right. He baffled hitters that afternoon using an array of effective fastballs, changeups, and curveballs. Joe D'Annunzio made two highlight-reel plays at second base. Baab hit an RBI double, and Ruggiero and Picardo hit RBI singles. Valerian fielded a ground ball flawlessly to record the last out as we defeated Parsippany 6–0. The team mobbed Raimondo, who had pitched a complete game shutout. He scattered three hits, walked two, and struck out four.

"Dom, the past two times out you got roughed up a little, but you didn't get discouraged. Instead you worked very hard the other day in the bullpen. That's what this program is founded on!" I said in front of the team. "Striving to be your best, and overcoming failure."

In his first two outings, he could not get out of the fourth inning. Now he had just pitched a complete game shutout. The changes that he made in the bullpen were not major changes, they were very subtle adjustments that had a very large effect.

"Sometimes it takes just one tiny adjustment; look at the difference," I said to our pitchers. "How could you not be motivated by that?"

On April 17 we were scheduled to play Dover at home. As I walked into the coaches' office, Renshaw was sitting there with his feet up, engulfed in reading a newspaper. He was reading an article about Seton Hall Prep baseball.

"Seton Hall Prep is loaded up again. They've won the *Star-Ledger* trophy as the number one team in the state for three out of the past five years, and they're favored to win again this year," Renshaw said.

"This team is loaded with studs. Have you seen this roster?" Renshaw asked.

"Loaded with studs to go along with Mike Sheppard Jr., the best coach in the state. He was National Coach of the Year back in '03," I answered.

"They have a kid on the mound named Rick Porcello, who throws in the mid-nineties and is projected to be a first-round pick next June when he's a senior. The funny thing is, he may not be their number one. Another kid, Mike Ness, has a full ride to Duke, and he is throwing ninety too. Check this out, their number three, a kid named Evan Danielli, is also projected to be drafted. He's six foot eight and throws ninety as well. Scott, we may never have one kid throw ninety miles per hour. They have three kids throwin' ninety all at the same time. Can you imagine? How do we compete with these private schools? They get the best kids from every town and assemble an All-Star team. We get whoever walks through the door, and we're supposed to go and compete with them?" he asked.

"That's why there's so much talk of putting these private schools in their own league and separating them from the public schools. You watch, this situation is going to escalate and wind up in court one day!" I said.

"We shouldn't have to play them. It's not even fair," he exclaimed. He held up the newspaper and continued reading.

"Two outfielders, juniors Steven Brooks and Nick Natale, are also expected to earn Division I scholarships." He lowered the newspaper so I could see his face.

"We've never had a scholarship kid in any position," he continued. "They have three scholarship kids on the mound alone—aside from all the others."

Again, he held up the paper.

"They've been to the Greater Newark Tournament finals nine straight years and won six. Scott, our best kid maybe throws eighty. Their kid is going to sign for over a million dollars. We have no business being on the field with them! We should just focus on trying to win the conference or possibly the section, because as long as they are in our county, we will have to beat them in order to win it," Renshaw complained.

"R. C., Seton Hall isn't just the best team in New Jersey. They may be the best team in the country!" I responded.

Rick Porcello, the best high school pitcher I have ever seen.
Photo by Richard Morris

We out-slugged Dover that afternoon 10–6. The victory was significant as our entry form for the Greater Newark Tournament was due after that game. We would enter the tournament seeding with a 4–2 record.

During that week we were off from school for spring break. This afforded us a chance to catch up on sleep, get more practice reps, and have a lengthy pregame on our game days.

I came in early each day. There was a lot of scuttlebutt in our locker room about an incident involving college students who played lacrosse at Duke University. Allegedly, the students had raped an African American stripper at an off-campus party, and the story grabbed national headlines. One of these students had grown up in Essex Fells but attended The Delbarton School instead of West Essex. Naturally, since many of our kids knew him, they couldn't stop talking about it. Eventually, the boys would be exonerated and found to be unfairly accused and innocent of all of the charges.

I felt that the situation could potentially be a very teachable moment, but then again, I wasn't sure if it was appropriate to even bring it up. What swayed me was something I once read by football coach Dick Vermiel, "Never pass up an opportunity to communicate your vision and passion."

I called my team in and candidly spoke to them about it.

"I'd be remiss if I didn't express a concern that I have. I'm sure you guys have seen the news lately and all the coverage with this Duke lacrosse incident. I understand some of you know one of the three boys who is being charged with raping a stripper. I'm not going to try the case in here, because I wasn't there, and I don't know all of the facts, but let me tell you what I do know. I know that those kids put themselves in a tough spot by hiring the stripper and throwing a blowout party. I get concerned about all of you. I'm not naïve to the amount of partying going on within this community and within society in general," I said.

Then I shared a story from when I was a senior at Cedar Grove High School in 1989. Our rival was Glen Ridge, so we knew most of the kids who played sports there. Some of them were wise guys. I thought there was a good chance that one day one of these kids would probably do something to somebody that would cause him to get the beating of his life. That's the type of kids they were. What I didn't know, and never expected, was that one day I would come home after practice, turn on the TV, and see all of them on channels 2, 4, 5, 7, 9, 11, and CNN.

"Some of you may have heard of the Glen Ridge rape incident," I said.

"A bunch of guys were hanging out at the local park where they lured a mentally retarded girl into the basement of a house owned by two twin brothers, promising her dates and things like that. Thirteen boys went into the basement. When they got down there, things started getting out of hand. Six of the boys knew that what was happening wasn't right, so they left. Seven boys stayed. The ones who stayed proceeded to sexually assault the girl with a baseball bat and broomstick. Eventually, after a long trial and appeal process, some of them wound up in jail. Their careless decisions during one given afternoon altered their lives forever!"

"How does this relate to all of you?" I asked. "The fact that thirteen boys entered the basement, and six of them had the presence of mind to leave."

I was remembering the nationwide shock and disgust that followed the story. The six who left did not get help for the girl—they should have. At least, they refused to participate, even in the face of peer pressure.

"They were able to recognize that they were at risk and chose to remove themselves from that environment. You can learn from that!" I explained.

"There are two types of experiences in life, boys. There is the expensive experience, and there is also the inexpensive experience. I call it the bargain of a lifetime! Expensive experience is when you do something to yourself, like crashing your car because you drove drunk. You then have to learn from your own experience and it costs you a lot. However, if someone else does something, like crashes a car and gets hurt, it costs you nothing, and you can learn from it just as easily."

"That's the bargain of a lifetime!" I yelled out.

"One day soon—either now, in college, or whenever—you guys are going to be at a party or in an environment that is not good for you. Maybe it will have to do with girls or maybe drugs. Think before you act! And by the way, the more you drink, the less likely you are to make good decisions. Now again, I don't know what happened in that house down at Duke, but I bet those kids could have gotten out of there before all hell broke loose. You can learn from their experience. However painful it may be for them, it is inexpensive to you."

The players didn't speak. They all nodded in agreement. Perhaps they were thinking about the boy they knew and what might happen to him.

I received a phone call from Tom Pengitore, who informed me that we had earned the number-fifteen seed in the Greater Newark Tournament. Seton Hall Prep was the obvious choice as the number-one seed, with Nutley earning the number-two seed, and Newark Eastside earning the number-three seed.

I was hoping for a higher seed, but as Pengitore pointed out, all four of the wins that we earned were against teams who had a sub .500 record.

"The committee felt we were lacking any real quality wins," said Pengitore. "You've got a tough draw because you have to win a preliminary play in game just to get in, and then you have to go to Nutley in the first round."

Nutley had been to the finals for five straight seasons. Their pitcher, Rob Gariano, was outstanding, having already accepted a scholarship to Fairfield University where he would go on to be drafted by the San Diego Padres in 2010. As a junior in 2005, he had pitched Nutley into the finals, where they would lose to none other than Seton Hall Prep. They expected a rematch in the finals again this year and with good reason. No one had beaten them at Nutley in the Greater Newark Tournament in more than five years. But in order for us to even earn that opportunity, we would first have to defeat Barringer.

That evening, I received a message from Al Williams. We were scheduled to play our nearby rival Caldwell in our annual "Mayor's Trophy" game. Since we had won the year before, we had the trophy in our possession. Williams said that he was calling to make sure that I would remember to bring the trophy to the game, and that he wanted to do a photo with the winning team, along with a story of the game. I chose not to return his call. A short while later he called my cell phone and left the same message. I chose not to return his call. The next morning I received a message from our athletic department that Williams wanted me to call him back about the "Mayor's Trophy" game. I chose not to return his call.

Williams' repeated phone calls had reminded me of the likelihood that I would be fired as head coach unless I were to produce a championship. I was becoming more and more nervous prior to each game, and the pressure was starting to affect me.

If we don't do it this year, this will be it, I thought to myself.

I was also concerned about our team. I knew we could play competitively, but I questioned whether or not we were actually good enough to win a championship. To do so, you needed a horse on the mound. Raimondo was far and away our best pitcher, and through three starts he had been shaky. Dalonges had made an error on a routine ball in the Morris Hills game, and I wondered if he could handle the transition from JV infielder to starting center fielder in big spots. I was even more concerned about our infield, which now consisted of a first baseman who couldn't throw, a fourteen-year-old second baseman, a second baseman playing shortstop, and a third baseman who was one conversation with his uncle away from not wanting to play at all.

"A good team could expose us," I said to Renshaw on a recent bus ride home.

I was also questioning myself. Another season without any sort of title would add to my legacy, as I had gone ten years without one and was now realistically looking at eleven titleless seasons. My insecurities were making me question my own system.

Have I done all I can? I asked myself. *Was somebody doing it better?*

Am I a good enough coach? I wondered. *Do coaches who have won championships know some secret that I don't?*

Were Doubleday and his ilk right? Was I a jinx?

I was becoming scared to lose. I was also hung up on what the kids thought. I knew they had read the papers where Williams portrayed me to be "The Biggest Loser."

What if they doubt me? I thought. I was asking them for a "buy-in" and a commitment to our system. If they were doubting me in any way, they won't give me the buy-in that we needed.

Again, I thought back to the teachings of Dr. Rob Gilbert. He placed a strong emphasis on the importance of acting as if you have already accomplished something, before you actually do accomplish it. He had told me a story about the "world's most confident fourth grader," who had asked his teacher for permission to draw a picture of God.

"No one really knows what God looks like," his teacher explained.

"Well, by the time I finish, everyone will know what God looks like," said the world's most confident fourth grader.

As mentioned, I had told the boys that Michael Jordan "acted as if" he was the greatest player in the world long before he ever was. I had repeatedly told the boys to "act as if" they were the best and to "act as if" no one could beat us, but now it was me having to take my own advice. I realized that if I did not exude confidence that they would not believe in me or follow my lead, and ultimately, they would not trust our system.

I knew that I would have to give an Academy Award performance. I didn't feel confident but decided to act like I did. I wasn't sure if I believed anymore but decided to act like I did. As I walked into our locker room prior to the Caldwell game, I told myself, *Act like the most confident coach in the world, even though you don't really feel it on the inside.*

"I need to talk to you about the article Al Williams wrote about us," I said as I turned the blasting stereo off. I explained that he had been after me for a while. I told them that I was a big boy and could handle anything that came my way. But in his effort to get me, he had taken a shot at them, and it was my job to protect them.

"If we win today, and you want to take a picture, I think that's great. You can keep it for your scrapbook one day, but I need you to know that I won't speak to him, and I won't be in any photos that he takes. If any of you have anything to say to him, you have the right to say what you want, but you also have the responsibility to do it in a respectful manner. Make sure you are first class, make no personal attacks, and use no profanity!" I said.

I started to walk toward the door and nearly walked right out of the room without even addressing the issue. Then I stopped, turned around, and "acted as if."

"As far as this title thing goes," I said. "I apologize to no one for my record here. We've always played up to our competition. I've had offers to take other jobs, to go somewhere else. Do you want to know the reason I haven't?" I asked.

"Because of all of you! We've had great kids here. Every so often I get a letter or an e-mail. A few weeks back, one told me, 'Coach, I'm a chiropractor now,' and another is currently in med school. None of these kids ever earned a scholarship, none of them have ever played professionally, but they call or write to say that what they learned here has helped them in their lives. They're all great professionals, great citizens, and some are now great fathers, and they all benefited tremendously from playing here. When you look back, that's what's most important, boys. Sure you want to win a title, but the journey that you make together and the lives that you touch along the way are really what matter most. It's true. I haven't won a title at West Essex—*yet!* I'm gonna see it through here, and one day we'll win a title, because there are no jinxes. There is no such thing!"

"When you get home later, take out an apple and cut it open. If you're persistent, you can count how many seeds are inside of that apple, but let me ask you this. How many apples are inside a seed?"

"You can't tell," answered Zurawiecki.

"That's right! Anyone can count the number of seeds in an apple, but you can't count the number of apples in a seed. This is not about fruit, boys, it's about potential! They're trying to define me permanently, but they can't because your past is not your future. Your focus is your future! These people who judge me say Scott Illiano didn't win a title at West Essex period. Well, I take that same statement and replace that period with a comma. I say Scott Illiano didn't win a title at West Essex (comma) and then won one in 2006. To them, it's the end of the sentence. To me, it's just a break in the sentence. Guys like Al Williams are nothing more than 'seed counters.' They base their evaluations on what was, not on what could be. Once you stop counting seeds, and you start counting apples, your potential changes from limited to limitless. Nothing is permanent, boys, nothing! As long as we never give up, never give in, and always give our best, we can determine our own future, regardless of what's happened in the past. Let's go get Caldwell today!"

I kicked open the door and walked out. Mark Ruggiero stood up in the locker room.

"Hey, guys, Coach has our back," he said. "Al Williams ripped us in the paper and Coach defended us. Well, where's our loyalty? Who's holdin' onto the rope?"

Then Mark outlined their plan. If we won, our team would line up for a picture and then walk away from Williams before he could take it.

"The way I see it," said Ruggiero, "if you take a shot at one of us, you take a shot at all of us! If we win today, I say we take a stand. Let's cold-shoulder 'em. We'll do to Williams what Chad Curtis did to Jim Grey when he trashed Pete Rose."

Caldwell jumped ahead 2–0. Then Anthony Cerza placed a bunt down the third-base side, which was overthrown down the right field line by the Caldwell pitcher, scoring Valerian and Zurawiecki. Joe D'Annunzio then drove in Cerza with a single giving us a 3–2 lead. We added three more runs in the fifth on a single by Lawrence Caprio, a triple by Vin Valerian, a double by Steve Zurawiecki, and a single by Cerza. Cerza also pitched a complete game, ending it with a ground ball to D'Annunzio. The Mayor's Trophy was ours to keep, at least for another year, but Williams was nowhere to be found. He never showed up. Perhaps my non-callbacks sent a message to him. Either way, it was flattering to know that was how the team had planned to handle the situation had he been there.

On April 19, we traveled to East Hanover to play Hanover Park. Led by their coach Dave Minsavage, one of the finer coaches and classiest individuals in the profession, they were a perennial Group II power in New Jersey, having won several championships in the past decade throughout the Iron Hills Conference, Morris County, and the state. They were also ranked number seven in New Jersey and were the odds-on favorite to win our conference this season. This was a big test for us as we had yet to beat a team with a winning record. With the first round of the Greater Newark Tournament scheduled for April 21, I had to keep Raimondo on hold and start Steve Zurawiecki on the mound.

Kevin Picardo clamped the rope to the visitors' dugout fence upon our arrival. After a combination of walks, hits, and two errors by Hanover's second baseman, Picardo singled in Nick Santomauro to give us a surprising 5–0 lead in the top of the first inning. It didn't take Hanover long to mount a comeback. After Ruggiero committed an error at shortstop, Hanover took a 6–5 lead in the third inning.

We roared right back. After a Santomauro double, Ruggiero singled home two runs giving us an 11–6 lead. Zurawiecki allowed three singles and a walk, so I removed him in favor of Mike Bustamante with the score 11–8. Bustamante struck out the eighth hitter to end the fourth inning. In the fifth, we scored one, but after Bustamante surrendered a home run, Hanover cut our lead to 12–11. Then we scored three in the sixth on a double by Valerian, a single by Zurawiecki, a double by Ruggiero, and a double by John Baab to take a 14–12 lead. In the sixth, Bustamante allowed three runs on a walk, a single, a walk, an RBI groundout to first, a double, and a single that gave Hanover the lead for good, 15–14. Caprio doubled to start the seventh putting the tying run at second but was stranded after Picardo popped up a sacrifice bunt attempt. Valerian then grounded out to first, advancing Caprio and bringing up Bustamante with the tying run ninety feet away at third base. He hit a fly ball to left that ended the game.

I felt sick to my stomach. I had thought of pinch hitting for Bustamante, who had never previously hit in our lineup, but I was reluctant to have Raimondo pitch and wasn't sure of who I would pitch in his place had we tied it. I rolled the dice that he might come through with a base hit.

Renshaw stormed across the field.

"Why did you have Kevin bunt? I was trying to signal you to let him hit," he said.

"I wanted the tying run at third with less than two outs so we could attempt to keep playing baseball," I said. "I realize we're on the road, but I wanted to extend the game."

I kept reminding myself to "rise above it," and "be like a hawk," but this was easier said than done. I was already getting it from all angles, and now I had to hear it from Renshaw too. I had always placed a lot of pressure on myself, but now, knowing that the Suits had it in for me, Williams' column had placed a pressure on me unlike anything I had previously experienced. The fact that my job was on the line, and that I was publicly branded as the guy who couldn't win the big one, was really taking its toll on me.

Former Mississippi State coach Ron Polk said that the worst moment for a coach is "when the scoreboard becomes God."

Jesse Owen's once said that on days when he had track meets, he "felt like he was being led to his execution." Game days were feeling a lot like that to me.

The games were supposed to be fun, but they weren't. The scoreboard was becoming God to me. As soon as the games started, my palms would begin to sweat profusely. I'd end up with black stains on my pants from having to constantly wipe the sweat off of them. There were times when I would go to spit and nothing would come out. My state of nervousness had eliminated any saliva in my mouth. Eating during the day was not even a thought until after a game. Even then, I could only eat if we won. I was reveling in turmoil and becoming increasingly miserable. I was getting headaches. I kept fruit-flavored Tums in the center consul of my car and ate them by the handful while driving to school. I had invented the most bizarre superstitions one could imagine, trying to gain control of something that I knew was well beyond my control. This was not healthy, either mentally or physically. I started to ask myself if high school baseball was really worth what I was putting myself through.

These types of symptoms are not completely uncommon for people in the coaching profession, even in those who are already proven winners. As a matter of fact, *Sports Illustrated* reported in January of 2010 that University of Florida football coach, Urban Meyer, decided to take a leave of absence from the nation's premier football program, citing a history of chest pains, headaches, post-loss desolation, and in-season weight loss. After hearing his decision, his daughter exclaimed, "I've got my daddy back!"

Something had to give! I had to find a way to cope with the situation. But, how could I keep my sanity knowing that my job depended on the outcome of each game? I had to somehow get a hold of my emotions, which were spiraling completely out of control.

The scoreboard can't be God to me, I thought. According to my beliefs, there already was a God, and we didn't need more than one. But resisting the temptation to become fixated on the score and the outcome of a game was the challenge of a lifetime. I had to fight it any way that I knew how.

I decided that the answer was what I chose to focus on. If I chose to focus on wins and losses, I would only get stressed. Focusing on the score and the outcome would only give me more bodily symptoms and that would cloud my judgment.

I also realized that focusing on wins and losses was causing me to commit what I construed to be a cardinal sin in coaching, which was to become a cheerleader who was rooting for his team during a game, rather than a teacher who was coaching and leading his team during a game. There were times I was rooting as heartily as a die-hard, season-ticket holder would, and it was paralyzing my ability to coach.

I placed a concentration on breathing, and just as I instructed my players to play the game one pitch at a time, I began to coach each game one pitch at a time. I wrote the phrase "Process Not Product" on the top of my lineup card each day, while making a concerted effort not to think about the outcome at all, but only the process of playing the game.

I also tried as best I could to take all of the emotion out of the game. I found that when I removed my emotion from the game, I was actually able to see things that I wouldn't normally notice, such as how far off the plate a hitter might be standing. When you focus on coaching, you become more observant and therefore more capable of teaching. When you stand there cheering, you reduce your role to that of a spectator.

Teach until the last pitch, I told myself. Ignoring the one thing that I wanted to know most—the final score—was the only way that I was ever going to make it through. I had to not think about the outcome and focus entirely on the process of teaching, coaching, and playing.

I also knew that I had to find a way to enjoy the kids more. I told myself that if I couldn't enjoy the kids regardless of whether or not we won, I should just quit and stop torturing myself.

I tossed and turned on that night we lost to Hanover 15–14. I should have done this, could have done that. They just can't handle the pressure, I told myself.

Then it hit me! Perhaps I was the cause of the enormous pressure that they were feeling. Was the tension that I felt causing me to project negative energy? Maybe the pressure had become evident in my body language and in my demeanor. That could be a cancer. Baseball, unlike football, required players to be relaxed. In football, you could bang your head against a locker to get ready, but baseball was different. In order to perform on a baseball field, you have to be intense without being tense. If I wasn't relaxed, how could my players be? If I seemed too uptight, they would be too.

I stood before the team the following morning. Then I did something I had never done before. I didn't want to seem superior to them, so I took a more submissive approach. Rather than stand over them, I sat down with them so that our eyes were on the exact same plane.

"Baseball is a tough game, boys. You can go from the penthouse to the outhouse real quick," I said. "As heartbreaking as yesterday was, on a positive note, each time they scored, we came back and scored. Good teams do that, and we're trying to become a good team."

I had their attention.

"What concerns me is that twice now we've had late leads against top-flight teams only to cave in and lose by a run. Why? Why are we playing our worst when the game is on the line?"

I asked them if they had been intimidated by Hanover Park because they were ranked seventh in the state. Why were we pressing so hard and trying to force things rather than just allowing them to happen for us? I pointed out that there were points in the game where we were beating up on the number-seven team in the state, just pounding 'em!

"Imagine if you were able to relax," I said. "Look at the way we're performing. Our pitchers aren't being aggressive. We're trying to be too careful, so we're walking hitters. Hitters are tentative and taking good pitches to hit. We're sitting back on our heels in the infield. Guys are throwing to the wrong base, because they don't know what to do when they get the ball. We're hesitant on the base paths. What is going on?"

Baab spoke up, "We had such high goals at the start of the season, and right away we've had some tough losses. I think the fact that we expected to do better is causing us to get uptight and tense up in big spots."

"We can play better, Coach," added Bustamante. "We're just playing nervous right now."

Some of the other players came clean too and admitted that they were afraid to make a mistake. A moment later, the rest of the team agreed with the others.

They were scared. We were banged up, out of position, undermanned, and now, worse than being injured, we were scared. Their fear was overcoming the desire that they had to play and causing them to become paralyzed on the field. This was preventing them from playing well and would assuredly guarantee further failures in the future.

What could I do to stop it? How could I get them to relax? The simple answer was there really are no magic words for a team that has collectively become afraid to fail. Hearing how afraid they were was the most alarming thing that I could have possibly heard. But, perhaps some good would come of it.

It was highly unusual for a group of teenage boys to admit their fears and openly communicate them to one another. I always believed that there was an indirect relationship between communication and conflict, whereas when communication goes up, conflict goes down, and vice versa.

Whether this sense of openness occurred because I sat down with them on their level and essentially became one of them, I'll never know. Maybe it was because John Baab had broken the ice by letting his guard down first. His peers respected and admired him. It was almost as if the players thought that if John could do it, then it was okay for the rest to do it. This was a real form of leadership, not the phony kind when a senior tells a sophomore to go grab the equipment and carry it.

They were communicating in a way that I had never heard teenage boys communicate. They were doing something that men aren't supposed to do: talk about their fears. They were admitting that they were scared. The only way that teenage boys could make themselves vulnerable enough to open up to one another and share their true feelings was through trust. Risking embarrassment in front of the group required great trust and faith in one another. They trusted each other. And they trusted me enough to be themselves and enough to reveal what they were struggling with. I had never had a group of teenage boys speak so candidly about how scared they were, speak so openly about how much pressure they felt and how it was adversely affecting them. This was unlike any team dynamic I was accustomed to.

We were completely torn asunder, and that was the reason that we were coming together. There was a closeness or intimacy that was uncommon for people their age, uncommon for boys, and uncommon for athletic teams. Actually, it was the groundwork and foundation for a cancer-free environment. There we were, sitting down together, feeling free to risk, while airing everything in the most honest way, talking about our fears and bringing them to the surface rather than continuing to deny or repress them. We talked about how we could best plan to deal with the pressure that we felt, together in a supportive way.

John Baab, seen here diving back to first base, provided our team with a form of open communication unlike any I had previously seen in team athletics. His leadership was genuine and real, as opposed to the phony kind that coaches often attempt to manufacture.

I was equally honest and candid in return. I explained to them that some of what they were feeling stemmed from the pressure that the game itself placed on them. I told them that, to a point, I couldn't help them with that, but I understand how hard the game was. I also told them that risking failure in front of a lot of people requires great courage. Then I reminded them of what they should really be judged by.

"Whatever is causing this, I just hope that it's not coming from me," I said. "Look, I want to win really badly. Lately, I've been concerned that you may be vibing on just how much I want to win and that it could only add to the pressure that you feel. I'm going to continue to push all of you as hard as I can, because I will never sell you short, ever. But, both myself and Coach Renshaw care for all of you very much, both as people and as players. The only thing we will ever judge you on is your effort. The effort that you make to do your best."

I knew that if we didn't stop holding back then, we could spiral completely out of control. "Do you know what you'll never hear anyone ever say on their death bed?" I asked.

They stared at me intently.

"'I wish I held back more.' No one will ever say that as they are about to take their last breath. Instead, they will say, 'I wish I had taken more chances.'"

I had recently videotaped an incredible story that was featured during halftime of a college basketball game on CBS. There could not have been a more timely moment to show it to my team.

The story was about an autistic high school student from New York named Jason McElwayne. The month before, he had stunned his teammates, his community, and ultimately the entire country. For four years, he was the team manager for the Greece Athena High School basketball team. He spent those four years cleaning up after the team and getting water for the players, so at the end of his final season, his coach let him suit-up for a game. It turned out that they had such a big lead at the end of the game that the coach decided to put him in. What happened next made national headlines. After missing his first shot, he sank six consecutive three-point shots and finished with twenty points in four minutes.

"How do you account for this?" I asked, after playing the video for them. "How do you explain that in spite of his autism, in spite of his disability, the manager of the team scores twenty points in four minutes after taking the court for the first time in his life?"

"Jason McElwayne wasn't lacking in ability. But could anyone see it? His lack of opportunity effectively blocked his ability. He wasn't lacking in potential. But did anyone see it? Did he see it? It was also blocked. But neither of these things mattered. Once Jason got on the court, he didn't freeze up or question whether he could or should shoot, he just did it. And when the first shot didn't go in, he didn't stop, he didn't question, he just tried again. He didn't hold back.

Why is it that people sometimes don't tap their full potential? Choices! They hold back. They hang out instead of going all out. They drive with their emergency brake on. That's what we're doing right now. We're all holding back! Don't hold back. Play this game like you're twelve years old in the backyard!"

"There's a Superman inside of every one of you!" I shouted. "All you have to do is let it out. There was a Superman inside Jason McElwayne all along. Stop blocking your ability, and let it happen for you. Stop telling yourself what you are lacking, and start focusing on the right strategy. Stop holding back. Lower that emergency brake! Remove the obstacles that you've created in your minds. Break down those barriers. Become unstoppable!"

After practice that day, Mike Cordasco would attempt to throw from the mound for the first time. We had begun our season during the first week of March. Now, in the third week of April, he finally received medical clearance from his doctor to participate.

After he loosened up, he climbed up on the mound in our bullpen adjacent to the football field. He proceeded to throw one pitch after another in the dirt. He had no strength. You could see how tight his neck and left side were. Understandably, he seemed very stiff. After another bad pitch, he stormed off the mound, kicked the dirt, and threw his glove to the ground. I walked over and put my arm around him.

"C'mon, Mike. Do you see that field over there?" I asked, pointing to the football field.

"When they carried you off that day, they didn't think you'd ever walk again. It's a miracle that you can even walk. Here you are, five months later, trying to pitch. It's not going to happen overnight."

He was teary eyed. "I know, Coach. I'm frustrated. I just want to pitch."

On the morning of April 21, I woke up feeling nervous over our scheduled rematch with Morris Hills later that day. My phone rang. It was my Dad. He informed me that he had prostate cancer, and he would be having it removed in a few weeks. I was shocked.

"I didn't want to distract you, but I went for some tests, and that's what he found," he said. "He thinks the prognosis could be pretty good, and he should be able to get it in time. We'll see. You just keep focused on your job, and keep doing what you're doing. I'll see you at the game later. Good luck."

"Okay, Dad. I love you," was all I could muster up. I hung up the phone. Suddenly the game didn't seem so important.

Prior to the game, Renshaw and I sat in the dugout as the kids stretched down the left field line.

"Scott, I can't do it anymore," he said. "It's always something. You know what we can never do? We can never field a ground ball with the game on the line."

His negativity was getting to me. I couldn't listen to it anymore.

"You know what, R. C.," I responded. "You're being really negative. If one of the kids was spreading this type of negativity, I'd throw him off the team. I wouldn't accept it from them, and I shouldn't be hearing it come from you. And I don't need you in my face, seconds after the game in Hanover, when my heart is in my throat. Call me later, or bring it up the next day and we'll hash it out. I get enough from parents. No one hurts more when we lose. I don't need it from you."

We had never before had words. I had coached him as a player, and we had always maintained that sense of respect.

"You're right," he replied. "I'm sorry. I'm just so damn frustrated. I'm sorry."

The scoreboard was becoming God to him too. I had to remind him what our role really was in all of this.

"Our role isn't to win," I explained. "Maybe if we recruited these kids it would be different, but we don't. We don't choose them. We happen to get whoever strolls through the door. Sometimes we will be more talented than other teams, and sometimes we will have less talent. That's the luck of the draw! But our role isn't to win. Our role is to teach them the game and prepare them as best as we possibly can for competition, while also being good role models. Don't ever lose sight of the fact that you're a teacher. That is your role! To teach, to educate, to instill good values, and to bring out their best, whatever that may be."

Renshaw agreed. We made up instantly. I knew that it was his competitive nature that was making him feel frustrated. In fact, I was frustrated too and it was taking its toll on both of us. I also appreciated the fact that he was remaining loyal in spite of his frustration by continuing to work as hard as he did.

We were scheduled to play Barringer in the preliminary round of the Greater Newark Tournament, so again I had to hold Raimondo back in spite of the challenge that Morris Hills presented. I gave the start to Mike Bustamante.

In the top of the first, Morris Hills scored twice off of him on a single, a double, and a two-RBI single. They scored two more in the third on a single, double, and two more singles. We scored one in the third as Nick Santomauro drove in Mark Ruggiero with a single. Our staff was gassed, and Raimondo was unavailable. I figured if I put Mike Cordasco in, he could begin to gradually break himself in. I also felt that he would be a different look from the right-handed Bustamante, so before handing the ball to Tundo, who was also right-handed, I put Cordasco in to pitch the fourth inning. I didn't know what to expect after his recent bullpen, but he looked a lot better. At least he was not bouncing everything in the dirt, and he worked a scoreless inning. We scored one in the bottom of the fourth as Picardo walked, moved to third on a double by Valerian, and scored on an infield error hit by Joe D'Annunzio. We added another run in the fifth on a single by John Baab, who moved to third on a single by Caprio and scored on an errant pick-off at first by the pitcher. We tied the game in the sixth after D'Annunzio doubled, moved to third on an infield error, and scored on a groundout to first by Ruggiero. Remarkably, Cordasco allowed no runs in the fourth, fifth, and sixth innings. I removed him with one out in the seventh after allowing a double and two walks to load the bases with the score tied at four. I replaced him with Anthony Tundo. After a pop-up to second, Tundo had two outs and an 0–2 count on the number-nine hitter, but then hit him with a pitch that allowed the go-ahead run. He then struck out the leadoff hitter to end the inning. Trailing 5–4, just like the game against Hanover Park, we had the tying run ninety feet away at third base with two out in the seventh. Valerian stepped in with a chance to tie it. He grounded out to second base to end the game.

Valerian threw a tantrum. He unraveled and went into a tirade by throwing his helmet, and then he abandoned the team by walking down toward our locker room without running his postgame sprints, which were customarily mandated for our team.

I once heard Boston Red Sox manager Terry Francona share three keys to playing championship baseball: 1) Attention to detail, 2) Handle frustration, 3) Stay in the moment. Vinnie's actions were a blatant disregard for at least two of them, and in the process, he compromised who we are as a program.

I intended to suspend him. Then, he came back. He was no longer in his uniform, already having changed into street clothes. He was wearing a black T-shirt, jeans, and a white hat, and he walked back up the hill leading to our field.

I had always believed that it was impossible to put the toothpaste back in the tube, so to speak. I often regarded apologies as an excuse to get away with bad behavior, but Vinnie's apology to me seemed very sincere. He was broken up. I accepted his apology and assigned him some extra equipment duties.

It was obvious to me that he had yet to get over his performance on opening day. Now, with the tying run ninety feet away in the seventh, he had had his chance to redeem himself, but he didn't get it done. He was carrying his failures with him, and the game was eating him alive. When I was in high school, my coach, Jack Lynch, would have referred to Vinnie's state of mind as having "gone in the tank."

"I'm sorry, Coach," he said. "I know I embarrassed you, and I'll never do that again. I wanted to tie the game so badly. That pitch was right there, and I didn't get it done. I just got really frustrated."

I explained to Vinnie what every baseball player comes to realize at some point or another—baseball screws everybody.

University of Texas coach Auggie Garrido once said, "Pitchers, hitters, the game doesn't discriminate. Everybody gets screwed."

Bart Giamatti said, "The game is designed to break your heart." Today happened to once again be Vinnie's turn. I often compared the game to a casino in Las Vegas or Atlantic City because more often than not, the house wins. That's why, when you succeed in baseball, it is the greatest feeling in the world.

I told Vinnie that we had a lot of baseball left and explained an all-important lesson that had come to me during my own time as a player.

"The game always comes back to you, Vinnie, always!" I said. "Any time you have a chance to be a hero and you don't come through, before you know it, either later that game or sometime down the road, you get another chance. What are you going to do? Cry, throw your helmet, or be ready for your next chance? Because if you dwell on your failures, you've got no chance. You'll never come through when the team needs you most."

He nodded. Little did I know that conversation was foreshadowing a much bigger moment down the road.

After practice the next day, I pulled Caprio aside. He had not been having the same quality at bats or even hits as he had the season before. He had batted .380 as a junior with four home runs, but with a few exceptions, he was struggling and didn't look right standing in the batter's box. I thought that maybe he was trying too hard, compensating for the frustration that he felt from missing his senior year of football.

"My knee is fine, Coach. But I can't see!" said Caprio.

"What? Whataya mean, you can't see?"

He had severe allergies, which were causing protein deposits to build up all over his contact lenses. At times, it was so painful for him that he would have to struggle to keep his eyes open, and he would uncomfortably turn away from the sun. At other times, it didn't hurt him so much, but he couldn't see because his contact lenses were so fogged.

"Forget about hitting," he said. "Sometimes I can't even see what sign you're giving me."

I asked him if he had been checked out. He had seen the doctor. The medication he received would minimize his allergies, but it would not eliminate them. Then I asked about glasses or sports goggles. He explained that he had tried both and had no peripheral vision without contact lenses. He was just going to have to battle his way through it.

I wanted him to know that I still believed in him.

"I'm going to stick with you in the four hole, L. I am not going to change your spot in the batting order. I know that in any given at bat that the potential is there," I said. "The most important thing right now is that you have to stay mentally tough. Maybe you're not having the same type of year this season that you did a year ago, but it only takes one to help the team. We may just need one big at bat from you in a spot, and you have to be ready to deliver."

"I will, Coach," he answered.

With Barringer scheduled for the next day, our season hung in the balance. Our success would be contingent upon how well we dealt with the second of Francona's three keys to playing championship baseball, which was to handle frustration.

It was hard to find anyone in our locker room who wasn't frustrated or feeling the pressure. Baab was distraught over our record. Bustamante had lost a couple of games. Zurawiecki was battling hard to keep his bases on balls down. Raimondo was struggling to become consistent. Ruggiero wasn't just plugging a gap for the time being, he needed to be good enough as an everyday shortstop. Dalonges wanted to bat in our lineup everyday as opposed to having a designated hitter bat in his place. D'Annunzio was trying to show that he really belonged, and that he was here to stay. Santomauro was hitting very well, but considered any out that he made to be like Armageddon. Picardo still couldn't throw. Now, Caprio couldn't see. Cordasco struggled to regain feeling in his back and neck. Renshaw was extremely frustrated. Valerian was more frustrated than Renshaw. For me, it was a state of constant emotional shock; I had already lost ten pounds without going on a diet. Worst of all, the fear factor was in full effect, as our team was admittedly scared and seemingly unfit to handle the pressure.

The night before the Barringer game I posted "The Champions Creed" on our locker door which read:

I am not judged by how many times I fail, but by how many times I succeed, and the number of times I succeed is in direct proportion to how many times I fail and keep going.

Could we overcome our fears in order to be successful, or would we give in to frustration? We would soon find out—but not before it rained.

CHAPTER 17
You've Still Got Value

When you get into a tight place and everything goes against you,
till it seems you could not hold on a minute longer, never give up
then, for that is just the place and time that the tide will turn!
—Harriet Beecher Stowe

I HEARD THE RAIN pounding on the roof above my bedroom. My phone rang. It was Tom Pengitore. The Greater Newark Tournament preliminary round game against Barringer was postponed until tomorrow. The following morning, I again heard the rain pounding on my roof top. The phone rang. It was Tom Pengitore. The game was now postponed until after school on Monday. This would now give us five games in six days if we were able to beat Barringer and advance to play Nutley in the first round on Saturday.

I was concerned that we just didn't have enough pitching to get us through that stretch. I was also kicking myself for keeping Raimondo on the shelf so long. I had kept him on the bench for our losses against both Morris Hills and Hanover Park in anticipation of a start against Barringer on Saturday. Now, he would not pitch until we played on Monday. This made me question whether holding him back had even been worth it. We had just lost two games in the conference. I estimated that we could have at least held on for a win at Hanover Park had I gone to Raimondo in relief.

"What are the chances of us winning the Greater Newark Tournament with Seton Hall in it?" I asked Renshaw. "Maybe we would be better off going after the conference championship instead."

"You're sounding like me," said Renshaw. "I know I've been down on our team lately, but I actually like the spot. You had to do this in order to give us a chance."

We had already been scheduled to play Mendham in a league game on Monday, but the Greater Newark Tournament bylaws stated that all tournament games must take precedence over any league games, so Pengitore moved the Mendham game to Thursday of that week. I had asked him to put it somewhere else, but he said we were too jammed up and had to play that day. However, Monday came and it was still raining. Pengitore reported standing water in our outfield and basically explained that "even if it stopped raining now, we'll still be too wet." The Barringer game was now pushed to Tuesday.

Postponing the game one more day may not sound like a big deal, but this was an enormous change. Raimondo did not bounce back well in between starts and often needed at least four days of rest, if not more, if he was to be effective during his next time out. Actually, I had found that most high school pitchers were noticeably different and less effective when pitching on only three days of rest, and that reality applied to Raimondo probably more than most other pitchers. If we were able to defeat Barringer on Tuesday and advanced to play Nutley, then Raimondo could rest on Wednesday, Thursday, and Friday. Given what we knew about him, we didn't think that he would be able to come back on Saturday. At least, we didn't think it was likely that he could be as effective as we would need him to be against a top-flight team. Our schedule also called for us to play Weequahic on Wednesday, the make-up game against Mendham on Thursday, and Parsippany on Friday, which meant that a win against Barringer would now give us five games in five days, two of which would be Greater Newark Tournament preliminary and first-round games.

Part of my daily routine at lunch was to call Dr. Rob Gilbert's *Success Hotline*. His hotline was highly motivating, inspiring, always thought-provoking, and best of all, it was free.

"Give me something, Doc," I said as a dialed the number.

Dr. Gilbert's voice kicked in: "Do something impossible this week. Then the next time you have to do something impossible, you'll know it is possible."

A moment or so later he shared the "never give up" quote from Harriet Beecher Stowe. Maybe it was the fact that we had to play five games in five consecutive days, or the fact that we would have to beat Nutley to advance beyond the first round of the tournament, but there was that word again—impossible. The word had already left an impression on me when I posted up the "Impossible Is Nothing" quote I had borrowed from the 1980 Lake Placid "Miracle on Ice" poster. Now, Gilbert was talking about doing the impossible. I paid attention to that.

Renshaw and I racked our brains in the coaches' office before Monday's indoor practice. We were attempting to figure out a pitching rotation for the next five days in which we could make our best run in the Greater Newark Tournament yet remain in contention in our league. Both of us struggled to finalize anything. After deliberating back and forth, we concluded that

Raimondo would pitch against Barringer, and come back for as long as he possibly could on Saturday against Nutley. Firavanti would pitch the Weequahic game on Wednesday, and he had to go the distance.

On Thursday, we would resort to a tactic that I felt would give us our best chance. We didn't think that any of our available starters were likely to throw a complete game, so my belief was that our best chance would be to give Mendham's lineup a combination of varied looks in order to confuse them and upset their timing. We would start Zurawiecki, a hard-throwing righty; and then go with Bustamante, a finesse righty; and then go to Cordasco, who was left-handed, to close. Cerza would pitch on Friday at Parsippany. Tundo would be in relief every day if we felt we were in a pinch. Whoever showed the most, and was rested enough, would come in to relieve Raimondo on Saturday.

It was still raining outside. The team was seated on the gym floor in our half of the gym. I held up a twenty-dollar bill.

Our record stood at 5–4. I felt at that moment that we were fighting for our playoff lives. Our season was on the line. There would potentially be two GNT games, but with five games in five days, we needed to have a good week in order to feel good about our chances to qualify for the state tournament, which required a minimum record of .500 or better.

"We're fighting for our playoff lives!" I said. As I paced back and forth I held up the twenty-dollar bill

"How much is this worth?"

The team responded, "Twenty dollars."

Then I folded the twenty-dollar bill in half.

"Now how much is it worth?"

Again the team responded, "Twenty dollars."

Then I crumpled the twenty-dollar bill up.

"How much is it worth now?

"Twenty dollars."

Then I spit on the twenty-dollar bill, threw it on the floor, stepped on it, and squished it with my foot.

"What's it worth?"

"Twenty dollars."

"That's right. It's been bent in half, knocked around, spit on, stepped on, and walked all over, and it still has value. This team has faced more adversity than any team I've ever had. The injuries to our pitchers. The injuries that caused four position changes. Some days Lawrence can't even see. We have a half of a gym to practice in. A reporter demoralized us in the newspaper. We've had three very close, very difficult, one-run losses, where one swing of the bat in either direction would have resulted in a different outcome. Now, if we beat Barringer tomorrow, we will advance and play five games in the next five days."

I paced back and forth.

"Well, adversities are wonderful character checks, aren't they?" I asked.

"Isn't this a chance to check our character? In spite of every adversity, we're still five and four through our first nine games."

I uncrumpled the now-wrinkly twenty-dollar bill and showed the team.

"We've still got value, boys! We're in a tight place right now, and as Harriet Beecher Stowe said, 'When you get into a tight place and everything goes against you, till it seems you could not hold on a minute longer, never give up then, for that is just the place and time that the tide will turn.'"

I held the twenty-dollar bill closer to their faces.

"No adversity, no matter how bad, can ever take away our value. Don't give up! Don't quit on each other before the tide turns. We've got five games in the next five days, and nine games in the next eleven days. This is our character check. We're just gonna have to grind it! Win or lose we have to come back twice as hard the next day, grind it, and fight for our playoff lives!"

On April 25, we hosted Barringer. The first two Barringer hitters reached on errors, one by D'Annunzio, the second by Picardo. Ruggiero recorded a force out on a flip from D'Annunzio at second, moving runners to first and third. The runner then scored on a sacrifice fly. We tied the game in the bottom of the second after Valerian doubled and scored on a throwing error by their shortstop. In the third, Barringer threatened with runners on first and third with two out. Raimondo threw to first on a pickoff attempt.

Bustamante alertly and enthusiastically grabbed our attention.

"Coach, he's leanin'. I'm tellin' ya, he's going," he said.

I looked at Renshaw, who flashed the pitchout signal to catcher John Baab. Raimondo pitched out, and Baab threw out the runner at second on an attempted steal. Our team, especially those in the dugout, celebrated wildly while mobbing Bustamante as everyone ran into the dugout. The score remained at 1–1 in the third inning. In the fourth, Nick Santomauro doubled and then scored on a two-out two-strike single by Lawrence Caprio. In the fifth inning, Valerian hit a sacrifice fly to score John Baab, giving us a 3–1 lead. As we took the field in the top of the seventh, Renshaw tapped me and pointed to his pitch chart. Raimondo needed three outs, and his pitch count was under seventy.

With two outs in the seventh, Raimondo walked the ninth-place hitter. With the tying run at home plate and a lefty pull hitter due up, I commanded Picardo to play behind the runner at first base. We positioned our outfield in a "no doubles" defense. Raimondo then hit the next batter, giving Barringer runners on first and second base.

I cautioned our guys that the tying run was now at first base and instructed them to pay attention and to keep both runners close.

Mark Ruggiero did not hold the lead runner at second base close, and Raimondo never checked him either. Our inattentiveness allowed Barringer to pull off a double steal. Needing only a base hit to tie the game, Raimondo struck out the number-two hitter to end the game. The team celebrated. I was disgusted!

On my very first interview to become the head baseball coach, Principal Jim Corino gave me a piece of advice that had stayed with me: "Never accept anything in victory that you wouldn't accept in defeat."

We had broken down and lost our focus with a critical mental mistake in the last inning. We hadn't used our acronym KTS—*know the situation*. With the tying run at first base in the last inning, they didn't know the situation. Raimondo's strikeout masked our blunder, for which we could have paid for dearly. They were elated that we won, but I let the kids have it in our huddle. This was about teaching!

When I finally simmered down, I praised Raimondo for a great outing. He had pitched well. He allowed no earned runs, struck out eight, walked one, and hit one, but more importantly, he also recorded the lowest pitch count of his career by throwing only seventy pitches. If he had ever needed a time for such a low pitch count, that was it. If he were to have any hope of bouncing back strong on Saturday at Nutley, this would give him the chance to do so.

I praised Bustamante. Little things really do mean a lot. He had picked up the steal in the third inning and was instrumental in our team calling for a pitchout. I felt that he deserved high praises for being so alert in spite of the fact that he was on the bench and not in the starting lineup.

I reminded Caprio about the reality that it only takes one to pick up our team in a big spot, and he did that for us with a two-strike two-out RBI. Before they all got up, I asked them not to think beyond tomorrow and take one game at a time.

"We gotta grind it!" I said.

As the team stood for their huddle, Renshaw walked to the center and motioned his hand forward from a flexed arm to it fully extended.

"Full steam ahead!" he said.

The team cheered, raised their hands together, and broke to a shout of "Hustle!" Mark Ruggiero made the sixth slash mark on the sledgehammer with a black marker and raised it in the air as his teammates enthusiastically clapped.

On April 26, Santo Barretta drove in four runs, and Frank Firavanti pitched a complete game shutout in leading us to a 26–0 win over Weequahic. We tried to emphasize a "midnight comes and it's over" mentality with the idea that win, lose, or draw, we must grind it each day.

Again, Renshaw did what was now becoming a patented postgame move of his as he motioned with his arm while saying, "Full steam ahead!"

Ruggiero was elated as he wrote slash mark number seven on the sledgehammer and raised it in the air. He passed it along, each player holding the sledgehammer high in the air, none more so than Pat LaConsole.

There were few players on our team who had as much personality as Pat. Pat was another player who was the oil that helped our motor run. He too had something to offer as an outfielder and a pitcher, but he had a few players in front of him. However, he was certainly one of the most popular players on our team. He was always arguing with teammates about how his favorite New York Mets deserved as much, if not more, recognition than the New York Yankees. He shared an incredible appreciation for Italian food and culture with his teammates and was known to tear up the dance floor with the best of them.

On Thursday, April 27, we traveled to Mendham. Nick Santomauro launched two home runs, and four different pitchers, Zurawiecki, Bustamante, Tundo, and Cordasco combined to beat Mendham. I thought the game was huge for our confidence because it was the only one of our eight season wins that was earned against a team with a winning record. Mendham was first in our league and ranked in the top five in Morris County. It was the first time all season that we had come from behind and held onto the lead, and we did it on the road. Being able to do that was, in my opinion, the mark of a championship team.

I complimented our pitchers. I couldn't recall the last time four pitchers combined to win a game for us, if ever. I got choked up while looking at Cordasco.

"What can I say? I never thought you would even make it back to school this year, and here you are. Three and two-thirds scoreless innings against that lineup. It's so good to see you healthy, Mike, and it's so good to have you back," I said.

After two outings on the mound, it was clear that Mike had recovered. It was hard for any of us to imagine what he went through, being immobilized and out of school for so long. He had made it back and was lifting our team in the process. It gave me chills!

Something changed on the field that day too. This team was gaining confidence, and now had a sense of belief that had been lacking earlier on. We were developing a swagger.

"Today means nothing if we don't come tomorrow," shouted Santomauro as we stood for our huddle. Renshaw did his "full steam ahead," and Ruggiero took care of slash mark number eight on the sledgehammer to a chorus of "Grind It."

On Friday, April 28, we traveled to Parsippany. While leading 4–2 in the fourth inning, Joe D'Annunzio singled to center field. Vin Valerian hustled around from second and was about to be tagged out by the catcher.

"Wham!" He plowed right into him, knocking him toward the backstop. Not only was he automatically out on the play for not sliding, but he was also ejected from the game and subjected to a mandatory two-game suspension as per the NJSIAA rules and regulations.

We managed to win that day, 15–5, ending on an offensive highlight—a two-run home run by Santomauro. For Santomauro, it was his fifth home run of the season and third of the week. As the season went on, he was becoming more and more relaxed. There was no doubt that he was a special talent. He just needed to let some of his outs go, as he tended to put a lot of extra pressure on himself—probably due to the fact that he knew how good he really was, and he wanted to get a hit every time up. As long as he didn't fight himself, there was no telling how dangerous a hitter he could be.

Ruggiero hit a triple and a double, and Baab hit a double to lead the way. Ruggiero made several fine plays at shortstop; he was looking more comfortable too. Cerza pitched a complete game to earn the win.

I was happy for Cerza. He had been cut at as freshman. He was in a sling on the first day of practice. He was nowhere on our radar screen on the first day of tryouts, and now he had won key games for us against Caldwell and Parsippany. His confidence as a young man had grown, and you could see in his expression and his demeanor how happy he was that he was making such an important contribution.

After the game, the boys were happy. We had won four straight and were now 9–4. But they were also subdued. They all knew the NJSIAA rule. They knew the consequences of what had happened.

Tomorrow, we would go to Nutley without Vinnie.

CHAPTER 18

It's Impossible, But I'll Do It!

I play my best nine, not my nine best.

—Skip Bertman
LSU Baseball Coach

As OUR BUS TRAVELED down Route 46 from Parsippany back to West Essex, I was deep in thought. *Who could play third base for Vinnie?* Our best candidate was Cerza, who was not only inexperienced, but he had also just thrown a little more than a hundred pitches. Who would our designated hitter bat for? I had planned the hitter for Raimondo, to just let him pitch, but now that Cerza was the likely third baseman, perhaps I should use the hitter for him, and let Raimondo bat for himself. I called Cerza to the front of the bus. I told him that we needed him to step up big for us. We had no one else. Then I told him that he needed to go for a long run as soon as we got back to school to get some of the lactic acid out of his body, so he could give his arm a chance to recover.

As the ride continued, my own wheels were spinning. The fact that Valerian would now be removed from the six hole in our batting order was a huge loss. How could we fill that void? I had concerns about our seven through nine holes in general, but now our lineup would be much thinner from number six through number nine, and we would be facing a scholarship pitcher. What should our batting order be?

I started thinking about the possibility of putting Cordasco in the lineup for Dalonges so that we could get his bat into the lineup. After all he was our everyday center fielder prior to his injury.

That night I paced back and forth in my kitchen, pondering both our lineup and batting order.

"What are you doing?" asked Jane. "Just do the best you can with who you have. What else can you do?"

Her comments made me realize that I had already decided. Dalonges had earned the spot in Cordasco's absence by stepping up big time. I owed

157

him some loyalty for that. It wouldn't be fair to bench him in the biggest game of the year after what he had done for us. Maybe it wouldn't be fair for Cordasco either if he were to make a mistake after so few practice reps. Besides, Dalonges was now one of our guys. His teammates loved him, and everyone respected him for the way he played.

Skip Bertman once spoke about the importance of playing "your best nine" players rather than "your nine best" players. His point was that sometimes certain players do things for a team that go beyond statistics. It could be certain intangible traits or perhaps a player might just have a way of rubbing off on others and making his teammates better. It was possible that Cordasco, the original starter, could have been a better option than Dalonges was at that time, but it was in between paces in my kitchen, I realized that Dalonges was part of our "best nine." I believed in this kind of synergy and was probably more aware of it than some other coaches, but that wasn't what swayed me entirely. I thought back to where Anthony was a season ago, when he hadn't made our team, and how he didn't let that deter him from coming back this season. Instead of quitting, he worked harder at a new position, and made rapid progress. Anthony had showed me that there was something inside of his heart, beyond any statistics, that should not be left on our bench. I didn't know it at the time, but this decision, or nondecision, to keep Dalonges in the lineup would turn out to be one of the more important decisions that I have ever made as a coach.

Nutley was the number-two seed in the tournament. Obviously, the biggest concern that we had about them was their pitcher, Rob Gariano. He threw in the upper eighties—and at times more than that. He had a tight curveball, and he knew how to pitch. Our kids were well aware of Gariano's capabilities and the fact that Nutley had been to the GNT finals for five straight seasons. We knew that Nutley fully expected to meet Seton Hall there once again. Beyond that, a lot of the talk among our players was about the fact that Nutley had not lost a GNT game at home in more than five years.

The aura and mystique of Nutley were a result of both the setting and the notoriously large crowds. The field was set down beneath surrounding sidewalks along Franklin Avenue located beyond left field and throughout the circumference of the field. In addition to the countless people lining the street, people also packed in the bleachers located on both sides of the infield. The field made for a cozy setting as a fly ball could easily reach Franklin Avenue for a home run, and people could watch the game from surrounding buildings. Their crowds were noisy, very unruly, and incredibly spirited.

I knew that the surroundings at Nutley would bring back the fear my players had spoken about so openly. I knew it would rear its ugly head the moment their fans began to rag on our team, as they were known to do.

Going into Nutley and beating them under the best of circumstances was highly unlikely. But, now being shorthanded without Vinnie, it seemed hopeless. In a way, it seemed impossible.

After hearing Gilbert's message about doing the impossible, I asked myself if there was anything that I could do. Was there anything that I could do to try to help my players eliminate their fear of failure so that they could achieve peak performance? We had practiced. We had emphasized not giving up. Was there something more I could do? Anything at all?

I drew upon what I believed was the greatest example of the incredible power of the human mind. It was a video made by the History Channel. Actually, it was a documentary about the World Trade Center that I had acquired shortly after 9/11. Interestingly, the scene that I showed them didn't have anything at all to do with the tragic attack. Instead, this powerful example of what the human mind was capable of would come from the great high-wire walker, Philippe Petit.

Petit's story actually began in the early '70s when he was sitting in a dentist's office in France. He just happened to pick up a magazine and began reading about the newly built twin towers in New York City. It was at that moment that his dream of walking on a high wire between the two towers, 110 stories in the air, was born. Petit traveled all the way from France to New York. He vividly recalled the moment that he first saw the towers.

"I got off the subway and emerged out of the darkness at the base of one of the towers and looked up. Like a slap in the face, I saw that my dream was impossible!" said Petit. "It was right there in aluminum and glass and steel and concrete. It was right there and said, 'Impossible!'"

Petit then trespassed as he snuck into one of the towers and climbed all the way to the top and outside in order to get a closer look. He was convinced even further that he could not do it. "Another time the word 'impossible' was etched inside me," Petit said.

But, maybe all Petit really needed was a different perspective. "Somehow I went back down and looked again from the street, and there, I realized: 'It's impossible, but I'll do it!'"

This was the point that I wanted my team to understand. Petit had been totally convinced that his dream was impossible. But then he looked again! Once he changed his vantage point, he changed his thinking. He began to look at it in another way. He now had a brand-new perspective. He no longer cared that it was impossible. He was going to do it anyway!

For several months, Petit became an imposter inside the towers, posing as a construction worker, a journalist, a maintenance man, and anything else that could get him inside to plot exactly how he could gain access to the roof in order to secure a high wire. He actually used a bow and arrow in order to connect the wire from one tower to the other.

"One thousand three hundred sixty feet below, Wall Street was just beginning to come to life at a little past seven on the morning of August 4, 1974. Petit stepped out onto the slender wire that stretched across the shimmering void," said the narrator.

"Hundreds of early morning commuters looked on in wonder and disbelief at what appeared to be a man walking on air," the narrator continued. For the next forty-five minutes, Petit made eight crossings across a one-inch steel cable, nearly a quarter mile into the sky and stretching 130 feet between the twin towers.

One security person, who went up to the roof to arrest Petit, described himself as "spellbound" when he witnessed him go down on one knee and then lay down on the wire. He could not believe his eyes when he saw him laughing and smiling as he danced across with both of his feet at times completely leaving the wire.

When Petit finally came down off the wire, he was arrested and then surrounded by an army of admiring reporters. It was there that he held court and described the incredible power of his mind.

"Whenever we are balancing on the boundaries of the limits of human condition, that's where life starts. That's where you feel yourself living," said Petit.

"So when I found myself one foot on the wire, one foot on the building, and I decided to shift my weight to become a bird, it was not something new. After a few steps, I was in my element. It did not even take a full crossing for me get to know the rigging and vibration of the building and the wire. It was then I was overwhelmed by a sense of easiness and simplicity, and smiling, perhaps out of disbelief, at how easy it was after all the months of ups and downs and detours. I was carrying my life on a path that was the simplest, the most beautiful, and the easiest."

"Why did you do it?" a reporter asked.

"When I see a beautiful place to put my wire I cannot resist," Petit replied.

"Were you afraid up there at all?" another reporter asked.

"I wasn't afraid," answered Petit. "I was just looking at what I had in front of me and living more than 1000 percent. So afraid not, and at the same time I was happy, happy, happy … happy!"

Petit's passion was unquestioned. "We need dreams to live. Dreams are as essential as a world to walk on and bread to eat. I would feel myself dying if this dream was taken away from me. The dream was as big as the towers! There was no way it could be taken away from me by authority, by reason, by destiny. It was really anchored to me in such a way that life is not conceivable without doing this," he explained.

Petit had referred to his preparation inside the towers as "getting into the belly of the beast." He was initially very fearful of the twin towers, but over time he had developed an intimate closeness with what was once his largest source of fear. He even said that he "married" them and that the towers "became his friends."

Amazingly, where most any person would view standing on a thin one-inch wire, more than 110 stories above the concrete pavement, as a place of certain death, somehow Petit viewed his most vulnerable position as a place where life began. He had initially thought that this feat was "impossible," but he had proven that he really was able to reframe his thinking. More importantly, he had proven how powerful the human mind can be when it becomes determined to do something.

This was the compelling lesson that I was trying to teach the boys! Does anyone ever really know what he or she is truly capable of achieving? Can we change our own beliefs about fear and failure? Could we stretch our own minds to the boundaries and limits of human potential?

I wanted my players to learn how to change their thinking the way that Petit did. I wanted them to reframe their biggest fears the same way—as a place where they could feel most alive!

I wanted them to adjust their thinking in such a drastic way that, instead of viewing Nutley as a place in which we had no chance to win, they would view it with the same sense of simplicity, beauty, and ease that Petit came to know while standing on the wire between the twin towers.

Just as Petit had first thought that the towers were a "beast" only to later consider them "his friends" and a "beautiful place to put my wire," why couldn't we view Nutley as a beautiful place to put our equipment and an even more beautiful place to play?

I knew that at Nutley, my team would be afraid to fail and scared to lose, perhaps more so than usual because this was a proverbial "big game." Rather than feel afraid to fail or scared to lose, maybe we could view tense moments in the game as a place where we could feel ourselves really living.

I spoke to my team inside the locker room that morning.

"When you get out there today, and you feel the pressure, when those butterflies start to creep in when the game is on the line, tell yourselves: *This is where living begins!*" I commanded.

Petit had minimized his fears by comparing them to the size of his dream, and I felt that we could do the same thing. What if our dream of winning the Greater Newark Tournament was as essential as a world to walk on or bread to eat? What if our dream was as big as the twin towers? What if our dream was so big that we simply could not see it being taken from us? What if our dream was anchored to us in a way that we could not conceive life without doing this? Maybe those thoughts would reduce our fears to a much smaller size. Maybe we could actually forget our fears by constantly focusing on something much larger—our dream!

Most people throughout the county thought that it would be impossible for us to defeat Nutley and even more impossible to beat them on the road in front of their own crowd. Many people even expected them to beat us so badly that they would have to stop the game after five innings for the ten-run mercy rule. I honestly felt that ingraining those Philippe Petit-type of thoughts into our own minds would permit that sense of simplicity and ease that we were hoping for while trying to perform.

Before we left for Nutley, I continued to reiterate the power of the mind. I distinctly recall Raimondo sitting there wearing his Saint Gerard T-shirt.

"Impossible is nothing!" I said.

Then I paced a little until I had eye contact from each player.

"When you get off the bus and walk into that park a half hour from now, tell yourself, 'It's impossible, *but I'll do it!*'"

Upon hearing that, the team erupted!

Our bus would be leaving shortly. Before we got on, I put sunblock on my face, neck, and hands, and sat on a large lime-green chair in our office and began to write out our lineup card. This chair was a throwback from the 1970s. It was big, bulky, and a discontinued bright lime-green color rarely seen in other pieces of furniture. It presumably had been in our office for decades, long before my arrival. In spite of its ugliness, it was probably the most comfortable chair that I ever sat in, as I would go out of my way to plop down there and write out my lineup.

The office door swung open. It was Whalen.

"What do ya say, Moose!" he said. "I feel it today, Moose. We're going to win today, because I got my lucky Munchos."

I looked up as he pulled a sandwich, a Gatorade, and a bag of Munchos out of a brown bag. I smiled, partially due to what he said, but also because I was envious that he could actually eat.

Rob Gariano ended the top of the first inning by blowing a fastball by Lawrence Caprio. In the second inning, we drew consecutive walks to Kevin Picardo and Steve Zurawiecki. Dom Raimondo then put down a sacrifice bunt that moved Picardo to third and Zurawiecki to second. Anthony Dalonges, who was removed and reinserted into the lineup three times overnight, placed a perfect safety squeeze bunt between the pitcher's mound and first base.

Gariano feeling hurried, overthrew the first baseman allowing both runners to score giving us a 2–0 lead.

"Moose, we just scored two runs without taking a swing, on two balls that didn't role more than forty feet," said Whalen at the end of the inning.

In the third inning, Santomauro doubled to left and scored when Kevin Picardo grounded to third and the third baseman committed a throwing error. In the fourth inning, Joe D'Annunzio, our number-nine hitter, walked and then stole second with help from Mark Ruggiero, who faked a bunt to distract the catcher from receiving the ball. Ruggiero then singled in D'Annunzio giving us a 4–0 lead.

In the bottom of the fourth inning, Raimondo allowed a double. The runner then moved to third on a passed ball and scored on a sacrifice fly by the number-three hitter, giving Nutley its first run. In the bottom of the fifth inning, Nutley scored twice, one on an overthrow by Ruggiero at short, which then placed the batter/runner at second. He then moved to third on a wild pitch and scored on a sacrifice fly. With two out, Raimondo hit the number-nine hitter with a pitch. The runner stole second and then scored on an error by Anthony Cerza at third base. They had cut our lead to one run at 4–3 going into the sixth inning. The game remained 4–3 into the seventh inning.

I called a team huddle to remind them that it was "Decision Time." Decision time to us was defined as any time after the fifth inning when the game was either tied or within a one-run differential. It was our goal to separate and distinguish ourselves during those moments.

I bent over, put my hands on my knees, and looked into my players' eyes.

"Hey, boys, the feeling that you have right now—this is where living begins!" I exclaimed.

The team got energized and huddled, with Ruggiero leading the call of "Hustle!"

Ruggiero singled and then stole second. With two outs, I asked him to attempt to steal third. This was against the book in baseball, and had Mark been thrown out, it would be the exact type of play that my detractors would call for my head over. In that situation, I was willing to go against the book if I felt that our chances were good to have the catcher overthrow the third baseman because of the pressure derived from the element of surprise. We got exactly what we hoped for, as the Nutley catcher overthrew the third baseman and Ruggiero scored, making it 5–3.

We needed three outs to pull off the upset. Nutley's eight hitter reached on an error by Ruggiero at short. Ruggiero came right back and made the next play as the number-nine hitter grounded out to him. That to me was a sign of mental toughness. Errors are always a part of any game, but to me, the guy who could come back after making a mistake and make a play under pressure was a tough guy. Mark had just done that.

Nutley had a man on second base and the tying run at the plate with one out.

The leadoff hitter singled, moving the runner to third. As the tying run, the leadoff hitter then stole second base. It appeared as if he was thrown out by our catcher, Baab, but the umpire ruled him safe. With the tying run at second and the winning run at the plate, Raimondo got the two hitter to pop-up to Ruggiero for the second out.

I thought about walking their number-three hitter, but at Whalen's urging agreed not to put the winning run on first base intentionally. I sent Renshaw to the mound to remind Raimondo that first base was open and to work him carefully.

With a 2–2 count, the hitter launched a fly ball skied high in the air to right field. Caprio settled under it, and it seemed to take a day to come down. I had my arm on Renshaw's shoulder. Caprio unsteadily made the catch, setting off a wild celebration in the West Essex bleachers.

I had told them on Monday that the next five days would be a character check, and they didn't just step up big that day. They had stepped up all week and showed tremendous character by winning all five games and advancing into the quarter finals.

"Impossible is nothing, boys," I said in the huddle. "You just shocked Essex County!"

"Full steam ahead!" yelled Renshaw as the team enthusiastically huddled, raised their hands, and yelled.

Something changed in me on the bus ride home that day. It dawned on me that this team was different. They weren't poodles. They couldn't be, because poodles could not have survived Nutley at all, let alone have survived that environment without Vinnie. Only a group of street dogs could have gone in there and won.

As our bus pulled into the parking lot, we were greeted with loud honking horns from students and parents. The entrance of the school was taped up with the letters "Go Home, Nutley."

Inside the locker room, Mark Ruggiero put slash mark number ten on the sledgehammer and raised it in the air. Then, he and Jon Baab began dancing in the middle of the locker room as the entire team surrounded them while "What You Know" by T. I. and "Pour Some Sugar On Me" by Def Leppard blasted on the stereo. They danced, reflecting the happiness they shared over the victory.

Part IV

Chapter 19

If You Have a Big Enough Why

Players must know you care, before they will care about what you know.
—Ken Ravizza
Sports Psychologist

SEVERAL MEMBERS OF THE team attended a Saturday night party. For roughly five dollars a person, one could get his hands on a red cup, which would typically serve as admission for unlimited trips to the beer keg. As they filed into a North Caldwell home with their money in hand, the "dream busters" greeted them at the door.

"Heard you guys got lucky today," said Glen Gloom.

"Nutley was the only team who could have beaten Seton Hall. Now that they are out of the tournament, Seton Hall has a cakewalk," added Donnie Doom.

"They won't even get a chance to play Seton Hall. They'll get knocked out next week, and it will be all over," added Gloom.

"Who do you guys play?" asked Doom.

"Montclair Kimberly Academy," answered Picardo.

Inside the party was heating up with a lot of dancing, drinking, and loud music. Mark Ruggiero appeared disturbed. He put down his red cup and glanced around. At the kitchen table a group of students were smoking marijuana and rolling more marijuana joints on the table. Mark went over toward John Baab and grabbed his arm.

"Let's get outta here," said Ruggiero.

Baab seemed confused, "Why, what's going on?"

Ruggiero also told Picardo. Then, Picardo told Santomauro and Barretta.

Within moments the team gathered outside.

Valerian felt deprived, "What was that about, Mark? I was chillin' with that girl I've been talkin' to!"

"Let's go. *Now!*" said Ruggiero

They left the party. The team started to jog. The jog turned into a run. As they reached Anthony Cerza's doorstep several blocks down the road, several cop cars sped down the street. As they watched from the porch, Anthony Tundo received a text message on his phone.

"Guys, Lawrence just texted me," said Tundo. "The party got raided. He made it out in time, but a bunch of people got arrested. He said they found everything in the house."

"Where was Lawrence?" asked Baab. "We couldn't find him."

"Where do you think he was?" answered Bustamante. "He was with a girl. What else is new?"

Had Mark brought them out of the house a minute later, they all would have been arrested.

"What made you do that?" asked Dalonges.

"Remember Coach talked to us about Duke lacrosse?" said Ruggiero. "I kept hearin' his voice as I was lookin' around. Coach said that the people on drugs are doing it because they're looking to fill a void—because they don't have what we have."

"I was thinking that too—when everyone was smoking in the kitchen," said Picardo.

"Thank God, you got us out of there. Whoever got arrested is going to get suspended at school," said Raimondo.

"Guys, what happened on the field today was one of the greatest moments of my life," said Ruggiero. "Imagine if we got suspended right now? We wouldn't be allowed to play. I don't know about you guys, but after today, I'm not doing anything to blow our shot. If we could beat Nutley, we could beat anybody."

The players stopped staring at the ground and looked up.

"Guys, we can beat Seton Hall!" shouted Ruggiero.

Some players nodded, and some just stared like deer in headlights.

They had left the party because they believed they had a purpose far greater than that of the party. They also had a leader secure enough in himself to call all of them out. Both were signs of a cancer-free team.

As much as Ruggiero was an outstanding leader, he was also evolving into one of the best players to come through our program. In the past, I had seen shortstops struggle offensively because of the tremendous pressure that the position of shortstop places on them. I saw other shortstops move to the outfield and instantly get better offensively. Conversely, Ruggiero had moved to shortstop, was handling the position, and as each day passed he was getting better offensively. His batting average was above .450 for most of the year. While Santomauro was our big bopper and our biggest offensive threat, Ruggiero was putting together the most consistent season of any player on our team, and he was doing so in the midst of transitioning to play the most difficult position on the field.

We were riding high at 10–4. On May 1, we beat Summit with Santomauro's towering three-run home run, his sixth of the season, leading the way. Just a week prior, we were 5–4, doubting ourselves, and staring at five games in five consecutive days. We had gained confidence, and we were building momentum.

I walked into the deli and picked up a newspaper. Right away the headline caught my attention: "Seton Hall Beats Hanover Park 17–1." The subhead read: "Game Called for Mercy Rule after Five Innings."

"That Seton Hall team is in a class by itself," said George. "They're like a damn college team! You guys don't play them, do ya?"

"We have to earn the chance to play them," I responded.

"No offense, Coach, but Hanover Park is the best team in your league, and Seton Hall Prep beat them by sixteen runs. Read it!"

George pointed to the newspaper in my hand.

"Hanover Park beat you guys, and Seton Hall beat them so badly yesterday that they had to call the game after five innings. If they beat Hanover by the mercy rule, what would they do to you guys?"

I put my head down.

"There's no shame in what I'm telling you, Coach. Seton Hall has been the number-one team in the state now for three of the past five seasons. And if they're not number one, they're always in the top five. Hey, if you ever get a chance to play them, I'll give you a free lunch if you beat them."

I walked toward the door, stopped, and looked back at George.

"Good luck, Mr. Gorsky!" I said.

He shook his head while looking over at one of the regulars seated at the lunch counter.

"I don't know where that guy's head is. At least get my name right. For some reason, he keeps calling me Mr. Gorsky. Ya know what? He probably thinks his team actually could beat Seton Hall. What a pipe dream!"

One of the challenges to advancing in the Greater Newark Tournament was that each game was played on Saturday, so there was a week in between each round, just as there is in the NFL playoffs. Normally your Saturday pitcher would be available for a brief stint in a game on Wednesday, but since Raimondo did not bounce back well, I didn't want him to do anything all week except run, condition, and throw a controlled side session in our bullpen on Wednesday. What made matters more complex was that teams were saving their best for us, especially after word spread that we had beaten Nutley. During the week we would have to beat our opponent's ace pitcher without Raimondo.

In one sense, that would make our upcoming games quite challenging, as we attempted to remain in contention for our league title. However, on the other hand, it would be great preparation for us, as the pitchers we would see in upcoming tournament games would be exceptional.

I was concerned about our swings. They were too big! We had won six straight, but I couldn't accept that approach to hitting in victory, knowing that I could never accept in defeat.

We needed to change our focus at home plate. In order to do that, I needed to demonstrate the importance of focus to them. I had picked up a cane at the Bombay Furniture Store and brought it to our next practice. It had a handle with the shape of a horse's head at the top of it. I asked Valerian to come up to the front and balance the cane on the tip of his index finger, focusing his eyes only on his fingertip.

He tried to balance the cane, but it kept repeatedly slipping off of his finger.

Then, I asked Vinnie to change his focus. I instructed him to balance the cane while staring at the horse's head at the top of the cane.

He tried to balance the cane again, this time while looking up at the handle of the cane instead of his fingertip. To his surprise—and everyone else's—he began to balance the cane without any difficulty for as long as he wanted to.

"Any of you can try this," I said. "Vinnie repeatedly failed to balance the cane when he focused on the wrong thing. But he was able to balance the cane once he changed his focus and began focusing on the right thing."

"Our focus at the plate is all wrong right now. We have too many guys who are trying to hit home runs, trying too hard to pull the ball. If you don't change your focus right now, a pro prospect like Rick Porcello will chew you up and spit you out. He'll eat you alive!" I explained.

Then I pointed to two orange cones on the field; one was placed in front of where the shortstop plays, and the other was placed in front of where the second baseman plays.

Skip Bertman had made reference to a "Hasselblad," which is a ten-thousand-dollar camera that the astronauts took to the moon. "Just before they snapped the picture, they would have to adjust and turn the lens. Even a ten-thousand-dollar camera requires sharp human focus," explained Bertman.

I told them that great hitters know how to focus and how to keep their focus in the middle of the field. I asked them if they wanted to be great. If they did, they would concentrate on improving their focus and stop trying to pull the ball! They were surprised when I informed them that our entire team would run ten sprints for every ball they hit to the pull side of those cones, which was to the left of the cone for a right-handed hitter or to the right of the cone for a left-handed hitter. We became better hitters that day with no mechanical adjustments. How did we do it? Fear of running!

On May 3, we got a firsthand look at the challenge of remaining competitive without having your ace pitcher available. After six straight wins, we were having a better year than our opponent, Parsippany Hills, but we had Anthony Cerza going against their ace, a kid by the name of Mike Halbach, who was being heavily recruited to continue his career at Montclair State University.

In baseball, your team could be stronger than another team in eight other positions, but that doesn't matter if the other team has a better pitcher on the mound than you do. Jack Lynch once said, "Montclair State could beat Florida State in baseball with the right guy on the mound, but they couldn't beat them in football, nor could they beat Duke in basketball either."

That was one of the beauties of our sport. The excitement and anticipation of that day's pitching matchup. As a matter of fact, based upon what I have described, baseball is the only sport where a last-place team could be a Vegas favorite over a first-place team because of the pitcher on the mound. I believe that actually happened sometime in the mid-'90s when Roger Clemens, then of the last-place Toronto Blue Jays, pitched against the first-place New York Yankees.

We were by far the underdog given the matchup of Cerza versus Halbach, a recruited college pitcher. "Anyone can win when their ace is on the mound," I said to the team. "Good teams find ways to win when they are deep into their pitching rotation, because it has to be win-win."

We fell behind 2–0, but battled back to take the lead 3–2. In the fifth, Tundo allowed a leadoff double, prompting me to insert Cordasco on the mound. He induced a pop-up, before allowing a game-tying single. After a pop-up and a strikeout, we were tied after four and a half innings. Cordasco was outstanding once again in relief, allowing no runs into the bottom of the seventh. Baab started the inning with a double. Santomauro was intentionally walked. Caprio was unsuccessful in attempting to sacrifice bunt the runners over for one out. Picardo then singled up the middle, scoring Baab for a "walk off" 4–3 victory.

We were behind, went ahead, relinquished the lead, and then walked off for our seventh straight win—twelfth of the season. Once 5–4, our record was now 12–4. Renshaw was perhaps the most enthusiastic person in our huddle as he gave his "full steam ahead!"

We were at practice on the day before we were to play Chatham, followed by Montclair Kimberly Academy, in the Greater Newark Tournament quarter finals. I didn't want them to look past Chatham for a second in anticipation of the big game on Saturday. We still had an important league game to play. I must have said, "We play Chatham tomorrow" ten times. Then I announced Anthony Tundo as our starter at Chatham. Bustamante threw a fit and walked over to the side as the team began to stretch. It was May of his senior year, and he had yet to record a win in his career. His frustration was building. He was slamming his glove against the fence, mumbling. I confronted him.

"What's the matter, Mike?" I asked.

"I thought this was my start, Coach. I'm sick of coming in relief. I've worked harder than any pitcher we have for three years. I don't get the start tomorrow? I've never done anything to help this team. I thought it was my turn," he snapped.

Prior to that moment, we had never had words, but I went back at him. He had a point that he had worked extremely hard, but I didn't think that any pitcher on our team besides Raimondo was likely to give us a complete game given what I had seen through sixteen games. I thought we were better suited to split games up and offset opposing offenses with a combination of different looks. We needed to do it as a staff, and he was someone who was used to coming in out of the bullpen, whereas some of our other pitchers were not. I explained this to him and then said very sternly, "Team needs come before personal wants!"

Reluctantly, he nodded.

For the second straight game, the matchup favored our opponent, as Chatham ace pitcher Pat Bocchino was an All-Conference-caliber pitcher. In the third, Ruggiero was on second base with one out as Santomauro came to the plate. I was certain that Bocchino would start him off with a slower curveball and give Ruggiero more time to steal third base. I flashed the signal. Bocchino surprised me. He was quick to the plate in his delivery and threw a fastball. Ruggiero was thrown out attempting to steal. I had guessed wrong and was painfully reminded of it by some loud groans in our stands.

Tundo took a 2–0 lead into the fourth before walking the bases loaded. I inserted Bustamante. He surrendered a base hit that scored one. The second run scored on a ground ball putout fielded by Valerian, who threw to D'Annunzio covering second. The third run scored when Valerian made an error at third. Bustamante then struck out the two hitter, looking to end the inning. All three runs allowed by Bustamante were charged to Tundo. We tied it at 3–3 in the fifth, and it remained tied until the top of the sixth. With two out in the sixth inning, we had runners on second and third base, with two strikes on Steve Zurawiecki. Bocchino had handled our lineup very well and seemed to be reaching back in a tough spot. It was time to go outside the box! I timed Bocchino from his windup. I felt that we could steal home. If we were to fail, the groans in the stands could get much louder, but as Joe Torre once said, "Once you start to manage according to what other people think, you're in trouble."

I gave Picardo the steal of home sign. Boccino's pitch went off the catcher's glove as Picardo slid in safely for a 4–3 lead. Valerian moved from second to third on the play. Zurawiecki drew a walk, as Bocchino was momentarily rattled. I then gave Zurawiecki a delayed steal sign from first. As the catcher threw down to second in an attempt to throw him out, Zurawiecki stopped short by design, allowing Valerian to stroll home unchecked. We now led 5–3. Bustamante retired the next six hitters for our eighth straight win.

I ran over to Bustamante. I knew what it meant to him.

"And you said, you haven't done anything to help this team? You couldn't have picked a better time for your first varsity win. Congratulations, Mike!"

I wanted our team to realize one thing. We were aggressive in the third inning when Mark was thrown out stealing, and we had failed, but we did not stop being aggressive. There is a difference between playing not to lose and playing to win. I wanted them to understand the difference between the two. I believed that aggressiveness wins out over the long haul, and as long as we continued to go all out without ever holding back that would prove to be true. We had gone outside the box and scored two runs with two outs without even putting a ball in play. If I hadn't let go of my fear of looking bad, I would not have been free to risk failure, and we would not have scored.

We could now begin to think about Montclair Kimberly Academy. They were the number-ten seed, five spots ahead of us. Their ace left-handed pitcher, Greg Harbeck, was signed, sealed, and ready to be delivered to Johns Hopkins University to pitch for them in the fall. They were a solid team led by their shortstop Jimmy Ruzich, who would later go on to star at the College of New Jersey.

Just as I had shared the story of Philippe Petit before our game against Nutley, I pondered if there was anything more that I could do that might inspire my players to achieve peak performance. Could we win again tomorrow? I asked myself, *How?* Perhaps we could, if we had a big enough reason why.

The following morning, May 6, I was standing in front of the mirror in the coaches' office wearing a long-sleeve black shirt and applying sunscreen when Whalen entered carrying a brown paper bag.

"Got my Munchos again, Moose," said Whalen. "You know what that means. I'm feeling good."

I took a seat in that same green chair I used before all the other games and wrote out our lineup card

"You know what, Moose?" I asked. "I haven't washed this undershirt or my uniform in eight games now, and I don't even care."

Inside the locker room, Baab and Bustamante were doing their best rendition of me reviewing our plan for reading a left-handed pitcher's pick-off move.

"We've gotta run, boys! We don't stop running just because we see a lefty," said Baab, in his best attempt at imitating my voice. "Maybe he is a head guy. If his head looks at you, he goes to the plate, but if his head looks at the plate, he throws over to pick you off," he added while demonstrating.

"No, John, it's like this," Bustamante said as he adjusted his hat to look like mine and placed his right-handed glove on the wrong hand. "Maybe he is a gap guy! If you see a gap between his legs, he is picking you off, but if that gap closes up, he throws to the plate," he added as he went through the motions.

The team erupted with laughter. As I entered the locker room, Baab and Bustamante nervously ran and sat at their spots in front of their lockers and put their heads down. Raimondo was again wearing his black Saint Gerard T-shirt.

"Before we go over our plan for stealing second off a left-hander—" I said.

Baab and Bustamante smiled at one another.

"You can have anything you want in life if you're willing to do just one thing," I added.

"*Anything*, anything you want in your life, can be yours—if you're willing to fight for it!"

Then I shared with them the story of the rabbit and the fox.

"One day a Zen master took his student into the woods for a lesson. They noticed a hungry fox eyeing up a rabbit as its prey. The Zen master turned to the student and asked, 'Do you think the fox will hunt down the rabbit?'

"The student said, 'Oh, of course, the fox is much quicker, faster, and stronger than that poor defenseless rabbit.'

"Just then, the fox began his chase, running and running and running until he was out of breath. He simply couldn't catch the rabbit. He rested for a moment and then began another chase. He was running and running and running, and he still couldn't catch him.

"The student turned to the master and said, 'I don't get it, Master, the fox is much quicker, faster, and stronger than the rabbit. Why can't he catch him?'

"The master replied, 'You are naïve, my young student; the fox is merely running for his dinner, but the rabbit is running for his life!'"

"If you have a big enough reason why you want something, you'll always find out how you can do it," I said.

I found this to be true, and I wasn't alone. Tom Peters, a long-time caller to Dr. Gilbert's *Success Hotline* was a leading salesperson. He credited a speech that his wife gave him for his tremendous success in sales. One day he came home, and his wife went into her speech. It was the shortest motivational speech he had ever heard. Actually it was only three words long: "Honey, I'm pregnant."

After learning the news, Peters found the "how," and he also found the "do."

During World War I, Allied Commander Ferdinand Foch said, "The most powerful weapon in the world is the human soul on fire."

"Imagine what it will be like if you had to compete against someone whose soul was on fire," I said as I paced across the locker room. "Our souls have to be on fire!" I exclaimed.

"Weak teams avoid challenges, but champions rise up and meet challenges!" I added.

"Are you willing to fight for it?" I asked. "See, if you just want something you won't get it. You'll be beaten out by someone who really really wants it. If their souls are on fire and ours are not, we will be beaten out by them. Wanting it isn't enough. We must hunger for it! We must compete for it!"

"There will be obstacles on that field today. Are you willing to fight through the emotional difficulty and the pressure?" I asked. "Are you willing to compete for every inch? Hannibal said, 'Find a way, or make a way!' Today, set your souls on fire, find a way, and *fight* for it!"

The team enthusiastically clapped, especially Baab and Bustamante, whose demeanors had changed. They were no longer laughing.

By encouraging my players to get their souls on fire and to really fight for something that they wanted, I was trying to emphasize and reinforce what might be the most important thing that they could ever learn—to compete.

The word *compete* stems from the Latin word *competere,* which means *to strive together.* Dr. Gilbert once shared with me what Boston Celtic Larry Bird attributed his Hall of Fame career to. I thought Bird was going to say the thousands of practice shots that he had taken, but his answer surprised me. He attributed his successful career to Los Angeles Laker Magic Johnson. Bird said that he always worked out twice as hard in the off-season, because he knew that if he didn't, there was no way that he could ever out-do Magic, and there was no way that his Celtics could ever beat the Lakers. Magic Johnson's greatness had brought out the very best in Larry Bird. They had strived together. They competed!

Teaching my players the value of competition was not just important for me to do, it might be the single most important thing that any coach will ever teach to his or her players. The United States is arguably the most competitive society in the world. The majority of all amateur athletes will never make their living while playing a sport professionally. Learning to compete on an athletic field can only better prepare an amateur athlete to someday function in our ultracompetitive society. While kids, parents, and the community at large would become consumed with whether or not we would win, this was not the true essence of what we did. Of all the games that I have coached and all the lessons that I have attempted to teach, the growth that a student athlete derives while learning to compete, truly compete, in every minute of every game, will ultimately prevail.

The field at Montclair Kimberly contained less seating than Nutley. Several hundred people lined up all the way down both the first and the third baselines. Kevin Picardo hung the rope on the backstop near home plate. Anthony Cerza carried the plastic toilet bowl and placed it on the West Essex bench. As each player followed in behind Picardo and Cerza, he grabbed the ball attached to the end of the rope and firmly tugged on it.

It was there that I first met Steve Tober of sidelinechatter.com. Steve is a good man, and he does an outstanding job covering sports in our area. He also had the foresight to sense that the print industry was changing and was ahead of the curve in founding his website, which remains the most popular sports site among people in the North Jersey area.

Mark Ruggiero led off the game with a towering triple to right center field. He then scored on a deep sacrifice fly ball by Nick Santomauro. Harbeck settled in and struck out six in the first five innings. Lawrence Caprio, Kevin Picardo, Vin Valerian, and Steve Zurawiecki placed their helmets down, walked over to the plastic toilet bowl, and "flushed it" after being sat down by Harbeck. Zurawiecki covered his face with both of his hands after his flush and then looked up.

Raimondo had only one strikeout through five innings, but he was outstanding, mixing fastballs, curveballs, and changeups, and not allowing a run in the first five innings. The score remained in our favor 1–0 in the sixth inning.

In the bottom of the sixth, the MKA two hitter led off with a single up the middle. The three hitter then singled to right, and Caprio bobbled the single, allowing runners to advance to second and third with no outs. A ground ball, handled by Ruggiero at shortstop with the infield back, tied the game at 1–1 with one out. Since Ruggiero had to go toward second base on the play, the runner from second advanced to third. With the infield pulled in, the five hitter hit a little swinging bunt squibber off the end of his bat toward first base. The runner from third got a great jump and scored as Picardo's only choice was to come in, field the dribbler, and tag out the batter/runner. MKA now led 2–1, as Raimondo struck out the seven hitter to end the sixth inning.

We were down to our final three outs in the seventh inning. Ruggiero and Baab screamed in the dugout.

"C'mon, boys. We want it more, right here!" shouted Ruggiero.

"Fight for it, boys! Keep fightin' now. Let's find a way how!" yelled Baab.

Caprio led off the seventh and grounded out to third. Our tournament hopes were down to our final two outs. Kevin Picardo then lined a ball that was a fraction of an inch above a leaping and outstretched second baseman for a single, putting the tying run on first.

I was going to give Picardo a steal sign, not too early, but not too late either. *Don't let me down*, I thought to myself. Valerian was the hitter. On the second pitch, he launched a towering triple to center field, scoring Picardo to tie the game at 2–2. Valerian slid into third, to the roar of an ecstatic West Essex crowd, and pointed to the dugout.

"Let's go! We fight for it, baby! We're not losin'. We're on fire! Let's go!" he screamed. I had nearly suspended him after the fit that he threw at the end of the Morris Hills game. Now, that seemed like a lifetime ago.

For the second time in the tournament, Anthony Dalonges placed a perfect safety squeeze bunt between the first baseman and Harbeck. As Valerian slid safely into home, Harbeck fell down without attempting a play on Dalonges. He brought Valerian in to give us a 3–2 lead, and he was also safe at first. Our bench and our crowd went crazy! I pumped my fist at third base. Dalonges then attempted a steal of second as Zurawiecki smacked a base hit to center field. The center fielder attempted to throw Dalonges out on his way to third, but threw the ball high over the third baseman's head into dead ball territory. Dalonges scored automatically, and Zurawiecki advanced to second. Ruggiero then hit a slow roller toward third. The third baseman charged in and fell over the ball. Zurawiecki was safe at third and Ruggiero was safe at first. Joe D'Annunzio then scored Zurawiecki on a sacrifice fly to right field.

John Baab reached on a single, and a throwing error on a ground ball to second by Santomauro then scored Ruggiero. We had been down to our final two outs, with no one on base, and scored five runs to take a 6–2 lead. Raimondo struck out their first hitter, before inducing a fly ball to Santomauro in left field. The game then ended on a pop-up to Picardo. The team dog piled on each other in the infield, before we got together for our postgame huddle.

What could I say? Raimondo was outstanding! Valerian, who nearly quit and who had nearly been suspended from the team for his conduct after the Morris Hills game, had given us a heart transplant. Dalonges, who was nearly pulled from the lineup before the Nutley game, had the game-winning RBI and now had three RBIs in two GNT games, all on safety squeeze bunts. He was being interviewed by Tober as a hero of the game.

"Coach told me as long as I don't bunt it back to the pitcher that we would score a run," said Dalonges. "I just held my feet and tried to place it away from the pitcher."

Ruggiero made slash mark number thirteen and raised the "ant killer." Renshaw gave his "full steam ahead!"

Back in our locker room, another dance party broke out as the players, in similar postgame clothing, broke out the same music while passing the sledgehammer back and forth. The main participants were once again Mark Ruggiero, John Baab, and Pat LaConsole as the team celebrated wildly. And why wouldn't they? We were headed to the Greater Newark Tournament semifinals.

CHAPTER 20

Cuidado de los Detalles (Attention to Details)

Sometimes when I think of what great consequences come from
little things, I am tempted to think that there are no little things.
—Bruce Barton
Author

THE GREATER NEWARK TOURNAMENT semifinals pitted us against Newark
Eastside. They were seeded number three in the tournament behind Seton
Hall Prep and Nutley, and ranked number fifteen in New Jersey's top twenty
according to the Newark *Star-Ledger*. On the other side of the bracket, Seton
Hall was set to square off against Bloomfield. The winners of each game would
meet in the next round. Seton Hall was attempting to reach the finals for the
tenth consecutive season, and their chances looked good behind one of the
best pitching staffs in the entire country.

Major league scouts were following junior Rick Porcello around all spring.
His fastball was routinely being timed at ninety-six miles per hour. He was
expected to be one of the first five picks in the first round of the major league
draft next season. Senior Mike Ness was headed to Duke on a full scholarship,
and junior Evan Danielli, a six-foot-eight right-hander, was already drawing
interest from Notre Dame; like teammate Porcello, he was expected to be
selected in the major league draft next year. But, Seton Hall didn't just have
pitching. They had other players around them too.

Center fielder Steven Brooks was being sought after by Wake Forest. Junior
Nick Natale was being pursued by Rice University. Joe Jamison had drawn
attention from Wagner, while Tim Shoenhaus and catcher Ryan Vandermay
had drawn interest from the University of Delaware. They had eight likely
Division I players, some of which were expected to sign pro contracts. Seton
Hall Prep was arguably better than a lot of college teams.

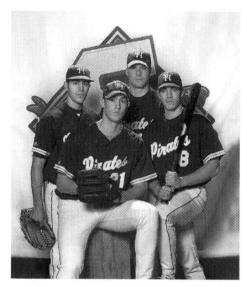

Clockwise from bottom. Rick Porcello (number twenty-one),
Nick Natale, Evan Danieli, and Steven Brooks (number eight) gave Seton Hall
Prep at least a quartet of Division I players/major league prospects in 2006.
Photo by Richard Morris

Valerian had been sky high since his big hit against Montclair Kimberly, but he had struggled at practice the next day. We wanted our players to pay attention to detail, handle frustration, and stay in the moment. All three were at times very difficult for Vinnie. After misplaying a few ground balls, he lost his focus and forgot to cover third base on a bunt coverage during a defensive situational drill. It was not the first time that he forgot this important assignment. No matter how many times we reviewed it, when it came time for him to do it, he wasn't covering third base. Instead, he would stand there staring into space. I jumped all over him.

"How many times do we have to go over it, Vinnie? With a man on first, the guy who doesn't field the ball covers third. Dammit, Vinnie! We've done it a hundred times already. What's wrong with you?"

"I know, Coach. I got it. I'll be there," he answered.

"Does it matter if you know what to do, if you don't do what you know? We're counting on you. Take your head out of your rear end and know the situation!" I hollered.

Then I called him in and explained that I didn't care if he finished the season with more than twenty errors. "We are who we are," I told him.

"I'm not changing anything. Stop looking back, Vinnie, unless that's the way you want to go. It doesn't matter how many errors you have right now.

In order for us to get through a tournament, we're going to need you to make a big play, so shake it off and step up!"

On May 8, we won our tenth straight game at home against Dover. I had to scratch Lawrence Caprio, as his battle with allergies was getting the best of him. Lawrence was voted as the individual having the "nicest eyes" by his senior classmates. When he came to me in the dugout, his eyes were far from nice. They were swollen, puffy, and completely red. He explained to me that they were burning so badly that he could barely keep them open. He was in pain! This had been a season-long battle for him, which adversely affected his play, and this was one of the worst days. We could only hope that his condition would improve in time for the weekend.

Mark Ruggiero, John Baab, Nick Santomauro, and Joe D'Annunzio led the way offensively. Steve Zurawiecki hit a home run and also struck out several hitters en route to earning the victory on the mound.

On the following day, May 9, we hosted Cedar Grove. Bustamante entered the game in the second inning to relieve Tundo, who wasn't sharp, and pitched six full innings to earn his second career win in as many tries. He struck out two and induced several pop-ups. Mark Ruggiero made several fine plays at shortstop. Our offense exploded early and took advantage of a few Cedar Grove mistakes. With an 11–3 lead, the game ended on a fly ball to Anthony Dalonges in center field. We had now won eleven straight games.

The next day, May 10, we hosted Hanover Park. As we were trailing 3–0 in the third inning, Renshaw turned to me in the dugout.

"These guys are as good as any team I've seen," he said. "They hit one through nine. There's not one weak spot in the order. They pitch, they run, play great defense. Hanover might be the best Group II team in the state."

"Seton Hall beat them 17–1," I said.

Renshaw's mouth dropped.

"Do you know how good you have to be to beat this team? And by a ten-run mercy rule? That's insane!" he answered.

"Beat them 17–1!" I repeated.

Ruggiero doubled, and Santomauro singled him in to make the score 3–1, but it wasn't enough. We never really got anything going after that and ended up losing 5–2. Our winning streak had ended. Hanover Park halted it at eleven and defeated us for the second time in two meetings that season. By comparison, they also left us little hope of competing against Seton Hall Prep, that is, if we were to even earn the chance to play them.

Our focus was now on Eastside. In the movie *Hoosiers,* Coach Norman Dale tells his players to "forget about the size of the school and the fancy uniforms." Coach Dale had given his players great advice. He didn't want them to be intimidated. He was encouraging them to block out all the distractions and focus only on playing basketball. However, it is one thing to merely tell your players to forget about distractions. I wondered, was there a way that I could teach my players "how" to forget about distractions?

Former New York Mets manager Bobby Valentine said, "Players become paralyzed by thinking about winning and losing. How do you get out of that? By thinking about playing!"

I knew that the size of the crowd at Verona could paralyze my players. They were used to playing in front of anywhere from twelve spectators to maybe forty. Come Saturday against Eastside, there would be more than fifteen hundred in attendance. There would be more reporters and more cameras than they had ever seen. I also knew that Eastside's reputation could intimidate them. They were led by junior Manny Melendez, who had hit thirteen home runs with fifty-five RBIs as a sophomore. He was also their best pitcher. He consistently threw in the upper eighties with a tight slider. He was quick to the plate, which made him tough to run on, and he could field his position too. Major league scouts were keeping an eye on him, as the biggest question seemed to be whether he would make a better pitcher or position player.

Coach Jerry Battaglini had Eastside well prepared. They had no weaknesses. They could hit. They had great arm strength at every position, and they had outstanding team speed too. They had just beaten Union High School by eighteen runs. Union was a large Group IV power that was comprised of several thousand students. We were a small Group II school with under 750 students. Pounding a large school like Union was the type of win that made me raise my eyebrows as I stared at the morning paper. But most of all, I was concerned about Eastside's passion and enthusiasm for the game.

A lot of the players on the Eastside team were Latin students who loved to play and really could play. When they got runners on base, they utilized momentum to their advantage. Once they got some momentum, they were like sharks circling in the water. When one of their players got a hit, they all wanted to hit. When a runner reached base, the entire team would all lean up against the dugout fence and cheer in support of the hitter. Their enthusiasm was second to none; they went beyond just rooting their teammates on. By the time their chanting reached its peak, the entire team would be standing up in the dugout singing, not in English, but in what was for many of them their native Spanish. Their intensity and spirit were unmatched and unlike any I had ever seen. I suppose if we weren't playing against them it would be a joy to see.

In particular, I was concerned about Raimondo. He had never pitched in front of a crowd that size. He had never encountered a team with that kind of tenacity. Was there a way to help him prepare for this?

I recalled a story that Skip Bertman told his team at LSU. It was about a fighter pilot in the Persian Gulf War named Dennis Krimble, who had taken off from the *Kittyhawk*. Krimble would have only a split second to decide whether to engage or to withdraw. The success of his mission, as well as his life, was contingent upon his reaction under pressure. In order to prepare for this, Krimble had spent thousands of hours in a flight simulator. His confidence stemmed from the fact that the simulator made him feel as if he had been there before.

At the start of practice, I held up a white board with the words: *Performance = Potential – Interference.*

"The crowd, the media, and the noise from their dugout are all forms of interference. If you can block out the interference and focus, you can perform to your potential," I said.

Just as Krimble went through his flight simulator, I wanted to put Raimondo in a similar situation. He would normally do his midweek side session in our bullpen, but I had him go out to the mound on our field. Baab was behind the plate. Hitters took turns standing in and tracking his pitches. The rest of our team was in our dugout.

At my local supermarket, they had bright orange dot stickers that people would normally use for garage sales. I stuck one of those orange dots inside Baab's glove.

Then I asked all the players in our dugout to try to distract Raimondo as best as they could. I wanted them to create as much interference as possible. As Raimondo went into his windup, the entire bench screamed as loud as they could, "Hey, hey now, hey pitcher! *Oooh, oooh!* He's feelin' it! Here we go!"

Raimondo threw a pitch high off of Baab's glove. As the team yelled louder, Raimondo threw another high pitch. He walked off the mound, visibly rattled, and kicked the dirt.

We used an acronym to help our pitchers slow the game down: AVCE. This meant they needed to: *analyze* the situation, *visualize* where they want to throw the ball, fine *center* their target, and *execute* the pitch.

The concept of "center" was an important teaching point. "Soft center" meant that the pitchers would look in and see the hitter, the catcher, the umpire, etc. But "fine center" meant that the pitchers wouldn't just use the catcher's glove as a target, they would try to hit a spot inside the catcher's glove.

"It's just you and the glove, Dom, nothing else," I said. "Close your eyes. When you open them, fine center on the orange spot inside John's glove. Don't see anything other than that orange spot. Don't forget to breathe!"

Again, Raimondo missed the target. Our players were riding him pretty good, but I wanted the situation to be even more similar. They were all sitting on the bench inside the dugout.

"Their players won't sit on the bench," I hollered. "They'll be standing up against the fence. Most of their players will be screaming and singing in Spanish, not English."

Most of our players were in college placement or honors Spanish. According to their progress reports, they were all doing well too. I asked them to duplicate exactly what Eastside would do come Saturday.

The team got off the bench and leaned against the fence and began screaming in Spanish. A couple of them were climbing the fence.

"El no tiene nada!" (He's got nothing!)

"Ten paciencia!" (Be patient!)

"No tira duro!" (He doesn't throw hard!)

"Rompe la cabeza!" (Bust his head!)

Screams were echoing from our dugout.

Raimondo checked the sign from Baab. As he delivered a pitch in the dirt, the noise in the dugout became even louder.

Pat LaConsole pointed at Raimondo and hollered out, *"El feo, el feo!"* (The ugly one!)

Raimondo understood Spanish too. He looked into the dugout and pointed at his chest. "I'm *Rico Suave!*" he answered, referencing a popular song title by that name.

"Dom, the bleachers are packed," I said. "Eastside's dugout is going wild. Manny Melendez is in the box with guys on base and there's nowhere to put him. Faze all of that out! Just focus on that tiny little orange spot inside the glove. C'mon, hit that spot!"

As the team sung in Spanish to a deafening roar, Raimondo delivered a perfect strike. Baab never moved his glove.

"Coach, can you believe they called me ugly?" he asked.

"Rather than you telling them that you're Mr. Rico Suave, the idea is to block out the interference and become so focused on that orange spot that you don't even hear them," I explained.

How this would go was anybody's guess. I didn't know if our "mound simulator" would help him to block out the distractions or if he would simply implode. The outcome was not something that we could control. However, our preparation was something that we could control. I felt that it was my job as a coach to duplicate as best we could exactly what he would experience when the pressure would be at its highest point.

That evening as I drove home from practice, I experienced the first of a series of omens that I would receive. I hadn't heard Gerardo's "Rico Suave" since college, perhaps as far back as 1992, but coincidentally, just moments after Raimondo had proudly declared himself Mr. Rico Suave, the song came on my car radio as I randomly flipped through the stations. I couldn't help but chuckle.

My fixation on superstitions—ranging from what I wore, to how I put certain things on, to the order or manner in which I did things—was bordering on an obsessive compulsive disorder, with the sole intent to somehow gain control over something that I had either no control or limited control over. Some would call this grasping at straws, but when you develop a belief in it, it becomes very real to you. The night before the Eastside game, I had this superstition in my mind that I had to do the exact same things that I had done the night before the Nutley and Montclair Kimberly games or else we would lose. So I continued my same exact routine of sitting on my patio after dinner. I had talked to my players about how many times a day they heard "that little voice in your mind" talking to them, telling them what to think. Now, I struggled to control my own.

I held the New Balance sneaker in my hand as my thoughts shifted back and forth. Each time I had a negative thought, I looked at the sneaker and tried to think of something positive.

We hadn't been to the semifinals at Verona since 2004 when the infamous botched safety squeeze play had occurred against Nutley. That little voice in my mind became quite loud as it reminded me of the voice in the stands, "What the hell is he doing? We'll never win with this guy!"

As I twirled the sneaker, that little voice began to recite random lines from Rudyard Kipling's "If."

If you can keep your head when all about you
Are losing theirs and blaming it on you.
If you can trust yourself when all men doubt you,
but make allowance for their doubting too …
If you can force your heart, and nerve, and sinew …
with sixty seconds' worth of distance run,
Yours is the Earth and everything that's in it …
And—which is more—you'll be a man, my son!

Then, that little voice knocked me into the corner, up against the ropes, and began to pound away. What if the voice in the stands was right? What if I was jinxed? What if there was some kind of hex on me? I held the sneaker by the lace as it dangled back and forth. That little voice blurted out the name of my idol: Mark Messier. Why, on the night before a game of such magnitude, would I be thinking of a hockey player? It wasn't about hockey. This was about the power of belief.

Messier was once asked about jinxes and the "Curse of 1940." He refused to believe that jinxes even existed. As Rick Carpinello wrote in *Messier—*

Hockey's Dragon Slayer, Messier said, "Nope, not one bit. If you're surrounded by enough talent and the people are all pulling on the same rope, you're going to be the master of your own destiny. This organization has been thinking along those lines since I've been here. Jinx is just another excuse for whatever, a lack of motivation or talent. If you push yourself you put an end to all those jinxes."

With the weight of the entire city on his back, Messier guaranteed victory with his team down three games to two and facing elimination in the 1994 Eastern Conference semifinals against the New Jersey Devils. A hat trick and an assist later, he had backed up his words. The rest is history, as the Rangers went on to beat the Vancouver Canucks in the Stanley Cup finals, ending a fifty-four-year supposed hex. Indeed, Messier had ended the "Curse of 1940" for the New York Rangers. He had slain the dragon, and in the process, he proved that hexes didn't really exist.

"We finally got a guy with balls," a Ranger season-ticket holder said to me in a deli the day the Rangers acquired Messier in 1991.

Having balls, or "a set of leather balls" to be more specific, was also the exact trait that Jack Lynch had described to us as kids as being essential for winning baseball teams.

The lesson that I learned from Messier was a compelling one: people who have balls do not believe in jinxes. People with balls believe in themselves. Other people will follow believers! Messier's overwhelming belief in himself gave him a strong sense of confidence that prevented him from having any notion of a jinx. His belief spread among his teammates, like an anti-cancer, and also among the fans. Messier inspired me to face challenges head on and to believe more in myself.

My balls felt like they were in my throat, but that little voice gave me some encouragement. I told myself, *If I want the notoriety that comes from coaching a team to a championship, then I have to show up and coach with balls in big games played in front of a lot of people.*

I couldn't coach it any differently than I would if there were only twelve people in the stands. I knew if we were to win, I was going to have to press some buttons, and with that, there would be great risk.

Anybody can buy a ticket to a bullfight, I thought. *But how many people have the balls to jump over the wall and fight the bull?*

My palms were sweating. I took my hat off and read what I had written weeks ago on the underside of the brim. It was from the book *Moneyball* by Michael Lewis: "Don't let the fear of looking bad be greater than the gain of making the best move."

I knew what had gotten us this far: aggressiveness. I also knew what we had to do: stay aggressive.

Do you want to be a lion for a day or a mouse for life? that little voice asked.

No one ever leaned over on his death bed and said, "I wish I held back more. I'm glad I played it safe."

I knew I'd have to make more than a hundred decisions tomorrow. My choices were that I could either go all out or hold back. That little voice assured me, *I don't care if there are a thousand people there, it's better to go all out and lose than to play it safe and win.*

I took a deep breath and looked down at the ground. When I looked up, I could hardly believe what I saw. It was another omen. It had to be! The most majestic hawk that I had ever seen, soaring high in the sky and circling in the air above all of the other birds.

"Rise above it!" I exclaimed.

On the morning of May 13, I was standing in front of the mirror in the coaches' office putting on my sunblock. Then, as to not dare break routine, I sat in the green chair and began writing out our lineup card. I began to wonder which opposing pitcher we would see from Newark Eastside. Dave Majias featured several off-speed pitches and could be sneaky fast. He had soundly beaten Newark Academy in their quarterfinal game, and the possibility that we could see him on the mound and Manny Melendez behind the plate was real. On the other hand, Melendez was more of a power pitcher, and given his size and velocity, he was certainly more intimidating.

As I continued writing, Whalen walked into the coaches' office.

"I hope you have your Munchos, Moose," I said as I greeted him.

Before I finished my sentence he pulled an orange Gatorade and a bag of Munchos out of his bag.

"I got the Munchos, Moose, and you know I'm feelin' a win when I bring the Munchos," he answered.

Our players were in our batting cage as we went through the process of our pregame and walk-through. Some of the parents of our players, including my father, were already at Verona to watch the other semifinal game between Seton Hall and Bloomfield. It was there that word spread: Eastside coach Jerry Battaglini had remained mum to this point but now announced Manny Melendez as his starting pitcher. My father called on my cell phone to give me a heads-up. I found the top of our batting order, who had finished their rounds in the cage inside our training room, and informed them that we would definitely be facing Melendez, not their previous GNT starter, Majias.

I had expected them to be intimidated, expected to see some negative body language, but on the contrary, upon hearing this, they seemed to get up an extra notch. They seemed turned on and fascinated with the opportunity.

"Allriiiiigghhht," was how Ruggiero and Santomauro reacted, high-fiving Caprio, Valerian, and Picardo as their eyes all widened. Their reaction was knee-jerk and could not have been phony or rehearsed. They genuinely couldn't wait to face the feared Melendez. White poodles would have been scared, but not them. These kids had balls!

Prior to getting on the bus, we met inside our locker room. As I opened the door, Raimondo's Saint Gerard T-shirt caught my eye again.

Arizona State coach Pat Murphy emphasized the importance of controlling your emotions during big games. I spoke to the team about doing just that.

"All the adversity! All the adversity that we have faced, and all the resiliency that we have shown, that's all in the past! Today! Today is about hustle! Today is about focus! You can get as emotional as you want right up to the point where you don't lose your focus. So before you get on the bus, find that point where you are emotional but not unfocused. Today is about the details, the little things, boys. Little things are going to mean a lot. Today, each at bat, each play, is like the lottery—you have to be present to get the prize. Keep your mind in the present on every single pitch. If you make a mistake, flush it right out, and stay in the moment. Come out when you're ready to play baseball the right way!"

As I walked out of the room, Ruggiero stood up.

"Hey, hey, guys. We got the semis today and the finals next week. For the next seven days, the most important thing on the planet is each other."

The team nodded, while looking intently at one another, and began to clap.

Paul "Doc" Goeltz Field at Verona was a picturesque setting for a baseball game. The field, for the most part, was wide open. It had a fence, but it was close to five hundred feet away from home plate. The infield was set down beneath beige concrete bleachers reminiscent of a Roman coliseum. The bleachers surrounded the entire infield. As we arrived, Seton Hall Prep was putting the finishing touches on Bloomfield in the first game, 4–0. Upon winning, they did not celebrate. This was expected. They casually strolled off and exchanged handshakes and high fives in a gentlemanly manner. They had done this before, ten times in a row to be exact.

As our team walked down the steps, our metal spikes against the concrete bleachers sounded like an army brigade marching in sync. Kevin Picardo hung the rope on the fence right in front of our dugout on the third-base side. Anthony Cerza placed the plastic toilet on the Knights' bench. A crowd of sixteen hundred people filed in, some remaining from the just-concluded Seton Hall game.

Both Raimondo and Manny Melendez looked outstanding in the first inning. Mark Ruggiero looked like a seasoned veteran, fielding a ball in the hole between shortstop and third base before throwing out a runner at first. In the bottom of the second inning, John Baab threw out a runner trying to steal second, as Raimondo held Eastside scoreless.

Nick Santomauro hit a long double in the third, but was stranded on second base as Picardo grounded out to third. Picardo flushed the plastic toilet as he returned to the dugout. Again, Raimondo kept Eastside in check in the third inning.

In the fourth, Melendez came up to bat with a runner on first base. Eastside was singing in Spanish from the dugout. Raimondo took a deep breath. He had thrown a steady diet of breaking balls to Melendez during his first at bat and got him to ground out to Valerian at third base. We normally played a shallow outfield and challenged opposing hitters to hit the ball over our outfielders' heads. This enabled us to take away shallow bloop singles. However, against Eastside, and in particular against Melendez, we played an exceptionally deep outfield. Since there was essentially no outfield fence at Verona, we positioned our outfielders close to four hundred feet away when Melendez stepped into the batter's box.

With a one and one count, Raimondo threw a fastball. Melendez hammered it. As the ball exploded off his bat, the Eastside dugout and crowd erupted. It was sure to be a home run. And at any ordinary field it would have easily been a two-run homer. But Dalonges, having been camped four hundred feet away from home, took a few steps back and caught a line-drive bullet that was still gaining momentum at the time of the catch. The West Essex crowd erupted, as the cheers from the Eastside crowd sharply turned into a collective groan of *"Aaawwwww."*

On the next pitch, Baab threw out another would-be base stealer attempting to take second base with two outs. The roar on the West Essex side escalated even further. Raimondo had made it through four innings of shut-out baseball.

We were headed to the fifth inning with the score tied at 0–0. I called the team into a huddle.

"Boys, we've got to be able to score a run here with one base hit," I said. I had noticed that Melendez was very quick to the plate with a runner on first, but was lifting his leg significantly higher and taking a lot longer to make his delivery with a runner on second. I told the team that if we got someone on, we might sacrifice-bunt him to second base and then look to steal third base.

"Look for it. I'm telling you it's there!" I explained as the huddle came together.

Our fifth inning ended with Santomauro grounding out to third base.

Eastside's fifth ended when their seven hitter hit a comebacker to Raimondo. The game was turning into a gem, as we had played six scoreless innings and remained deadlocked 0–0. As Eastside took the field for the sixth inning, there was a buzz in the crowd on both sides, as the sixteen hundred in attendance seemed overjoyed with the quality of play, as well as the performance being turned in by both pitchers.

Caprio led off and got hit by a pitch. Kevin Picardo sacrifice-bunted him to second. I gave the steal sign to Caprio. He nodded. Then he dug his feet in the dirt.

Eastside's coach, Jerry Battaglini, alertly called time and took a trip to the mound to talk to Melendez and his infielders. I called Caprio over. I felt that Battaglini went to the mound specifically to tell them to watch for the steal, so I took it off, but I told Caprio to watch for when I put it back on.

The cat and mouse game was on.

Valerian drew a walk as ball four skipped a few feet away from the Eastside catcher. Caprio aggressively advanced to third base. Dalonges walked to the plate. In that split second of an instant, that little voice again reminded me of the voice in the stands: "What the hell is he doing?"

I can't coach scared, I assured myself. I flashed the sign to Dalonges and then leaned over toward Caprio to make sure that he gained momentum toward the plate on Melendez's delivery.

I took a deep breath as my heart pounded faster. "Can't hold back," I said under my breath. "Here we go, fasten your seat belt!"

As Melendez delivered, Caprio crept down the third-base line. Dalonges showed bunt and placed it perfectly between Melendez and the first base line. Caprio darted for home plate. Melendez went for the ball, fielded it, and shuffled it to the catcher. Caprio slid safely under the tag. Dalonges was also safe at first, as the ball went to home plate.

I pumped my fist as we took a 1–0 lead.

Simultaneously, the West Essex crowd rose from their seats and let out a deafening roar. A few even screamed out, "Great call, Coach!"

Two years prior, I had put on the same exact play in the same game against Nutley. When it failed, my detractors portrayed me to be a buffoon. This time it had worked, so now I was being hailed as a genius.

With Valerian at second and Dalonges at first, Steve Zurawiecki stepped in. Realizing Eastside was still reeling from the safety squeeze bunt, I gave Valerian the steal sign. He and Dalonges pulled off a double steal. Zurawiecki then walked. Joe D'Annunzio stepped in with one out and the bases loaded, looking to add more.

D'Anunzio's hit was a hard one-hop ground ball right at the shortstop, who flipped to the second baseman, who threw to first for the 6–4–3 double play. We had a chance to add more but were not able to do so.

Mark Ruggiero handled a ground ball for the first out of the bottom of the sixth. Then, he made an error. Vin Valerian followed with another error. Eastside's two hitter then hit a ground ball to D'Annunzio, who tossed to Ruggiero for a force-out at second, but he could not convert the double play at first with the speedy Majias running.

Trailing 1–0 with two out and runners on first and third base, the Eastside crowd rose to their feet as Manny Melendez walked to the plate. There was nowhere to put Manny as he now had a chance to tie the game, if not more. I took a trip to the mound to talk to Raimondo and the infielders.

I told them that if they were to try to steal second base, we were going to throw it right at Raimondo's cap and try to pick the runner off of third base. If that didn't work, the runner would steal second uncontested. Then, I intended to intentionally walk Melendez. I looked at Domenick.

"Dom, he can't beat us! Every pitch has to be approached like your ahead in the count 0–2, with nothing out over the plate," Raimondo nodded.

Melendez stepped in after crushing a four-hundred-foot line drive for an out in his last at bat. There are defining moments in any game, and with us leading 1–0 with runners on first and third, and two outs in the sixth inning, undoubtedly, this was one of them.

The Eastside players leaned against the fence in their dugout. Some partially climbed up the fence and shook it on their way up. They were all screaming and singing loudly in Spanish.

"Ahora aqui, Manny, numero uno, ahora!"

Raimondo came set and took a deep breath.

"Analyze! Two outs, 0–0 count. Best hitter up," he said to himself.

Baab flashed two fingers down indicating the sign for curveball.

"Curveball," Raimondo mouthed to himself. "Visualize. See that glove. Center. Orange spot."

Raimondo lifted his leg, let loose, and delivered a curveball on the outside corner for a called strike.

Baab did not have to move his glove.

The Eastside dugout was intense. They tasted it! They continued singing and chanting in Spanish.

Raimondo looked in at Baab's glove.

"Count 0–1," Raimondo muttered, analyzing. "Changeup down. C'mon, right to that orange spot."

Melendez checked his swing and grounded softly to Picardo at first base. Picardo fielded the ball, stepped on first, and ran off the field, pumping his right fist in the air.

Raimondo had fooled Melendez on the changeup and pitched out of the jam. We would go to the seventh leading 1–0.

Picardo walked toward Raimondo in the dugout. Raimondo was sitting on the bench, wiping the sweat from his forehead. Picardo patted his head and sat down next to him.

"Great job, Dom! Way to shut 'em up," said Picardo

"Shut who up?" Raimondo asked.

"Their entire bench. Didn't you hear them screaming at you and taunting you?

"When?" asked Raimondo.

After winning the 1988 World Series, Los Angeles Dodgers pitcher Orel Hershiser described a state when a pitcher is entirely focused on his target and does not hear anything, not even crowd noise—a place when he is "totally relaxed and confident." He referred to this state as being "in the zone." When Hershiser reached this state, the only thing he saw was catcher Mike Soscia's glove, and he knew that he was going to hit it. Raimondo had reached that frame of mind. We were now three outs away from the finals.

Ruggiero led off the seventh and got hit by a pitch. He moved to second on a ground ball to third by Baab. Caprio stepped up with two outs. He had struggled practically all season with vision problems, but we needed one hit from him in that moment. Melendez threw. Caprio ripped a line-drive base hit between first and second base. He had come through and given us an important insurance run; we now led 2–0.

The number-four hitter from Eastside grounded to Valerian, who threw to first for the first out. Valerian, like Caprio, had had his share of struggles throughout the season but was now there when we needed him and stepping up in a big way. Raimondo struck out the next hitter looking on a curveball. The number-six hitter grounded to Ruggiero.

On the day nearly two months earlier when I removed Picardo from shortstop because of his torn shoulder and replaced him with Ruggiero, most fans would have said it would be impossible for us to be doing this. But, here was Ruggiero at shortstop, throwing over to Picardo at first base for the final out.

Ruggiero ran toward his teammates with his hand raised in the air, signifying number one. Our team mobbed each other in a dog pile in the middle of the infield.

Unlike Seton Hall, we were in uncharted waters heading to the Greater Newark Tournament finals. The bleachers seemed to shake as we looked into the sea of red, white, and black in the bleachers. The crowd was going wild!

Bob Behre of the Newark *Star-Ledger* requested interviews with Raimondo and Dalonges. Dalonges now had four RBIs, two of them game-winning, in three Greater Newark Tournament games, all on safety squeeze bunts.

"I knew I would get it done for two reasons," Dalonges said to Behre. "I had already done it against Nutley and Montclair Kimberly, so I didn't feel any pressure, and I knew that was what the team needed me to do."

Raimondo spoke of his strategy. "We practiced locating down and away all week. If you bring it in against those guys, they can really crank it on you."

A short while later, inside our locker room, Ruggiero put slash mark number seventeen on the sledgehammer and raised it in the air. Another dance party broke out with the players in their customary attire and music. The main participants were once again Ruggiero, Baab, and Pat LaConsole, who passed the ant killer back and forth as the team celebrated wildly.

7S7001560514 RACE 7S1001560514 ZALLCALL 01:22 05/14/06

HIGH SCHOOLS

Quinones leads Science, 25-7; Lyndhurst rolls

SOFTBALL

Jacquelyn Quinones finished 4-for-5 with seven RBI to pace a 24-hit attack for Newark Science during a 25-7 victory over Montclair Immaculate yesterday in Montclair.

Quinones, a junior shortstop, hit a two-run homer and scored three runs, while Wendy Quincaloia went 4-for-5 with a triple, an RBI and three runs and Allyson Buldoka went 4-for-5 with a double and four runs for Science (7-12). Lizzie Menendez went 3-for-4 with two runs for Montclair Immaculate (0-14).

Lyndhurst 11, Union Hill 0: Freshman righty Melinda Martin pitched a perfect game with 10 strikeouts in her first varsity start and classmate Francesca Gaccione went 2-for-3 with a three-run homer and four RBI to spark Lyndhurst (8-13) in Lyndhurst.

Raritan 20, University 0: Melissa Mancuso pitched a one-hitter with seven strikeouts and two walks and Samantha Helmstetter went 4-for-4 with four singles, four runs scored and two RBI for Raritan (7-13) in Hazlet. Jazmin Collazi singled for University (4-14).

Kittatinny tops Morris Knolls, 4-3

Ninth batter Kate Muller singled in the go-ahead run with two outs in the top of the sixth inning to lift Kittatinny to a 4-3 victory over Morris Knolls yesterday in Denville.

Sara Stocklinski (4-1) allowed five hits for Kittatinny (16-3), striking out three and walking two. Mandie Pierson added a two-run triple for Kittatinny. Sara Gilmore singled twice for Morris Knolls (15-6).

West Milford 3, Lakeland 1: Kristina Jimenez pitched a three-hitter with six strikeouts and two walks for top-seeded West Milford (18-4) in the quarterfinal round of the Passaic County Tournament in West Milford. Kait Bailey hit a two-run double in the fourth inning to break a 1-1 tie against ninth-seeded Lakeland (15-8), which defeated West Milford, 3-1, in a regular-season game earlier in the week.

Fietkiewicz, Brown lift Westfield, 7-0

Kristina Fietkiewicz used her bat to make a powerful statement for Westfield yesterday.

The senior shortstop slugged a home run, tripled and finished with four RBI and two runs to support the one-hit pitching by Lindsay Brown when ninth-seeded Westfield upset top-seed and defending champion Brearley, 7-0, in the quarterfinal round of the 31st Union County Tournament in Kenilworth.

The tournament continues with the two semifinal round games Friday at 6 and 8 p.m. at Memorial Field in Linden.

Fietkiewicz blasted a two-run homer to deep left-center with two outs in the first inning to give Westfield a 2-0 lead and added a run-scoring triple in the third to make it 3-0.

"There've been games we've had trouble getting started and have played from behind, so those early runs were huge,"said Fietkiewicz, who came up with five assists in the field. "Maybe nobody expected a lot from us, but we were confident we could win."

Brown, a junior right-hander, employed a deceptive drop curve effectively and finished with nine strikeouts and three walks. Vanessa Muniz singled with one out in the first for Brearley (14-3).

Westfield extended its lead to 6-0 in the fifth after three runs scored on Jenny LaSpata's sacrifice fly. LaSpata lofted a shot to deep right-center, where Brearley right fielder Mallory McElroy made the catch after a long run but collided with center fielder Lisa Reilly. McElroy held the ball but went down with an injured left knee and all three runners tagged and scored. Fietkiewicz drove in the final run with a sacrifice fly in the seventh.

Scotch Plains-Fanwood 1, Roselle Park 0: Elaine Piniat, who scattered four hits, singled and later scored on a single by Allie Brown in the second inning for second-seeded Scotch Plains (17-4) in the Union County Tournament quarterfinal round in Scotch Plains. Piniat struck out five and walked none. Brandy Guarnaccio allowed 11 hits with three strikeouts and two walks while Michelle Rose singled twice for 10th-seed Roselle Park (13-10).

Gov. Livingston 5, Union Catholic 0: Nicole Ruggiero ground out drove in Christine Bennett, who tripled, in the first inning to give third-seeded Gov. Livingston (17-4) a 1-0 lead in the Union County Tournament quarterfinal round in Berkeley Heights. Capri Catalano threw a one-hitter with 16 strikeouts and one walk and Kerry Havas went 3-for-3 with a triple and two runs for Gov. Livingston.

New Providence 5, Holy Family 1: Kelly Marchisio drove in two runs in the first inning when New Providence (13-5) took a 2-0 lead in New Providence. Tara Alberse contributed an RBI double for New Providence. Caitlin Ross scattered three hits, struck out six and walked none for New Providence. Holy Family of Bayonne is 15-6.

Bailey, Jimenez key West Milford, 3-1

Kait Bailey stroked a two-run double in the fourth inning and Kristina Jimenez pitched a three-hitter to lead defending champion West Milford to a 3-1 victory over Lakeland yesterday in the Passaic County Tournament quarterfinal round in West Milford.

Top-seeded West Milford (18-4) gained a 1-1 tie in the second when Hope Van Dyke's double scored Jamie Chalkley. Jimenez (17-4) struck out six and walked two. Samantha Tempe of ninth-seeded Lakeland allowed five hits, struck out three and walked.

Amanda Smith singled home the run for Lakeland in the second inning. West Milford, which has won the tournament title three of the last four years, will face fourth-seeded Passaic Valley next week in the semifinal round.

Lewis, Reidy lead Woodbridge, 1-0

Brittany Lewis lofted a sacrifice fly in the sixth inning and Kelly Reidy tossed a two-hitter to lead Woodbridge to a 1-0 victory over North Brunswick yesterday in Woodbridge.

Lewis delivered Beth Fenton, who reached on an error and took third on a single by Lynda Ha for Woodbridge (13-8). Reidy, a junior right-hander, walked one and struck out four for her third shutout. Halley Weinstein allowed five hits with two walks and six strikeouts for North Brunswick (2-15).

Kinnard propels Lawrenceville, 3-2

Rashonda Kinnard clubbed a two-run homer and pitched a five-hitter as Lawrenceville edged Blair, 3-2, yesterday in Lawrenceville.

Lindsey Ciresa, who tripled, scored to give Blair (8-9) a 1-0 lead in the top of the second. Christian Barber's RBI-double tied the game in the bottom of the second for Lawrenceville (11-8).

Metuchen 12, Timothy Christian 0: Christina Mantak went 4-for-4 and drove in a run and Liz Marquard had two hits and scored three times for Metuchen (14-6) in Piscataway. Amanda Hermes collected two of the three hits that Timothy Christian (8-7) managed off of Metuchen's Caitlyn Zahn.

Hun 4, Hill 1: Alyssa Fares and Morgan Cawley each drove in a run in the fifth inning while Nikki Caplinger and Alex Their both scored on passed balls in the sixth as Hun (11-5) rallied to defeat Hill (4-11) of Pennsylvania in Princeton.

BOYS VOLLEYBALL

ESSEX COUNTY TOURNAMENT QUARTERFINALS

Livingston def. Barringer
25-11, 25-20

Livingston (12-8): Brandt Grobes, 15 assists, 4 kills, 4 aces, 1 block; John Me 6 kills, 1 block; Harry Xu, 6 kills, 2 blocks; Johann Kim, 19 digs, 5 kills; Tim Kim 19 digs.

AARON HOUSTON/FOR THE STAR-LEDGER

After making the play for the last out yesterday, West Essex shortstop Mark Ruggiore celebrates his team's 2-0 victory over East Side in the Greater Newark Tournament semifinal.

Ness paces Seton Hall, 4-0; Raimondo leads West Essex

BASEBALL

BY BOB BEHRE
FOR THE STAR-LEDGER

Mike Ness of Seton Hall Prep was virtually unhittable and Dom Raimondo of West Essex was simply unbending.

The sparkling pitching performances of the right-handers propelled their teams in the semifinals of the 74th Greater Newark Tournament yesterday to set up an intriguing match-up in the championship game.

Ness threw a 69-pitch one-hitter to stifle Bloomfield, 4-0, and Raimondo needed just 73 pitches in a tidy three-hitter that gave West Essex a 2-0 victory over East Side before 1,000 at refurbished and manicured Doc Goeltz Field in Verona.

The victory for top-seeded Seton Hall (19-2), No. 8 in The Star-Ledger Top 20, gives the West Orange school its 10th straight berth in the championship game. It will be just the second appearance in the GNT final for West Essex (17-5), the 15th seed.

The North Caldwell school, which fell in the 1993 final to Nutley, had already picked off second-seeded Nutley before taking out third-seeded East Side (18-4), ranked No. 15 in the state.

"It's a great feeling," said West Essex center fielder Anthony Dalonges. "I've never felt anything like this. This is my first final in anything."

Dalonges should feel good. It was his perfectly executed safety squeeze bunt that delivered L.J. Caprio with the game's first run with one out in the top of the sixth. Caprio would single home Mark Ruggiero with an insurance run in the seventh.

Caprio led off the sixth by getting hit with a two-strike curveball by Melendez. He was bunted to second by Kevin Picardo and moved to third when a ball-four pitch to Vin Valerian got past the East Side catcher.

That set up Dalonges, who had already layed down successful squeeze bunts for West Essex in GNT victories over Nutley, in the first round, and 10th-seeded Montclair Kimberley, in the quarterfinals.

"There was no doubt in my mind I would get it done for two reasons," Dalonges said. "I had done it against Nutley and MKA, so I didn't feel any pressure. And because all I wanted to do was what the team needed."

Dalonges dropped Melendez's first pitch down the first-base side on the infield grass. Melendez attempted to make a quick, backhanded throw to catcher Alex Sepulveda, but Caprio slid across the plate ahead of the throw.

AARON HOUSTON/FOR THE STAR-LEDGER

Lawrence Caprio of West Essex scores a run on a bunt yesterday as East Side catcher Alex Sepulveda takes the throw.

The loss snapped East Side's 11-game winning streak. The victory was the 12th in the last 13 games for West Essex.

That West Essex could win such a low-scoring game against a very good hitting team like East Side is a direct result of Raimondo making a living on the outside corner all afternoon.

"We practiced working the outside corner all week," Raimondo said. "If you bring it in to those guys they'll crank it on it you."

The only cranking was done by losing pitcher Manny Melendez, who jumped on a Raimondo fastball out over the plate in the fourth. But the long shot to center field went for a fly out to Dalonges at least 380 feet away in the spacious and fenceless, Doc Goeltz Field outfield.

"Dom was throwing three pitches for strikes," West Essex coach Scott Illiano said. "We wanted to work fastball down and away and go inside when we wanted to. Boy did he compete."

Raimondo (5-0) struck out three and walked one and faced just three batters over the minimum. Melendez battled gamely, limiting West Essex to five hits, struck out four, walked two, but hit five batters. That caused him to battle with runners on base in six of his seven innings but he was able to strand 12 West Essex runners.

Ness' performance was even better than Raimondo's. The Duke-bound Ness struck out seven, walked none and did not go to a three-ball count on any batter. In fact, Ness didn't throw a ball out of the strike zone against the aggressive Bloomfield squad until the second batter of the third inning.

Bloomfield's only hit was a slow rolling grounder to second by Luis Gonzalez leading off the third. Seton Hall second baseman Matt Kenney bobbled the ball as he charged the grounder, but it was clear Gonzalez had the play beat.

But Ness and Seton Hall found themselves in a tight duel with 12th-seeded Bloomfield (13-12) as left-hander Billy Salvato (3-1) kept the 2005 Non-Public A champions at bay. He permitted eight hits and three earned runs.

Joe Jamison doubled leading off the second, moved to third on a sac bunt and scored on a two-out sac fly to left field by Nick Natale. Seton Hall struck for two more in the fourth to take a 3-0 lead when Rick Porcello and Natale singled with two outs and came around on Ryan McCrossan's booming double to left-center field.

Seton Hall tacked on an unearned run in the seventh on a two-out single by Adam Gomez.

Bloomfield Tech 10, Glen Ridge 0: Hector Santiago (5-1) threw a six-inning no-hitter, struck out 12 and walked four and Burt Reynolds hit a two-run homer, his 13th of the season, for Bloomfield Tech (10-0) in Glen Ridge.

Arts 11, Shabazz 2: Ricardo Martinez (1-6) threw a three-hitter, struck out 13 and walked five and Stanley Rosario's two-run single in an eight-run fourth gave Arts (1-18) an 11-2 lead in a Newark Public Schools Tournament preliminary game in Newark. The victory ended a 40-game losing streak for Arts, which last won, 7-5 in eight innings, over University on May 17, 2004. Sunni Ali had an RBI single for Shabazz.

Belleville 3, Caldwell 2: Mark Balbach (6-0) worked 6⅔ innings for the victory and David Caruso came in to snuff out a Caldwell rally in the top of the seventh for the save for Belleville (16-6) in Belleville. Jonathan Serrano (3-for-3) hit his fifth home run of the year, a two-run shot in the sixth that gave Belleville a 3-0 lead. Matt Dorting had two hits, including an RBI single in the seventh for Caldwell (7-18) that cut the deficit to 3-2.

Passaic Valley 5, Wayne Valley 2: Adam Christopher's three-run homer in a four-run top of the seventh erased a 2-1 deficit for Passaic Valley (12-11) in the first round of the Passaic County Tournament in Wayne. John Kruse hit a solo shot in the bottom of the sixth to tie the game at 2-2 for Wayne Valley (13-9).

Hawthorne 5, Passaic 3: Matt Goitz (5-0) worked six innings for the win and was 3-for-3 with two runs scored for Hawthorne (14-4) in the first round of the Passaic County Tournament in Hawthorne. Passaic was limited to five hits and fell to 4-14.

Clifton 5, West Milford 2: Mike Vinciguerra threw a four-hitter, struck out five and walked none and singled in the middle of a three-run rally in the top of the sixth for Clifton (10-10) in the first round of the Passaic County Tournament in West Milford. Albrich Perez had an RBI single in the rally and Clifton added two runs on a throwing error. West Milford is 14-7.

Petrillo (4-for-4) lifts Newark Academy, 6-5

Dan Petrillo went 4-for-4, scored twice and drove in two runs for Newark Academy, which edged Montclair Kimberley, 6-5, yesterday in Montclair.

Dave Hardin and Chris Russo each had an RBI single as Newark Academy (17-2) built a 6-3 lead in the top of the seventh. Charlie Gray went 4-for-4 and scored two runs for Montclair Kimberley (12-9), which pulled within a run on Greg Harbeck's two-run single with two out in the bottom of the seventh before Andrew Del Colle induced a fly ball to end the game.

St. Benedict's Prep 11, Rutgers Prep 0: T.J. Valentin cracked a three-run homer in the first inning and added a solo shot in the fifth for St. Benedict's (10-5) in Somerset. Casey Epps had the lone hit that Rutgers Prep (10-11) managed off of Trevor Reckling (2-3), who struck out 11 and walked one.

Morristown-Beard 13, Montclair Immaculate 1: Mike Betz drove in four runs with a three-run homer and a triple while John Gianis doubled twice and brought in three runs for Morristown-Beard (13-5) in a five-inning contest. Montclair Immaculate took a 1-0 lead in the first on an RBI-single by Jon Dominguez, its lone hit of the game.

CHAPTER 21

He's Got the Same Agent as A-Rod

The bigger the conflict, the more glorious the victory. And if we
don't win, we hope that at least we were a worthy opponent.

—Ralph Purdy
Former West Essex Teacher/Coach

I STARED AT THE ceiling. My head was pounding.

"What's wrong?" asked Jane.

"He has the same agent as A-Rod," I answered.

"Who?"

"His name is Rick Porcello. He throws ninety-seven miles per hour.
His agent is Scott Boras, the high-profile sports agent who handles Alex
Rodriguez. Next year, some major league team will draft him in the first
round, and he'll be a millionaire."

"Really? Right out of high school?" she asked.

"They are one of the best teams in the country, Jane. We are not even
ranked in the top twenty in New Jersey. After Porcello, they've got at least five
other Division I players, maybe more. They are bigger, stronger, and faster.
They have studs at every position! Athletically, we don't even belong on the
field with them. We need a miracle. That's the only way!"

She tried to encourage me that at least we had made it this far, but that
was my biggest fear. It had taken me eleven years to get to the finals, and
now that we were there, we had to face a major league pitcher. In our culture,
people wear T-shirts that say "Second Place Is The Best Loser!" If we lose, no
one would say that we overachieved. They would forget that we even made
it to the finals.

"You don't think you've proven yourself already? Look at you," Jane
scolded as she became irate.

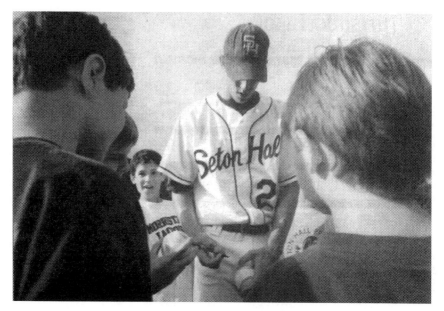

Rick Porcello was already signing autographs in high school.
Photo by Richard Morris

"You can't even enjoy what you did yesterday! You were seeded fifteenth. Fourteen other teams were supposed to be better than you. You weren't even supposed to beat Nutley, let alone make it to the finals. Everyone sees what you've done; so what is your problem?"

"It's the label. I'm the guy who can't win a title, and it's ... it's a life that I can't accept."

"Are you kidding me?" she asked. "On the second day of practice your shortstop got hurt. Overnight he became a first baseman, and your second baseman became a shortstop. That little fourteen-year-old boy is at second base; the JV infielder took over center field. On most days your right fielder can't even see. Two months ago you weren't even sure that your pitcher would get over his sore elbow. Should I go on? How about the All-Stater who graduated? Despite it all, you are going to the finals—the GNT finals—and you're still not happy? What the hell is wrong with you?"

It was the label. If I could only shake that label, I would feel I could enjoy it more. It wasn't fun. It was sheer hell. I couldn't eat. I was nauseous for half the day. Forget about sleeping. I felt if we could win this thing, in the future I would be able to enjoy it more—the practices, the kids, the bus rides—everything about it could be better without this pressure to win.

Again, Jane set me straight. She acknowledged that coaches are judged by wins and losses but pointed out that she had often seen some really lousy coaches win titles because they were blessed with great talent.

"It's hard for me to know what you're going through right now," she said, "but no matter what happens next Saturday, I think that you need to see this through, because this is where your heart is. This is something that you're good at. I've been to almost every game. I watch how they look at you when you speak to them in the huddle. You have this immeasurable trait to reach and connect with those boys. Not everyone has that, but you do, and that goes a lot further than wins and losses. Watching you reach and connect with them makes me proud. It shouldn't matter if you ever win a title. If you bring out their best, that's all that anyone can ask of you. Can't you just stop being so concerned about what other people think?"

I knew she was right, but I just couldn't stop obsessing with the outcome. This was a quest! I had six days to get my kids to believe that they could win. Six days seemed like an eternity.

"You're just feeling the stress that comes with the job right now," said Jane. "If you want the rainbow, then you have to put up with the rain!"

That evening my phone rang. It was Trongone.

"Scott, I'll throw my arm out for this team! I'll do anything to get them ready," he said.

His offer to throw batting practice was a prime example of the single most important trait you could look for in an assistant coach: loyalty. As a young coach, I was introduced to Elizabeth High School's football coach Chet Parlavechio, who advised me that when choosing my coaching staff, "Take a little more loyalty for a little less circle and *x*," meaning give an edge to loyalty over strategy and logistics, as they can be taught over time.

Loyalty was paramount to knowledge in assistant coaches. But in Trongone, I had a guy who was evolving as a teacher of baseball and, even more important, a guy who was loyal to our program. How loyal? He would literally throw his arm out to help us get ready.

Our players had never even seen a ninety-seven-mile-per-hour fastball, let alone tried to hit one. Just as we had adopted the Dennis Krimble flight simulator premise with Raimondo to overcome the distractions from Eastside's dugout, we would somehow have to put our hitters in a similar situation prior to facing Porcello. We could use a pitching machine, but that would not compare to a live arm.

Trongone threw in the mid-eighties when he was in his prime at Montclair State University. That was prior to tearing his elbow, an injury that ended his career. It had been a while since he had thrown, but he could probably still bring it in the low eighties for a short period of time. That would only be equivalent to a Porcello changeup. But, I thought, what if we moved him up to the Little League distance of forty-five feet away from home plate and protected him with an L-screen? Maybe eighty miles per hour at forty-five feet could simulate the reaction time of a fastball at ninety-seven miles per hour at the regulation distance of sixty feet six inches away from home plate. Perhaps that could duplicate what our hitters were about to encounter. But would it even be safe to do?

CHAPTER 22

Do You Believe in Miracles?

When your heart is in your dreams, no request is too extreme!
—Jiminy Cricket

I PACED BACK AND forth in the lobby at Hackensack Hospital. My mother had gone downstairs for a cup of coffee. My brother Dan read through the rankings in the *Star-Ledger*. For the first time in weeks, I wasn't thinking about baseball. The only thing that could take my mind off the game was the condition of my father. He was in surgery to remove his cancerous prostate.

"Wouldn't the doctor have come out by now if everything was okay?" I asked.

"These things take time," Dan answered.

I was anxious. The surgery was definitely taking longer than we had expected. And there wasn't anything to do other than to pace or sit around and wait. Mostly as a distraction, I began talking about the upcoming game.

Dan put down the paper and said, "Look, you got to stop doing this to yourself. You have done everything you can with this team. The fact that you've made it to the finals is a tribute to the job you've done."

"I'm afraid we are going to come this far for nothing. We finally get here and have to play a private school that's comprised of an All-Star from every town."

"When I saw your team piling on each other in the infield the other day, that wasn't nothing; that was something! You never know, Scott. This Seton Hall team, they're still kids."

He pointed to the paper and slapped it down against the chair next to him.

"I don't care what these rankings say. You guys have heart!" he said adamantly.

"But they're reading the papers too, Dan. Somehow, I've got to find a way to get them to believe that they can win."

The doctor came out. It was a relief when I saw him smile. He informed

197

us that Dad had done great. He said the cancer was larger than he thought, but they had gotten it all. He expected him to be just fine.

Having been assured that my father would be okay was like a weight being removed from my chest. For the first time in a long while, I actually felt like I could eat, as my brother, mother, and I walked down to the hospital cafeteria for lunch. Then, my thoughts shifted back to the game.

I felt that I had to do two things in the remaining days leading up to the game. One was to get them ready to face a ninety-seven-mile-an-hour fastball. The other was to get my players' minds off of what they were reading and hearing in order to believe that we could actually win. The first we could attempt on the field. The second would require us to put time in off of the field too.

By now, the "dream busters" had come out in full force. Every person they came in contact with, every newspaper, every website, and the NJ.com chat forum predicted that Seton Hall would beat us soundly. Many said that Seton would even beat us by the ten-run mercy rule in five innings. The kids were hearing it from their peers too.

"I give you guys props," Gloom said to a large group seated at the cafeteria table. "I didn't think you guys were good enough to beat Eastside, but Seton Hall is going to pound you!"

"Me too," added Doom. "Props to you guys, but now it all ends next week against Seton Hall. I mean, c'mon, guys, their pitcher is going to be a major leaguer. You don't have a chance!"

I had my own doubts too, but that didn't matter. It was my job to get them to believe that they could win. How could I get their minds off what all of the "dream busters" were saying and turn them into believers?

I had to sell them on the fact that with the right perspective, problems could actually be a good thing. They could be a chance to do something great. As soon as I arrived at school, I went to work on their psyche.

"I've got a tough job to do today," I said. "I've got to get you to love something that you hate. I bet you hate problems!"

I asked them to think about any great movie that they had ever seen. Then, I told them that I bet the one thing that they all had in common was a big problem.

"What was the problem in *Rudy*?" I asked.

"He had no talent," answered Picardo.

He was right. If Rudy was six foot two, two hundred and forty pounds, athletic, and bright, they would not have made a movie.

"What was the problem in *Titanic*?" I asked.

"They crashed," replied Zurawiecki.

"The Atlantic Ocean," I said. "No iceberg, no problem. No movie, case closed!"

The players laughed.

"See, the bigger the problem, the more interesting the story," I added. "What do you want your life to be? No drama, no problems? Or do you want your life to be like *Rocky* or *Harry Potter*? Imagine if a Hollywood film crew was going to make a movie about the West Essex baseball team. Who would we have to play?"

"Seton Hall," the players answered.

"No disrespect to Bloomfield High School, but no one would ever watch our movie if we played them in the finals. The only way people would ever watch is if we have a nationally ranked team with the best pitcher in the country standing in our way. Boys, we need Seton Hall! They're our opportunity to do something great! Without them, we are just another team that no one will ever remember. The bigger the problem, the bigger the opportunity!"

They had been subjected to so much negativity and so much doubt. The prevailing wisdom throughout the community was that it was impossible for us to win, that it would take a miracle. I wanted to give them hope. The best way I could do that was to tell them a story about a person or a team who had faced similar odds and persevered.

Before our very first practice, I had posted the "Impossible Is Nothing" quote that I borrowed from the Nike poster with the 1980 US Olympic Hockey Team, but I ran the situation by my former assistant and current Saint Mary's coach, Charlie Giachetti. He was adamant that I show the team the movie *Miracle*, starring Kurt Russell, which chronicled the 1980 United States Olympic hockey team's triumph at Lake Placid.

We had had work to do on the practice field, but after previewing *Miracle*, I realized that I didn't have to show them the movie in its entirety. I only needed to show them a few key highlights, namely the famous speech that Team USA coach Herb Brooks gave his players just prior to taking the ice against the Russians.

"What was Team USA's problem in the movie *Miracle*?" I asked the team.

"The Russians," said Baab.

Baab was exactly right. There never would have been a miracle at Lake Placid without the Russians. Team USA needed the Russians in order to achieve greatness. Without them, Team USA's players would just be a bunch of insurance salesman who no one remembered.

I hit the play button. The players tuned into the television monitor. Russell depicted Coach Herb Brooks to a tee.

"Great moments are born from great opportunities, and that's what we have here tonight. If we play these guys ten times, they beat us nine out of ten—but not tonight. Not this time! Tonight we play with them! Tonight we skate with them! Tonight we shut them down, because we can! They've had their moments, and they've had their time, and their time is over! This is our moment. This is our time!"

I paused the video.

"Let's be honest here," I said. "If we play Seton Hall ten times, they beat us nine out of ten times. But it's a one-game series, boys. It doesn't matter that they're better than us. We just have to play better than they do on Saturday night. Seton Hall has had their moments. They've had their times. They'll have many more—but not this time! We haven't come this far and defied the odds for nothing. We were meant to be here. This moment is ours. This moment belongs to us. *This is our time!"*

I forwarded the video to the next part that I thought was key. The Russian goaltender Vladislav Tretiak was removed from the game. As he skated to the bench, his coach, Victor Tikhonov, screamed at him.

Herb Brooks encouraged the American players, "You guys just knocked out the best goaltender in the world!"

As Tretiak skated to the bench, the Russians were unnerved and visibly shaken. I believed this point was critically important for our preparation. Seton Hall, like the Russians, were used to dominating their opponents and expected to do so. I felt that if we could manage to keep the game close, and stay close late, the pressure would be entirely on them.

Two weeks earlier, the Russians had beaten Team USA by ten goals. They had expected to easily do it again. I continued playing the tape as the camera panned in on the Russians.

"Look at the expressions on their faces when they expected to win but it wasn't happening," I said. "Now their goalie gets yanked. Stunned disbelief, boys!"

I paused the tape. I felt this was the key to our game.

"Seton Hall expects to beat us by ten runs," I said. "If we can play with them through five innings, we will put the fear of God in them. You will see that look in their eyes—the fear of God!—if you can just stay close to them. They are not used to being pressed! If you can press them, they will know that you have made it a ballgame."

The team was staring at me and nodding. I hit play as the tape continued. The broadcaster Al Michaels counted down the final seconds, "Do you believe in miracles? Yes!"

Team USA began mobbing each other on the ice! I stopped the tape.

"The problem isn't the problem," I said. "How you handle the problem, that's the problem! Do you get turned on or turned off by difficult things?

Do you get frustrated, or do you become fascinated? If you are a surfer, do you want to surf ten-foot waves at Seaside Heights or fifty-foot waves at the Bonzai Pipeline in Hawaii?"

"The Bonzai Pipeline," answered Caprio.

"If you're a mountain climber, do you want to climb the Ramapo Mountains or Mount Everest?" I asked.

"Mount Everest," the team answered in unison.

"Well, if you're goal is to beat the best high school baseball team in New Jersey, who do you want to play?" I asked

"Seton Hall!" they said, enthusiastically.

"Some people will tell you to run from your problems," I added. "I'm telling you to seek out the biggest problem that you can find and meet it head on. The bigger the obstacle, boys, the more joy in overcoming it!"

CHAPTER 23

How Am I Not Wet?

Einstein's Theory of Relativity can be summed up like this: If you spend two hours with someone you love, it feels like two minutes. But, if you stick your finger on a hot frying pan, two seconds feels like two hours.

—Mike Tully
Head Volleyball Coach
Motivational Speaker/Author

THE ANTICIPATION LEADING UP to Saturday's Greater Newark Tournament final was agonizing. The days seemed to take forever. We still had two games to play, one against Columbia and another against Summit, but it was hard to think about anything other than Seton Hall Prep. Two more times that week we watched Herb Brook's speech: "If we play these guys ten times, they beat us nine out of ten, but not this time!"

In the meantime, we were waiting, we were hoping, and we were praying.

The third week of May was when the Saint Thomas Moore Church in Fairfield held its annual carnival. Raimondo, Valerian, Ruggiero, Picardo, Tundo, and Bustamante were all taking in the rides, games, and concession stands when they saw Father John, a priest from their church. They greeted Father John, who was elated to see them. To the best of his recollection, he had not seen the boys since they had been confirmed. He asked how they had been doing.

"Good," said Raimondo. "We're playing Seton Hall Prep in the county finals this Saturday night. Maybe you can send a word upstairs for us, Father. They're one of the best teams in the country, so we can use all the help that we can get."

Father John then inquired which arm Raimondo pitched with. Raimondo told him that he was right-handed. Father John reached out and grabbed his right arm. While holding Raimondo's arm, he knelt down and said a prayer.

The other players bowed their heads. Then Father stood up and made the sign of the cross over Raimondo's right arm.

"Thank you for blessing my arm!" said Raimondo.

"Thanks, Father," the other players said.

"Good luck, boys! God bless you."

It was Tuesday, and Saturday seemed like a lifetime away.

I looked for omens, both good and bad, and desperately hoped that they would somehow give me a hint that things would work out our way.

While making my daily call to Rob Gilbert's hotline at lunch, I perceived his message to be another omen, one that I had hoped to hear. He began the message by stating that a miracle was about to happen. The gist of his three-minute message was that most people are not afraid of failure. Instead they are deathly afraid of success. They wonder if they are truly worthy enough to be successful.

"There is no reason to be afraid of success," said Gilbert. "Of course you're worthy enough. You are one of God's children. God shares his love with everybody! You are worthy enough!"

Raimondo, in the meantime, had felt that he had experienced his own omen. He and his father had gone to the city of Elizabeth to purchase a used 2002 grey Toyota Camry, his first car. The two of them drove the car home together. While trying to familiarize himself with his newly purchased car, Raimondo had taken a wrong turn onto McCarter Highway. While attempting to get back to Route 3, he pulled up in front of Newark's Bears and Eagles Riverfront Stadium where we would be playing in the finals. Both he and his father were so awestruck at the beauty of the stadium that they could hardly believe that he was going to get to pitch in it.

"What are the odds, Dom?" his father asked him, "that we pull right up to where you're going to be playing?"

Wednesday was supposed to be the day we traveled to Columbia for a game. As I came out of the coaches' office in uniform, Tom Pengitore informed me that we were cancelled. I was baffled, as it was eighty degrees and sunny. He explained that Columbia had somehow forgot to book umpires. I had never previously heard of such a thing. However, their mishap would provide us with an important practice opportunity. I called Trongone and informed him that because of the cancellation, today was the day for him to throw batting practice rather than later in the week. He showed right up.

When I announced to the team that Coach Trongone would be throwing live to them, they erupted, especially Santomauro. When I then explained that he would be throwing from forty-five feet away, their grins turned to frowns as they sat silently. They had never seen a ninety-seven-mile-an-hour fastball, let alone try to hit one. This was the only way.

Trongone gave a Herculean effort that day. I knew he would only have so many throws in his arm, but he aired it out to the nine hitters in our lineup for over an hour. At first, I was concerned that he was so close, that one of our hitters could get hurt as a few of them fouled a few off dangerously close to their own feet. Mark Ruggiero convinced me that it was okay. I was also concerned that Trongone might hurt his arm.

What I couldn't believe was how focused our kids were and how tough they hung in on fastballs thrown at them with everything Trongone had at forty-five feet. They were getting a piece of him and at times more than that.

After our starters hit, I put them out in the field and let the remaining players on our roster take their batting practice in a game called "twenty-one outs." The rules were simple. Our reserves stayed up to bat and hit batting-practice fastballs until the starters got them out twenty-one times—good enough for seven innings. Again, the focus was incredible, as they played close to flawless defense with great communication. Afterward, we went over to our football field and turned the lights on so that our outfielders could get used to fielding fly balls at night as our final was scheduled to be played at 7:00 p.m.

Later, after practice, I was in the coaches' office and heard someone scream out in pain, *"Aaaaaaahhhhhhhhh."*

I opened my door and walked around the corner. There was Trongone, standing in the hallway, shirtless, holding his right arm out in a bent position against the ice pack in his left hand. When he told me that he would throw his arm out for our team, he was not lying. That was exactly the kind of staff loyalty that Coach Parlavecchio had spoken of so many years before.

On my drive home, I called my father to see how his recovery from surgery was going. My mom picked up on the other receiver. They asked me about the team. I told them what I had just observed, which was quite simply the best practice I had ever witnessed by a West Essex team. The focus, the concentration, the competitiveness, the communication, the intensity, all were second to none. But most of all, there was a confidence that I had not previously seen from any of our teams.

Jack Lynch had once posted a sign in our high school locker room that said: "When a player gets his confidence, good things can happen."

The same can be said for a team. I did not know if we would win on Saturday, but I knew for sure that this was not the same team that had stumbled out of the gate. Our team at that time was fragile, visibly shaken, and filled with doubt. But this team had gained confidence. I can't say exactly how. Maybe it was just the feeling that was derived from winning. We had been "acting as if" for several weeks, but after beating the number-two, number-ten, and number-three seeded teams, we were no longer acting. We were now believing!

We had also prevailed in many tightly contested games, which seemed to magnify our confidence. An 8–7 win in our final tune-up at Summit the next day made the losses against Morris Hills seem like a distant memory. While this team had begun the season 5–4, we were now 18–5, and with one more day to go before the finals, we were ready.

However, I was not ready for the impending media frenzy. I did more interviews over the next twenty-four hours, with a variety of media outlets, than I had done in my first ten years combined.

Steve Tober asked what I thought in anticipation of the biggest game of my career and also the biggest game in the history of the school.

I explained that when I look back, I think I will remember our journey more than our destination. I didn't think that I could find a more committed group of young athletes—athletes who had made a daily commitment since March 3 and even earlier, to be the best that they could be. Regardless of what would happen the next night, I thought that the daily journey and the relationships that had been formed were what would ultimately be remembered most.

Another reporter asked me what I attributed our turnaround to.

"Defeat may test you, but it need not stop you. We are believers, and we have refused to quit," I said.

The next reporter referenced Seton Hall's experience and proven track record. Over the past four years, Seton Hall was 108–10–1. They had been the number-one team in New Jersey for three out of the past five seasons. They were expected to finish number one again, which could make four number-one rankings in the past six years. They were also ranked high in the nation.

"How can you guys, who aren't even ranked in the top twenty in New Jersey, compare to a nationally ranked powerhouse like Seton Hall? I mean, you've had a great run, but don't you think that facing a national power will bring your magic carpet ride to an end?" he asked.

"We have great respect for Seton Hall and their ball club," I said. "They are incredibly well coached, well prepared, and talented. They are confident in their abilities, and they've been here before. They're going to get their share of hits, but we can't give them anything for free. At the same time, we don't expect them to give us any freebies either. We'll have to earn everything we get."

Another reporter brought up the comparison of common opponents,

Hanover Park had beaten us twice during the season. Seton Hall had beaten Hanover by sixteen runs in a game stopped short after five innings due to the ten-run mercy rule.

"Do you think that it would be an accomplishment just for you guys to finish the game?" he asked.

I told him that if we had to play Seton Hall's reputation, then we might as well just not show up. But we were not playing against Seton Hall's reputation. We were playing against Seton Hall.

"Shug Jordan of Auburn football said, 'Always remember Goliath was a forty-point favorite over David,'" I explained. "In a one-game series, anything can happen, and it usually does. We're going to show up and see what happens."

The next reporter did a "tale of the tape" between our teams. Raimondo was five foot eight and 170 pounds. He normally topped out at eighty-one miles per hour. Porcello was six foot five and 205 pounds and topped out at ninety-seven miles per hour. Mike Ness was six foot four and 195 pounds and topped out at ninety-three miles per hour. Offensively, Seton Hall's team batting average was .410, almost one hundred points higher than ours. They had hit thirty-nine home runs during the season. All of our players combined had only hit nine home runs. That equated to thirty more than we had hit. Rob Vogt, their leadoff hitter, was batting .435, with nine home runs. His home run total alone equaled that of our team. Steven Brooks also had nine home runs and was hitting .322. That made two players in their lineup who had matched our team total for home runs all by themselves. Joe Jamison was hitting .457 with eight home runs, and Tim Shoenhaus, arguably their most consistent hitter, was batting .526.

"Realistically, Coach," he asked, "do you honestly think that you can compare to a nationally ranked power like Seton Hall?"

Before I could respond, he asked another question.

"Coach, by the time they all graduate, at least six of their players are expected to earn Division I scholarships, perhaps even more. A few of them will even be drafted by major league teams. You don't have even one scholarship player. Give me something here, Coach. Where do you think you stand?"

"I'm standing in the middle of a special team!" I answered.

Coach Mike Sheppard Jr. addresses his potent lineup during a postgame huddle.
Photo by Richard Morris

On Friday, we were rained off the practice field. Our final preparations would be made in our tiny half of a gym. Whalen threw in our cage from a shortened distance, and then we moved the machine up and cranked it. Again, I was concerned about someone getting hurt.

After our reps, we got together in the center of the gym.

"Do you know how you find your passion in life, boys?" I asked them.

The team sat silently.

"Goose bumps!" I said. "That's right, goose bumps! What do you see, what do you hear, what do you do, that gives you goose bumps? This is what does it for me, boys. Baseball! If you're wondering what it is you should do when you're my age, figure out what gives you goose bumps and go and do it for a living. When we get out there tomorrow night, and we hear the roar of the crowd and feel the excitement and the pressure of competition, it's going to make the hair on the back of my neck stand up. I know I will get goose bumps!"

The team was nodding back at me.

"Everyone has already written us off," I added. "They say we're going to lose by ten runs, that we'll be lucky to even finish the game. Well, I've got news for you, I know who's going to win tomorrow."

"Do you mind telling us?" asked Bustamante.

"Everyone always thinks that the best team wins. But the best team does *not* always win. It's the team who plays best that wins. That's who's going to win. The team who plays the best. Whoever performs best will win. Let's go out there tomorrow night and perform the best as a team, through our hearts. Dominick, it starts with you."

Raimondo looked up at me.

"You can't throw, you have to pitch! You have to locate and read your movement patterns. We have to play defense like we've never played, and I don't care if the other pitcher is throwing ninety-seven miles an hour."

"You know what Lou Brock told himself when he faced pitchers who threw real hard? He would step into that batter's box and tell himself, *I don't care how hard he throws. Once that ball leaves his hands, I'm the only one in control of what happens to that ball!* That's how you have to reframe it in your minds. Personalize it for yourself. Once it leaves his hands, you are the one who has control! If he's going to be a major league pitcher, then let's go out and beat a good major league pitcher!"

I paused. I leaned forward and put both hands on my knees. I waited for eye contact.

"Boys, if you win this thing, you'll walk together for the rest of your lives!"

Every player's eyes widened!

As the rain poured down, I opened the door to my patio. There was no way I was going to break my ritual of sitting out on my patio after dinner the night before the big game. I had done it every round, and at this point, I wasn't about to leave that to chance.

"I'm just going to have to suck it up and get wet," I said to myself as the rain began coming down harder.

I was wearing a light grey, long-sleeve West Essex baseball shirt and light grey sweat pants. Again, I was holding the New Balance sneaker. For a second, I chuckled as I watched my clothes turn dark grey, almost black, as I quickly became drenched. As I sat there, I took a deep breath. My first thought was that I hoped the weather would clear by tomorrow night. *I can't bear to wait another day*, I thought.

Then, I looked into the sky. "C'mon, give me a sign," I pleaded, hoping that I would receive some sort of omen like seeing the hawk the night before the Eastside game.

All I want is this one. I won't ask for any others, I thought. This one could be so big, it could cover all of my losses put together.

I looked up at the sky to my right and then to my left. Drops of water dripped off the brim of my cap onto my cheeks.

"*Hmm.* Nothing," I said to myself, while looking for an omen that we could in fact pull off a miracle.

I didn't expect to receive an omen that in itself would seem like a miracle.

I reminded myself to stay aggressive, no matter what. Then, I got up to go back inside. I didn't want to step on the hardwood floor with soaking-wet socks, so I figured it was best for me to take them off. Then, the omen came—an omen so miraculous that it took me a little while to tell people that it actually happened out of fear they would think I was cracking up.

As I began to take my socks off, I realized that I didn't need to. They were dry. I stood still, completely in shock. Then I felt my shirt. It was dry. Then I felt my sweatpants. They too were bone dry. I looked down and examined the light grey color of my clothes.

"What the hell? My clothes are dry!"

I looked out the window of my door and saw the rain as it continued pouring down. Again, I felt my socks.

I looked at the rain outside the window a second time. I had been looking into the sky for an omen, not realizing that I was wearing one. I smiled.

6SA203860520 Page 40 Baseball 6S1003860520 ZALLCALL 01:27 05/20/06

HIGH SCHOOL SPORTS

West Essex, Seton vie for title

GNT BASEBALL FINAL

BY BOB BEHRE
FOR THE STAR-LEDGER

Only six times in the previous 73 years of the Greater Newark Tournament has a Group 2 or Group 1 school won the championship. Each of those titles earned by small schools occurred since the tournament became an Essex County-only event in 1973.

However, that historical obstacle appears small for West Essex (18-5), a Group 2 team, to the physical roadblock presented by top-seeded Seton Hall Prep (20-2-1), No. 2 in The Star-Ledger Top 20, and the defending champion.

The 7 p.m. start tonight at Bears-Eagles Riverfront Stadium in Newark is believed to represent the first GNT final played at night since the early years of the tournament.

Seton Hall, playing in its 10th straight GNT final and intent on winning its seventh championship over that span, boasts two pitchers ranked among the finest in New Jersey in right-handers Rick Porcello (9-0, 0.21 ERA), who'll get the start, and Mike Ness (7-1, 1.75 ERA), ready for relief. Porcello is a junior and has dazzled pro scouts with a fastball that has touched 94 miles per hour. Ness, a senior bound for Duke, is a control pitcher. He has issued just 24 walks to go with 79 strikeouts in 52 innings.

"They both have outstanding command," West Essex coach Scott Illiano said. "We don't expect any freebies." West Essex, ranked No. 19, is seeking its first GNT title. It lost to Nutley in its only other GNT-final appearance in 1993.

The North Caldwell school answers with junior right-hander Dom Raimondo (5-1, 0.88). He also has outstanding control, surrendering just 10 walks in 43 innings, and enjoys the benefits of a solid infield anchored by senior shortstop Mark Ruggiero (.471, 20 runs).

Seton Hall's typically gaudy offensive numbers include 39 home runs and a team batting average of .410. But the West Orange school has been contained, at times. Morris Hills handed Seton Hall a 4-1 defeat on Thursday, its first loss since April 21. Seton Hall, in fact, has scored just seven runs in its previous three games.

Morris Hills owns a pair of one-run victories over West Essex (18-5).

"I don't put too much stock in Seton Hall's loss to Morris Hills," Illiano said. "It's a question of what type of club Seton Hall is with Porcello or Ness on the mound. Plus, the team is so confident and proven in pressure spots."

The game represents an all-Iron Hills Conference final. Seton Hall is in the big school Iron Division and West Essex is a member of the smaller school Hills Division, which

arguably has more pitching depth than the Iron this spring.

"We have a lot of respect for West Essex," Seton Hall coach Mike Sheppard, Jr. said. "It's a well-coached team. We are going to have to keep our heads up on defense, make the routine plays and anticipate what could happen in certain situations. At the plate we'll have to be patient and prepared to make adjustments."

The big hitters for Seton Hall have been leadoff batter Rob Vogt (.435, nine HRs), No. 3 hitter Steven Brooks (.322, nine HRs) and cleanup man Joe Jamison (.457, eight HRs). But No. 3 hitter Tim Schoenhaus (.526) has been the team's most consistent batter.

West Essex counters with Ruggiero at leadoff, No. 2 hitter John Baab (.396, 18 RBI), a masher at No. 3 in Nick Santomauro (.371, six HRs) and a dangerous cleanup hitter in Lawrence Caprio, who has stepped up since resolving a vision problem caused by allergies.

AUTO RACING

MARK J. REBILAS/US PRESSWIRE

Defending champ Mark Martin makes what is supposed to be his final appearance in the Nextel All-Star Challenge tonight in Concord, N.C.

Martin will be back for one last hurrah

ASSOCIATED PRESS

Amid confetti and champagne after last year's All-Star win, it became abundantly clear that Mark Martin was already having second thoughts about ending his Nextel Cup career.

"Thank you guys! Thank you!" Martin screamed as he crossed the finish line. "I'll be back next year if you give me a ride!"

At that moment, Martin was only considering coming back for another Nextel All-Star Challenge. But as the months dragged on and his car owner struggled to find a suitable replacement, Martin was talked into postponing his retirement for another year.

So here he is a year later, in his second farewell tour with time running out on an illustrious 20-year career. He'll make what is supposed to be his final appearance in the Nextel All-Star Challenge tonight, when he'll attempt to defend his title. He qualified 14th out of 18 last night.

Then he'll finish out the season, which he's certain will be his last of full-time Nextel Cup racing.

"I never say never because how many times can you get away with that?" he said. "But I will say I am not going to run another full schedule. I have 13 more weekends off in 2007 than I will have in 2006, and no event is going to get those — no racing."

His family isn't so convinced that Martin will be able to walk away so cleanly.

"All this changing his mind, he's starting to look like an idiot" his 14-year-old son, Matt, said yesterday. "He said last year was going to be his last, then he came back this year. Now this year is going to be his last, but then he says maybe not.

"I think the problem is how much he knows he's going to miss it."

Perhaps that's what happened to Martin last year, when Jack Roush twisted his arm to return to the No. 6 Ford.

Roush didn't have anyone ready — or worthy — to step into one of the most respected rides in NASCAR, and Martin refused to leave his longtime car owner in a lurch.

The only problem was that Martin already committed to running a significant portion of the Craftsman Truck Series schedule.

NOTEBOOK

He also agreed to some Busch Series races, and to the IROC schedule.

So, instead of scaling back, Martin is doing more than ever. So much so, that his wife is eager to find the light at the end of the tunnel.

"I told him 'No more,'" Arlene Martin said. "I'm ready for him to be home and I think he will be unless something really, really exceptional comes along."

A full truck schedule has already come along for 2007, and few people would be surprised if Martin isn't talked into another race here or there. It can sneak up on a guy like Martin, who is passionate about racing and winning.

"I'm no Kenny Schrader, but I am racing quite a bit this year — that's for sure," he said. "I just wound up involved in a lot."

Kasey Kahne's pit crew lost its title as the best in NASCAR, but bounced back by putting the driver on the pole for the All-Star Challenge.

Kahne's crew serviced his Dodge in 13 seconds to help put him in the top starting spot for tonight's race. His crew was dethroned earlier this week in the Pit Crew Challenge, finishing second in the competition that spotlights NASCAR's unsung heroes.

"They stepped it up tonight, and they showed they didn't care about finishing second," Kahne said.

The qualifying format for the All-Star event is unlike any other race, in which the fastest lap wins the pole. In this race, the field is set by the combined speed of three laps and a pit stop.

Jimmie Johnson, winner of the 2003 All-Star race, qualified second and actually had the fastest pit stop of the day at 12.2 seconds.

Kyle Busch made it 3-for-3 at Lowe's Motor Speedway by driving away to an easy victory in the Craftsman Truck Series.

Busch, who became the youngest series winner in series history last year when he won the race at the age of 20, crossed the finish line an impressive 3.154 seconds ahead of runner-up Terry Cook.

Series points leader Todd Bodine finished third, his lowest finish in the nine races this season run on 1.5-mile tracks. He has a 17 point lead over Ted Musgrave, who was fourth.

REVISED STATE PAIRINGS

■ BASEBALL

NORTH JERSEY, SECTION 1
GROUP 4

1-Hackensack over 8-Bergen Tech; winner of 1-Memorial (W.N.Y.) 11-West Orange at Ridgewood; winner of 4-Kearny, 11-Hunts Knolls at 6-Livingston; winner of 3-Belleville, 10-Bloomfield at 7-Vernon; winner of 2-Randolph

GROUP 3

3-Piscataway at 6-North Hunterdon; winner at 1-Newark East Side, 5-Union at 4-Phillipsburg; 6-Watchung Hills at 3-Westfield, 10-Elizabeth at 7-J.P. Stevens; winner at 2-Bayonne

CENTRAL JERSEY
GROUP 2

5-Hanin Kennedy at 8-New Providence; winner of 1-Spotswood, 12-Carteret at 5-Rahway; 13-Ayerson at 4-Shore Reg; 14-Roselle at 3-Roselle Park; 15-Delaware Valley at 6-Raritan; 10-Manasquan at 7-Somerville; winner at 2-Gov. Livingston

NORTH JERSEY
NON-PUBLIC B

9-Gill St. Bernard's at 3-Montclair Kimberley; winner at 5-St. Mary's (J.C.), 5-Oratory at 4-Morristown-Beard; 13-Paterson Catholic at 6-St. Anthony; winner at 3-St. Mary's (Ruth); 10-Eastern Christian at 7-St. Joseph (N.Y.); winner at 2-Newark Academy

NORTH JERSEY, SECTION 1
SOFTBALL

3-Sparta at 5-Wayne Valley; winner at 1-Sparta; 12-Northern Highlands at 5-Ramsey; 14-Pequannock at 4-Ramapo; 14-Garfield at 3-West Milford; 11-Lakeland at 6-Passaic Val. Reg; 13-High Point at 7-Montville; winner at 2-Glen Rock

NORTH JERSEY, SECTION 1
GROUP 2

3-Mountain Lakes at 6-Emerson Boro; winner at 1-Wallington; 12-Wood-Ridge at 5-Verona; 13-Pascack Hills at 4-Pompton Lakes; 14-Bogota at 3-Park Ridge; 15-Hasbrouck at 6-Cedar Grove; 10-Becton at 7-New Milford; winner at 2-Newark Brook

SOUTH JERSEY
GROUP 4

8-Triton at 6-Absegami; winner at 1-Washington Twp; 12-Williamstown at 5-Toms River North; 13-Shawnee at 4-Cherokee; 14-Lenape at 6-Mainland; winner at 2-Cherokee; 10-Eastern at 7-Millville; winner at 2-Toms River North

SOUTH JERSEY
GROUP 1

8-Penns Grove at 1-Pennsville; 5-Pitman at 4-Palmyra; 6-Salem at 3-Gloucester City; 7-Burlington City at 2-Woodbury

SCHOOL SCHEDULE TODAY

■ BASEBALL

749-GREATER NEWARK TOURNAMENT
FINAL
At Bears-Eagles Riverfront Stadium, Newark
West Essex vs. Seton Hall Prep, 7

GREATER MIDDLESEX CONFERENCE TOURNAMENT
SEMIFINALS
At Middlesex CC, Edison
At Bridge on South Amboy, 11
Piscataway vs. St. Joseph's, 1

PASSAIC COUNTY TOURNAMENT
QUARTERFINALS
At Clifton at Hawthorne, 11
Passaic Tech at DePaul, 11
Passaic Valley vs. Paterson Cath., 1

SUSSEX COUNTY
COACHES TOURNAMENT
SEMIFINALS
At Kittatinny at Lenape Valley, 11
Pope John at Vernon, 11

UNION COUNTY TOURNAMENT
CHAMPIONSHIP
At Memorial Field, Linden
Roselle Catholic vs. Westfield, 11

PREP B TOURNAMENT
FINAL
Montclair Kimberley at Newark Acad., 11

HUNTERDON-WARREN TOURNAMENT
CHAMPIONSHIP
At HealthQuest Field, Flemington
Warren Hills vs. Phillipsburg, 7:15

REGULAR SEASON
ESSEX
Millburn at Milburn, 11

HUNTERDON
Delaware at North Hunterdon, 11

MIDDLESEX
Timothy Cr. at Highland Park, 11

MORRIS
Whippany at Lakewood Prep, 11

NON-CONFERENCE
Paramus at Paramus, 11

BERGEN COUNTY TOURNAMENT
SEMIFINALS
At Ivy Hill Park, Newark
Bloomfield vs. Livingston, 7

HUNTERDON-WARREN TOURNAMENT
At All Saints, Bayonne, 11

REGULAR SEASON
ESSEX
Columbia at Chatham, 11

MORRIS
Delbarton at Chatham (N.Y.), 11

PREP
Dwight Englewood at DePaul, 1

NON-CONFERENCE
North Hunterdon at Peddie, 10
Moorestown at Somerville, 11

GIRLS LACROSSE
NJSIAA TOURNAMENT
PRELIMINARY ROUND
NORTH A
East Brunswick at Verona, 10

NORTH B
Verona at Madison, 1

SOUTH A
Dwight-Eng. at Oakland, 12

MORRIS
Vernon (at) Chatham, 11

SOMERSET
Roxbury at Chatham, 10

PASSAIC
Wayne Valley at Wayne Hills, 11

SOUTH JERSEY
St. Weatherich at Agnes, 11

REGULAR SEASON
At Moorestown, 11

VOLLEYBALL RESULTS

NJSIAA TOURNAMENT
FIRST ROUND
Bayonne def. Moffair Academic
25-21, 25-14
Bayonne (24-2): Mark Shultz 5 points, 22 assists, 4 digs; Dave Lopez 5 kills, 6 points, 11 kills, 2 blocks, 6 digs; Danny Szeferski 2 service points, 12 kills, 4 blocks, 5 digs; McKeel 13-12); Steven Tilen 27 assists; Christopher Orsini 7 kills, 6 digs; Aaron Thomas-4 kills, 5 digs

GREATER MIDDLESEX CONF. TOURNAMENT
FIRST ROUND
25-13, 25-11
Old Bridge def. Piscataway
Old Bridge (21-4): James Herman 7 points, 1 dig; 2 assists; Mark Mather 5 aces, 1 dig, 2 kills; Alfonso Singh 2 aces, 4 digs, 2 kills; McEl-roy (N.J.): David Wheeler 4 kills, 2 digs, 2 kills; James Cambrel 20 kills, 6 digs, 2 kills; Dan King-2, 2 blocks, 2 kills

J.P. Stevens def. South Brunswick
25-21, 27-25
J.P. Stevens (15-8): Brian Seide 12 kills, 3 blocks, 7 digs; Chris Seide 8 kills, 7 digs, 7 l; Tung 5 kills, 2 digs, 8 Blocks, 4 digs, 21 assists; South Brunswick (8-12): Patty Tsotao 23 kills, 2 blocks

STATE VOLLEYBALL PAIRINGS

17-Passaic Valley at 16-Lincoln; winner at 1-Fair Lawn; 8-Livingston at 9-Bloomfield at 12-Memorial (W.N.Y.); winner at 5-Manalapan at 13-Paramus; 14-Wayne Hills; winner at 4-West Morris; 7-Paterson Kennedy at 10-Elizabeth; winner at 2-Paterson Eastside; 18-Cliffside Park at 15-North Bergen; winner at 3-Ridgewood

COLLEGE SPORTS

Cosgrove, Kropp lead CNJ past Kean, 3-1

ROUNDUP

■ Baseball

Andrew Cosgrove doubled home Rich Kropp, who had singled, and then scored on a ground out in the seventh inning to guide top-seeded The College of New Jersey for a 3-1 victory over Kean in the NCAA Division 3 Regional tournament yesterday in Boyertown, Pa.

TCNJ (38-6) made it 3-0 in the eighth when Blake Bullis doubled and scored on a single to center by Chris Wilson. Brad Kittle scattered five hits in 6⅔ innings. Bill Opiel came in for 28 innings, yielding a home run by Mike Styrzanski in the bottom of the ninth for Kean (31-16).

CNJ, unbeaten in the tournament, needs one victory in the final round to advance to the NCAA Division 3 World Series May 26-30 in Appleton, Wis.

Montclair State 7, Thornburg State 2: Tim Stringer kicked a three-hitter with 14 strikeouts and one walk as second-seeded Montclair State set up an all-NJAC final in the NCAA Division 3 Regional tournament in Boyertown, Pa. Montclair State will face third-seeded Kean today for the right to meet CNJ in the final round. Kevin Cuozzi's two-run double capped a four-run burst in the fourth that gave Montclair State a 5-2 lead. Montclair State also was led by Scott Evangelist, who was 3-for-4 with one run and one RBI and Andrew Vicaro, who was 2-for-4 with one run and one RBI.

Rowan 9, Salisbury 3: Matt Errano went 2-for-4 with a homer, two RBI and one run, Tim Eidimeads was 3-for-5 with three doubles, two RBI and one run and Shawn Counard was 3-for-5 with

a double and one run as third-seeded Rowan (39-14) advanced to the final round of the NCAA Division 3 Regional tournament in Rocky Mount, N.C. The victory was the 350th for coach Juan Ranero, who has a 250-191-1 record in 10 seasons, the last six with Rowan. To advance to the double-elimination tournament, must win twice today against North Carolina Wesleyan, the unbeaten fifth seed.

Connecticut 7, Rutgers 4: Rutgers (27-23-1, 13-13 Big East) scored two runs in the first inning on Ryan Hill's two-run homer and went ahead 4-3 in the third on Todd Frazier's two-run shot in Storrs, Conn. Connecticut snapped a 4-4 tie on Josh Farkes' three-run homer in the seventh inning.

Le Moyne swept Rider, 10-4, 5-3: James Hayes went 5-for-7 with three doubles, two RBI and one run for Rider (25-29, 17-9 Metro Atlantic Athletic Conference) in Syracuse, N.Y.

Niagara swept St. Peter's, 14-3, 3-2: Santo Maerta finished 4-for-6 with a double in each game, three RBI and one run for St. Peter's (10-40, 3-22 MAAC) in Niagara Falls, N.Y.

■ Softball

TAYLOR LIFTS RUTGERS CAMDEN

The NCAA Division 3 softball tournament opened with a familiar pairing as Rutgers Camden defeated Ramapo, 3-1, on pinch-hitter Heather Taylor's two-out double in the bottom of the sixth inning yesterday in Raleigh, N.C.

Michelle Schlebring pitched a four-hitter with seven strikeouts and three walks for top-seeded Rutgers Camden (44-8). Katie Norton also yielded four hits with one strikeout and seven walks for Ramapo (36-12) in the double-elimination nation competition.

Ramapo took a 1-0 lead in the third when Ginny O'Brien doubled and two batters walked before Becky Pollak poked the ball to right with no outs to bring home a run. Pollak was thrown out at first by Autumn Milleti, and Schlebring got a strikeout and a ground-out to end the threat. Rutgers Camden pulled even in the bottom of the inning when Alaina Giles drew a two-out walk, stole second and scored on Marissa Van Cleef's single. The tie was broken when Megan Parrell singled and Amber Parker walked before Taylor's double.

Brookdale 5, Monroe 0: Erin Covell (15-5) threw a three-hitter with seven strikeouts and two walks and also singled home the first run in a two-out first inning to lead defending champion Brookdale (39-13) into the final round of the NJCAA national tournament in Rochester, Minn. Brookdale added a run in the second on Suzanne Gorezynski's RBI single and made it 3-0 in the third on back-to-back doubles by Jenna Criscolo and Mandy Kap-sales and an RBI single by Lynn Oleski.

Unbeaten Brookdale has two chances to pick up one victory today against the winner of a Monroe-Rowan Arundel matchup for its third title in five years.

LSU 5, Princeton 0: Erin Snyder of Princeton allowed just four hits and two earned runs with four strikeouts and no walks on the NCAA Division 1 regional tournament in Baton Rouge, La. Vanessa Soto and Andrea Smith each had a solo homer for LSU, which also took advantage of three errors to score three runs. Princeton past second base until three were two outs in the sixth.

■ Men's golf

SAWIN PLACES 80TH

John Sawin of Princeton was tied for 80th in a field of 141 with a 154 when he landed three of the last five holes to finish his second straight 6-over par 77 in the NCAA Regional golf tournament at Sand Ridge Golf Course in Chardon, Ohio.

■ Women's golf

FELDMAN PLACES 55th

Sarah Feldman of Middlesex shot an 87 to finish with a 162 for 58th place in a field of 80 in the NJCAA national golf championship at Halifax Country Club in Daytona Beach, Fla.

NASCAR ALL-STAR CHALLENGE

Tonight's lineup at Lowe's Motor Speedway at Concord, N.C. (TV: FOX, 7 p.m.). Lap length: 1.5 miles.

POS.	NO.	DRIVER	MAKE	MPH
1.	(9)	Kasey Kahne	Dodge	132.465
2.	(48)	Jimmie Johnson	Chevrolet	131.774
3.	(2)	Kurt Busch	Dodge	131.456
4.	(24)	Jeff Gordon	Chevrolet	130.858
5.	(12)	Ryan Newman	Dodge	130.507
6.	(48)	Greg Biffle	Ford	130.286
7.	(17)	Matt Kenseth	Ford	130.235
8.	(20)	Tony Stewart	Chevrolet	130.045
9.	(29)	Kevin Harvick	Chevrolet	129.538
10.	(5)	Kyle Busch	Chevrolet	129.374
11.	(43)	Bobby Labonte	Dodge	129.214
12.	(88)	Dale Jarrett	Ford	127.132
13.	(99)	Carl Edwards	Ford	127.121
14.	(6)	Mark Martin	Ford	126.024
15.	(16)	Greg McMurray	Ford	125.632
16.	(8)	Jamie McMurray	Dodge	124.984
17.	(6)	Mark Martin	Ford	125.389
18.	(19)	Dale Earnhardt Jr.	Chevrolet	112.725
19.	(15)	Jeremy Mayfield	Dodge	111.543

ASSOCIATED PRESS

CHAPTER 24

Sunblock for a Night Game?

If people aren't laughing at your dreams, then
your dreams aren't big enough.

—Willie Jolley
Motivational Speaker

BY EARLY SATURDAY MORNING, the rain had cleared.

Vin Valerian parked his car in front of Saint Moore Church and walked inside. An usher stopped him.

"Hey, you can't be in here. We have a wedding about to start."

"Sir, I have to do this. I'll only be a few minutes. Please?" asked Valerian.

Sensing desperation in his voice, the usher let him in. Valerian knelt, blessed himself at the pew, and began to pray.

Raimondo was driving around in his Camry, listening to music. Realizing that we had hours to go before meeting at the school, he pulled into a gas station.

"Hey, are you the kid in the paper? You're pitchin' tonight," the attendant said.

"Yeah. I feel like this is the longest day ever. I wish it was time to go to the field already. I've just been driving around trying to relax, ya know," answered Raimondo.

I had asked Tom Pengitore to arrange for our team bus unusually early. I knew that our kids would be enamored with Bears Stadium. I wanted them to take in the dugouts, the seats, the scoreboard, the ads on the walls, the music. I felt that if we arrived early enough, it would give them some time to get some of that out of their systems. We planned to meet at 3:00 p.m., four hours before game time. We intended to hit and do a situational walk-through at our school, meet briefly in our locker room, and then bus over to Newark.

I figured I would get there by 2:00 p.m., but even that seemed like a lifetime away.

It was 10:00 a.m., and as I paced throughout my house, my phone rang. It was my father. He was still in pain, recovering from surgery. He wished us luck and explained that he was going to try as hard as he could to be there. I told him that if I didn't see him there, I would know why, and I asked him not to push it too much.

Then my brother picked up the phone and insisted that "you're beating this team today." I thanked the two of them and hung up. I picked up the New Balance sneaker and took a deep breath.

I couldn't eat out of fear that I would not be able to keep any food down. Then I thought that not eating could possibly effect my ability to think later on, so I opted for the most bland food I could find: two lightly toasted slices of wheat bread with a slice of yellow American cheese on the top of each. That was all the food that my body would allow for the entire day.

A few hours later, I stood before the mirror in the coaches' office and rubbed some sunblock on my face. Jim Whalen entered the office. It was after lunchtime, but he took a bag of Munchos, a Gatorade, and a sandwich from a brown bag. He was not about to defy superstition. Neither was I.

"What are you putting sunblock on for, Moose? It's a night game."

I had put sunblock on in front of that mirror before all of our other GNT games. I was not about to fool around with that one now. After the sunblock, my routine called for me to sit in the green chair and write out our lineup card. Whalen purposely avoided the green chair, leaving it for me as he sat in the less comfortable grey metal chair.

"As long as I have my Munchos, I'm feelin' it," Whalen said.

My hand began to shake as I attempted to fill out our lineup card. The first few names were barely legible. I literally attempted to get a grip.

"You know what Mark Messier said the morning of game seven back in '94, Moose?" I asked Whalen.

"No, what?"

"'This is no time for the faint of heart.'"

"Well, it isn't," he answered.

I finished writing the lineup card, put my uniform on, and headed down the hall to meet with the boys one last time before we boarded the bus.

CHAPTER 25

The Struggle Is within the Self

Compete against the game, not your opponent!

—Ken Ravizza
Sports Psychologist

I WALKED INTO THE locker room. You could hear a pin drop. Most of the players were in full uniform. Raimondo was wearing the black Saint Gerard T-shirt.

I stood in my usual spot, in the center of the room. Then, I told the players that the University of Michigan basketball team once ran into Muhammed Ali in the airport.

Their coach went over to Ali, and said, "Hey, Champ, what advice can you give to young athletes?"

Ali looked at him and said, "Shock the world!"

I paced a little.

"Wherever there is great vision, there will always be opposition," I said. "A lot of people have been laughing at us lately—dream busters saying that we've got no chance tonight."

I continued pacing.

"For every dream buster out there telling you that you can't, there's a hundred other people rooting for us to win. Do you know why? Because at one time they had the same dream that we have, but they became too scared to ever finish."

Several players nodded, others stared intently.

I wanted to remind them of one of the most important concepts in all of sports, that a player should always focus on competing against the game that they are playing rather than focus on their opponent. In the DVD, *Inning by Inning,* University of Texas coach Auggie Garrido said to his team before the NCAA regional tournament, "Don't worry about who we play. We get to play baseball. We're good at it. We know that."

"People say Sir Edmund Hillary was the first man to ever conquer Mount

Everest," I said. "Well, he wasn't! Yes, he was the first person to reach the top of the summit, but he didn't conquer the mountain. That mountain is still there. What he really conquered was himself! Most people think that the battle is against others, but the winner understands that the struggle is within the self. Boys, this isn't about Seton Hall. It's got nothing to do with them. The feeling that we have right now, that feeling in our stomachs, that's what this is about. If you want to reach the top of the mountain, you don't have to beat Seton Hall. You've got to beat that part of yourself that is fearful. You've got to beat that part of yourself that is doubtful. You've got to beat that part of yourself that is unfocused or undisciplined. This is about you conquering whatever stands between where you are right now and where you want to be. That's what tonight is about!"

I could see the intensity in their eyes as I paced back and forth.

"Now, how you do that? I don't have any perfect answer for you. What I do know is that nobody ever shocked the world by holding back. After watching all of you come around these past few months, I know you've got what it takes. You can be as fearless as you want tonight, boys. You can conquer any demon you've ever had, because you've got what it takes!"

By now I was practically foaming at the mouth. I pointed to my forehead with my index finger.

"Right now, touch your forehead and tell yourself, 'I've got what it takes!'" I commanded.

The players pointed to their own foreheads. "I've got what it takes!" they yelled.

"Louder!" I yelled.

The team repeated the act of pointing to their foreheads and yelled, "I've got what it takes!" noticeably louder.

"Let's shock the world!" I hollered as I walked out of the room. The players clapped it up. It was time for us to go.

We arrived before Seton Hall. As expected, the players were enamored by their surroundings. They were in awe of the stadium. Kevin Picardo hung the rope from a hook in the dugout. Anthony Cerza placed the plastic toilet on the top of the dugout bench. Bustamante, Nichols, McCullough, and Buonomo went out to the warning track to get a better look at the wall and all of the billboards on it. Then, they pretended that they were trying to rob a home run. Anthony Tundo was staring inside the dugout.

"I can't believe how big these dugouts are," he said.

Having the chance to play in the GNT finals at the Bears and
Eagles Riverfront Stadium in Newark was a thrill in itself, so much
so that somebody suggested a pregame team photo.

Suddenly, Seton Hall made their arrival. There were twenty-one players
and three coaches. They walked in like a military group, marching in tandem.
Each player was wearing a blue team pullover and carrying a gym bag with
their name and number on it. They were physically much bigger than we
were.

Rick Porcello was cheered loudly by Seton Hall's crowd as he made his
way out to the bullpen. The bullpens were located right next to one another
in left field. Porcello towered over Raimondo as the two warmed up side by
side.

Their assistant coach, Frank Gately, was another phenomenal coach. He
called Seton Hall's pitches. He was also responsible for hitting Seton Hall's
pregame infield and outfield fungoes and always did so to perfection.

Their pregame infield looked like an Olympic tryout. As we watched,
Whalen commented, "Their outfielders' arms are so strong, they don't need
a relay man."

One of the staples of Seton Hall's pregame routine was that each infielder
would stretch out his arm and make a long throw to first base from the
outfield grass.

Again, Whalen chimed in, "Their shortstop and third baseman can throw
us out from the warning track."

Renshaw looked at me, "Scott, their backups throw better than our starters."

Trongone then added, "They throw better than my college team, and we were national champions."

We stood along the third-base line, opposite Seton Hall, as the national anthem was played. The turnout, at least a couple of thousand people, was the largest crowd I had ever seen attend a West Essex baseball game. Beyond the right-field wall of the stadium, something caught the attention of our players, particularly Bustamante.

Jane had explained to me that if I wanted the rainbow, I had to put up with the rain. The rain had poured throughout the previous day and into the night. But now, as the sun set around 7:00 p.m., the most beautiful rainbow appeared in the distance.

Perhaps this was another omen. Some would say it was a bridge between what was real and what was imagined, or maybe Bustamante's grandfather was making good on his promise.

As Father Kilcarr of Seton Hall threw out the first pitch to the delight of the large crowd, the rainbow loomed over the stadium in all its majesty.

The umpire yelled, "Play ball!"

Seton Hall and West Essex players eagerly await the start of the big game.

CHAPTER 26

Hold onto the Rope!

Whatever you vividly imagine, ardently desire, sincerely believe,
and enthusiastically act upon must inevitably come to pass!
—Paul J. Meyer
Founder, Success Motivation International

THOROUGHBRED WAS THE WORD that came to mind as I watched Rick Porcello take his warm-up pitches. He reminded me of one of those kids from Stanford who I would always see on ESPN during the College World Series. Porcello had great height, a nice lanky build, and very muscular legs. He had the perfect pitcher's build. He seemed effortless as the ball just exploded out of his hand.

After Porcello's first few warm-up pitches, I remember thinking
that perhaps Coach Trongone was too far from home plate when he
threw batting practice to our hitters at forty-five feet.
Photo by Richard Morris

The West Essex girls' softball team didn't just like baseball, as athletes themselves, they understood it. Led by their All-State pitcher, Danielle Bertscha, one of New Jersey's all-time strikeout leaders, they were incredibly spirited and our biggest supporters. They were seated above our dugout, halfway up the third-base line, wearing West Essex jerseys that they made with T-shirts that included our players' names and numbers on the back. As Ruggiero stepped in to face Porcello, they broke out with a chant reminiscent of a Brazilian soccer game, *"Olay, olay, olay, olay, ooolaay, ooolaay."*

Porcello uncorked a blazing fastball for a called strike one, and my first thought was that Trongone wasn't close enough at forty-five feet; we should have moved him even closer. Porcello's velocity was unlike any I had ever seen at our level. With a 1–2 count, the girls softball team continued chanting, *"Olay olay olay olay, olaaay olaay."*

As Porcello blew Ruggiero away with a fastball, within a split second the chant of *"Olaay"* turned into a groan of *"Oooohhh,"* followed by dead silence. Our girls' softball team was seldom quiet, but a ninety-seven-mile-an-hour fastball from Porcello had turned their voices off like a light switch.

As Ruggiero walked back to the dugout, he looked at Baab, "He's tough! Hang in there."

Moments later, Porcello blew Baab away with a swing and a miss.

Baaab turned and walked to the dugout and looked at Santomauro, "Hang in there."

We had had to beat some very good pitchers—some heavily recruited and scholarship pitchers—to get there, but we had never seen a pitcher of Porcello's caliber. Quite frankly, there weren't any other high school pitchers of his caliber. He was by all expert accounts, the single best high school pitcher in the country. The crowd was in awe of him. We were in awe of him. He was absolutely popping the catcher's glove. It sounded like an explosion!

Santomauro drew a walk, and then stole second. Caprio struck out to end the inning.

In the bottom of the first, Raimondo started their leadoff hitter with three straight balls. He came back from the 3–0 count and struck him out on a high fastball. He was obviously a little nervous, falling behind 3–0 before pulling it together without any harm. The next hitter singled. He struck out their three hitter and induced a ground ball to Rugggiero, who tossed to D'Annunzio at second base to end the inning.

Our biggest fans were the West Essex softball players. The Lady Knights were also the 2006 North Jersey Section II Group II state champions.

The Knights get ready to defend the field in the bottom of the first.

In the second inning, Picardo led off and got hit by a curveball. Vin Valerian then hit a ground-ball single up the middle. Vinnie's hit seemed to change the demeanor in our dugout. Not one of the first five hitters in our lineup had made contact against Porcello, not even a foul ball, but Vinnie's hit showed us that it was at least possible to put the ball in play off of him.

Dalonges, who by now was clearly our best bunter, sacrifice-bunted Picardo and Valerian to second and third for the first out. Steve Zurawiecki unsuccessfully tried to safety squeeze twice, while bunting through the ball each time. Porcello struck him out. Then, he struck out Joe D'Annunzio to end the inning. D'Annunzio flushed the plastic toilet bowl inside our dugout.

Through two innings, Porcello had struck out five out of a possible six hitters as he easily pitched out of trouble.

Seton Hall's Matt Kenney hit a bloop pop-up between Caprio and D'Annunzio to shallow right field. Somehow, through miscommunication, they let it drop between them. Porcello followed with a ground ball that went right through Ruggiero's legs for an error.

Nick Natale singled to give Seton Hall a 1–0 lead with runners on first and second. Ryan McCrossin then hit a tailor-made double-play ground ball to Ruggiero at shortstop. He fielded it, but was late getting it out of his glove. He tossed to D'Annunzio for the force out at second, but D'Annunzio hurried and threw errantly off Picardo's glove, scoring Porcello. McCrossin stayed at first and did not advance on the ball off Picardo's glove. Seton Hall now led 2–0 with runners on first and third and only one out.

Are my kids really ready for this? I wondered to myself. We had never been to the finals before. The stadium, the size of the crowd, the aura of Seton Hall, the entire girls' softball team in the stands, the loud music blaring from the speakers—maybe it was all too much for them to handle. What could and should have easily been two outs with no one on base to start the inning instead resulted in two Seton Hall runners on base with no outs. What could and should have been a routine double play that would have left a runner on third without any runs against instead resulted in a run scored for Seton Hall, and a great chance to add more with a runner on third and less than two outs. Of the four misplays in the inning, there were only two official errors charged to our team. The other two mishaps, the missed pop-up and the botched double play, were not official errors but were plays that we were certainly capable of making but failed to do so. Was the pressure too much?

Let's not fall apart, I secretly hoped. I don't want to embarrass ourselves by losing in a shortened game owing to the ten-run mercy rule.

Let's just keep it close here. Please don't unravel and fall apart now, is what went through my mind.

Raimondo induced a comebacker that he fielded, threw to Ruggiero at second for one out, who threw to Picardo for an inning-ending double play. It was a "momentum shift" that we desperately needed and one that would hopefully loosen us up and allow us to play more relaxed.

Mark Ruggiero roles over a 1–6–3 double play that allowed us to settle down and overcome some of the intimidation we were feeling.

Porcello sat us down in order that inning. Caprio grounded to third base for the third out. The score stood at 2–0 Seton Hall as we went to the bottom of the third inning. Rob Vogt, the leadoff hitter for Seton Hall, led with a single. Tim Shoenhaus put down a sacrifice bunt. The bunt was picked up by Baab, our catcher, who threw to Picardo at first for an out. Without breaking stride, Vogt, a plus runner, wheeled around second and headed for third,

Valerian alertly retreated back to cover third base. Picardo threw a dart across the diamond to Valerian, who applied the tag. The umpire, Johnny Jones, asked for Valerian to show him the ball, while pointing at Vogt. He then and only then called Vogt out in enthusiastic fashion to complete the double play. The West Essex crowd erupted!

We had practiced and drilled that play hundreds of times, and far too often, Valerian had failed to remember that he was required to hustle back and cover third base. If there was one time that we could handpick, when he would actually remember his responsibility, that would have been that time. Just as he had during other big moments, Vinnie came through for us again.

Picardo had not let loose and thrown a ball with a full effort all season long. If his injured arm only had one throw in it, and we could also handpick when we would need it from him, that too would have been the time. Instead of Vogt standing on third base with only one out, Valerian had hustled back to cover third, and Picardo cut it loose and aired out a perfect strike across the infield. There were no Seton Hall runners on base. We had our second double play of the game. We had two outs, and now, we had gained confidence to play in this unfamiliar setting.

As Steven Brooks flied to right field, ending the third inning, Whalen patted Valerian on the way into the dugout.

"That a boy, Moose. You finally remembered to cover third base."

I walked up and down in the dugout and reminded them of a mantra that we had adopted throughout the tournament, one I had learned from Boston Red Sox pitcher Curt Shilling: "They're not going to quit, so we can't!" I asked them to keep playing hard. It was now the fourth inning, and surprisingly, we were still in the game.

Equally important was the fact that we were having better at bats against Porcello. We didn't score in the fourth inning, but Santomaro drew another walk on his second time around. Of the twelve outs we had made through four innings, we managed to put five balls in play as Porcello ran his strikeout total to seven. As our players saw him more, we were going deeper into the count and hitting more foul balls against him. We had yet to make a dent, but our kids were really battling him and competing in their at bats. As a result, he was throwing a lot of pitches.

In the bottom of the fourth, Porcello hit a ball down the left-field line. Santomauro momentarily disappeared in the left-field corner of the stadium. Suddenly, a ball seemingly shot out of a cannon reached Valerian on a line that held Porcello to a double. Santomauro's strikingly strong throw drew a chorus of "*oohs*" and "*ahhs*" from the crowd. Nick Natale then grounded to Valerian, who fielded the ball and threw to first to end the inning.

Trailing 2–0, Joe D'Annunzio walked to lead off the inning. Mark Ruggiero then hit a bullet line-drive single to right field that went through the right fielder's legs for an error. The error was costly and perhaps a turning point in the game. Instead of having men on first and second with no outs, we now had runners on second and third with no outs.

Baab followed with a ground ball out to shortstop that was productive in more than one way. Not only did D'Annunzio score on the play, but because of the placement of the grounder, which was hit more toward second base, Ruggiero was able to advance safely from second to third base with one out. Santomauro hit a ground ball to second that was mishandled by the second baseman as Ruggiero scored. The West Essex crowd erupted, and our players went wild in the dugout. Amazingly, we had only two hits but had managed to tie the game at 2–2.

It was getting late too as we played on in the top of the fifth. Caprio hit a ground ball to shortstop that forced Santomauro out at second, but he was safe at first as he beat the next throw. Caprio then stole second. Picardo had deepened up in the batter's box and pulled back a fake bunt that aided in Caprio's steal.

The tip about deepening up in the box was something that Seton Hall coach Mike Sheppard had previously shared with me. He did that with the knowledge that I could one day use it against them, but he respected the game so much that he unselfishly gave me advice.

Next, Picardo hit a swinging bunt that rolled down the third-base line. Rob Vogt gambled that it would roll foul, but it hit the third-base bag for a hit. Picardo was safe at first. With runners on first and third base, Picardo stole second base without a throw. With runners on second and third and two outs, Porcello actually appeared to be tiring as Valerian stepped in.

Mark Ruggiero paced up and down in the dugout.

"Fear of God!" he hollered. "They've got the fear of God, boys! Look at their faces. They can't believe they're not beating us. They've got that look like they're gonna lose. They've got the fear of God in 'em!"

Valerian hit a bullet up the middle. Before he could even react, it hit Porcello in the leg and rolled to the right of the mound. Porcello picked it up and just nabbed Valerian at first to end the inning. Porcello had just demonstrated superior athletic ability in making that play to pitch out of the jam and end the inning. If it hadn't hit his leg, we were sure to have scored two more runs. The score was now tied 2–2, but you could hear a pin drop on the Seton Hall side. Meanwhile, our crowd was buzzing with enthusiasm.

Raimondo lifted us by retiring three straight hitters in the bottom of the fifth. That was crucially important as he needed to hold them down in the inning after we had just scored, a very underrated aspect of pitching.

As the sixth inning began, Mike Ness took the mound and relieved Porcello. Through five innings Porcello had struck out seven, allowed three hits, two walks, and a hit batsman. Regardless of the reason for his departure, I saw it as a choice opportunity to try to motivate our team.

After knocking out Russian goaltender, Vladislav Tretiak, Herb Brooks told the US hockey team that they "just knocked out the best goaltender in the world."

I, in my zeal to rally our team and build their confidence, told them in our huddle, "You guys just knocked out the best pitcher in the country!"

This was already a moral victory for our team, but could we actually finish? Ness, a first-team All-State pitcher, was another tall right-hander who had already accepted a scholarship to Duke University. He had superior control, and his fastball was timed at ninety-three miles an hour, so turning the game over to him was something that Seton Hall was certainly comfortable with—and justifiably so.

I reminded our team not to think about who was on the mound and to keep having disciplined at bats. Then, John Baab completely took over the huddle.

"This is our time! Let's go! This is our time! IT'S OUR TIME!" he screamed.

Dalonges led off the sixth with a base hit to right field. Zurawiecki failed to bunt twice, and with two strikes, also singled to right field. D'Annunzio attempted to bunt twice, and with two strikes, I kept the bunt on. D'Annunzio bunted it hard, right back to Ness, who threw in time to Vogt at third base for the first out. The sacrifice attempt had failed, as we now had runners on first and second base with one out. Ruggiero then grounded to shortstop Matt Kenney, who tossed to second baseman Eric Bergman for the second out. Bergman threw to first, but Ruggiero, who showed tremendous hustle on the play, just barely beat the throw to keep the inning alive.

Baab walked toward the plate. Ruggiero was standing on first base. He shouted to Baab.

"John! *John! Hold onto the rope!*" he yelled.

Baab made eye contact with Ruggiero. Zuraweicki was standing on third base. He looked in at Baab.

"Hold onto the rope, John! Hold on!" screamed Zurawiecki.

Baab made eye contact with Zuraweicki. I flashed a series of signs. Our dugout, reacting to hearing Ruggiero and Zurawiecki, all rallied together. Kevin Picardo tugged on the rope clamped to the dugout.

Each player in the dugout began to holler out, *"Hold onto the rope! C'mon, John! Hold onto the rope!"*

Baab heard his teammates. He took a deep breath and stepped into the batter's box.

As Ness delivered, Baab hit a line drive that sliced down the right-field line. Nick Natale hustled after it and dove fully extended to his glove side. The ball fell just perfectly, perhaps an inch from Natale's glove and maybe an inch within the foul line, and rolled all the way to the wall. The crowd roared as Zurawiecki scored, and Ruggiero, who would later say that he knew by seeing the reaction of our crowd that the ball had to be fair, came around to score.

Baab made it to third with a stand-up triple. I smacked him on his butt upon his arrival.

"Thaaat a boyyyyyyy!" Moments prior he had commanded our team: *"This is our time!"* Perhaps it was his time. We had just taken the lead, 4–2, as a result of his two-out two-run triple.

Santomauro followed with a single up the middle. The West Essex crowd was electrified and essentially took over Bears Stadium as we took a 5–2 lead.

Raimondo cruised through the sixth as both Shoenhaus and Brooks flied deep to right field. Caprio, who had gone to his left, his right, and even up against the wall, turned in stellar defense and recorded his fifth putout of the game. We were three outs away.

We went quietly in the seventh.

As we took the field in the seventh and last inning, Renshaw climbed out of the dugout with his pitch chart.

"Wait, what inning is this?" he asked

At first I was stunned by his question, but then it dawned on me that he was completely honed in and focused on the pitch chart. He was concentrating at the highest level to doing what he did best: call pitches. Renshaw was not only a phenomenal all-around coach, he was also one of the most masterful pitch callers that I have ever known. He had been frustrated at certain times throughout the season but stayed true to his ideals and really gave everything that he had both to me and, more importantly, to the kids.

"R. C., we need three outs!" I answered.

He had become completely focused on his specific plan for each hitter who was due up. He was studying his chart and considering what pitch patterns we had used so intently that he momentarily lost sight of the inning. The fact that the inning was not even in his thought process was actually a great thing. He was doing what I had been striving to do all along, which was to not even think about the outcome or results and just live in the pitch-by-pitch process, engulfed in the moment of each situation. As he stood next to me, Rob Nichols made an important observation.

"Coach, you've been standing at the bottom of the dugout steps for six innings, you can't change now. Get back down here," he said as he pulled Renshaw back down into the dugout. Renshaw nodded and agreed.

After the double by Porcello in the fourth, Raimondo had retired the next seven hitters in a row. In order to do the unthinkable, he would have to get three more.

Matt Kenney popped the ball up toward our third-base line. Valerian made it to the wall, reached up, and made the catch for out number one. Our crowd erupted. I don't think, prior to that moment, that I realized the size of our crowd and just how loud they really were. My father, who had made it to the game, was battling through his pain in the bathroom. While holding the wall, he also heard a deafening roar and hoped that we had recorded an out. Upon exiting the bathroom, he saw the scoreboard and realized we were just two outs away.

Porcello had stayed in the game at shortstop after being relieved by Ness. He was due up next. He hit a soft blooper to right field. Joe D'Annunzio back peddled, reached out, and made the catch for the second out.

The noise from our crowd escalated even further. Coach Trongone was hollering to Raimondo, "C'mon, get tough. Get tough right here!"

Whalen yelled out, "Haven't done anything yet. Keep getting better, Moose. Keep getting better!"

I looked at Trongone and Whalen to my right and then at the crowd to my left. I heard Al William's voice, "Are you not the winningest coach at West Essex who never won a title?" Then I heard Doubleday's voice, "We'll never win anything with this guy."

I saw the New Balance sneaker; followed by Ruggiero at our first practice, "To win the GNT, Coach!"; followed by Santomauro, "No, to beat Seton Hall, to win the GNT."

Raimondo took a deep breath and delivered. Nick Natale hit a bullet right at Ruggiero. The ball took a big hop as he gloved it chest high. Our dugout began to empty. Ruggiero took a crow hop and threw to Picardo, who he had replaced at shortstop, for the final out.

We had begun our magic carpet ride five weeks prior, and now, we had literally gone over the rainbow and found a pot of gold at Bears stadium. We had done the impossible! Miraculously, we had beaten Seton Hall Prep, and for the first time in school history, we were Greater Newark Tournament champions!

As he completed his throw, Ruggiero dropped to his knees with his hands on his head looking at the sky. Picardo hurled his glove sky high into the air. Valerian tackled Ruggiero at shortstop. Baab leaped into Raimondo's arms, and the team sprinted from the dugout and dog piled on top of one another.

Whalen, Trongone, Renshaw, and I embraced in a group hug as we jumped up and down. All I remember is telling them, "I love you guys!"

Ruggiero's sister hugged his aunt, who was holding his grandfather's watch. "He wanted this so badly," she said.

Picardo and I embraced, as he handed me the game ball. "Here, Coach. You deserve this."

Pat LaConsole and Anthony Dalonges incited the crowd as the cheering escalated.

A reporter named Greg Lernerr was the first one to get to me. "How does it feel right now?" he said.

"We believe in miracles. We believe in winning against the odds, and we believe in the power of the human spirit!" I said, fighting back tears.

I went over toward the crowd to seek out my family. I looked up and saw my mother, father, brother, and Jane. They all had tears in their eyes too, as they smiled and clapped.

I shrugged my shoulders in half disbelief.

I had played on a team that had won the GNT back in high school. At that time, it was the happiest moment ever, but I didn't recall being this happy.

Just then, a local fan yelled out, "Hey, Coach, where's Al Williams?"

It was the biggest win in the history of the school, and Williams was conspicuously absent, as were the Suits.

Gloom and Doom, to their credit, were respectfully cheering as the celebration continued.

The same could not be said for Doubleday. There is a German term, *schadenfreude*, which means to revel in the misfortune of others. Doubleday attended that night, I am certain with that exact purpose in mind. He stood among the onlookers in the postgame crowd with a scowl on his face, clapping half-heartedly.

West Essex players celebrate after the game (top and below).

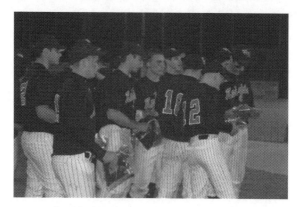

Wayne McCullough (front) and Anthony Tundo (left) were among
the West Essex players holding their championship plaques.

From left to right: Pat LaConsole, Santo Barretta, Kevin Picardo, and Nick Santomauro savor the moment.

As Raimondo and Ruggiero flash huge postgame smiles, Valerian bends down and picks up a souvenir that he will cherish forever: dirt from the Bears Stadium infield.

Champions!

When things settled down, we all went out to right field to take a team picture in front of the scoreboard. As we lined up, there was a momentary lull in the noise level as we waited for the picture to be taken. It was during that brief lull that Ruggiero summed up the moment, "It's impossible, *but we did it!*"

7S7001560521 7S1001560521 ZALLCALL 01:06 05/21/06

HIGH SCHOOLS

Rothenberger, Rehm power Livingston, 5-3

ECT SOFTBALL FINAL

BY JOE BATTAGLIA
FOR THE STAR-LEDGER

In recent years, Livingston has been strong on the field, but has lacked the off-field camaraderie that often makes the difference between being a championship team or not.

But that has changed.

"We are so close as a team," senior Kelli Rehm said. "We have awesome chemistry, which is something that we haven't always had. The seniors, the juniors and the sophomores all get along. It doesn't make a difference whether someone is a year or two older or younger."

As a result of that bond, the players have a strong confidence that anyone on the team can come through when needed.

Such was the case last night when sophomore Danielle Rothenberger went 3-for-3 with a pair of doubles and an RBI, senior Kelli Holota delivered the go-ahead run, Rehm pitched a three-hitter and drove in a run, and Tara Writt singled in a run and scored to help Livingston, No. 19 in The Star-Ledger Top 20, earn a 5-3 victory over No. 20 Bloomfield for its first Essex County Tournament title since 1992 at Ivy Hill Park in Newark.

"Winning this is a tremendous accomplishment for the team," Holota said. "We're going to remember the family we've created and what we've accomplished together with our coaches for the rest of our lives."

For the second straight game in this tournament, Livingston (22-3) found itself playing catchup early as Bloomfield opened a 1-0 lead on an RBI single in the first by Lindsay Karwowski. But as she did in her team's semifinal victory over Nutley last week, Rehm settled in and remained unfazed.

"I have so much confidence in my teammates that I was pretty comfortable being behind," said Rehm, who struck out four and walked three. "I knew if I took a deep breath and settled down, we had the hitting to get back into it."

Livingston bounced back in the third. Rothenberger led off with a single, stole second, and was sacrificed to third by Ashleigh Ayars. Rehm followed with a bloop over third base and the diving reach of Karwowski to tie the score 1-1. Holota then jumped on the first pitch she saw, a hanging curve, and drilled it to the fence in left-center for an RBI double and a 2-1 lead.

"When Rehm tied it, the entire bench felt like a victory was tangible and you could feel the excitement," Holota said. "We scouted them four times, and I knew she liked to throw her curve and screwball outside for strikes early. The first pitch she threw was kind of flat and I just ripped and it worked out where I was able to help the team."

Livingston tacked two more runs onto its lead in the fourth when Danielle Massa singled, went to second on a groundout and scored on a single by Writt. Writt went to third on a double by Rothenberger and scored on a passed ball to make it 4-1.

But Bloomfield (22-4) did not go down quietly. It cut the deficit to two in the top of the fifth when Nicki Veneziano doubled, was sacrificed to third and scored on a passed ball. Pitcher Cara Swerdlow doubled to lead off the sixth, and her courtesy runner Lori Weiss was sacrificed to third and scored on an error at third to make it 4-3.

"We've been that type of team all season," Bloomfield coach Bob Mayer said. "The kids stayed focused and kept scoring. We were confident we would be able to hit and score. We probably should have scored a little more, but it didn't work out that way."

Livingston added insurance in the bottom of the sixth when Writt reached on a two-out fielder's choice and scored on Rothenberger's second double.

"I was really nervous coming into the game and was hoping to be able to help the team and show myself well as a sophomore on a team of seniors," Rothenberger said. "To be a part of this is just an incredible feeling."

Passaic V reaches Passaic County final

SOFTBALL

BY MIKE LAMBERTI
FOR THE STAR-LEDGER

The semifinals proved to be a round of the upset last night when Passaic Valley and Wayne Valley each won at Main Memorial Park in Clifton.

Sixth-seeded Wayne Valley opened the semifinal doubleheader with a 2-0 victory over second-seeded Hawthorne, No. 18 in The Star-Ledger Top 20, and then fourth-seeded Passaic Valley rallied to post a 3-2 victory over West Milford, the top seed and defending champion.

Wayne Valley and Passaic Valley will meet for the Passaic County title at Main Memorial Park this afternoon at 3.

Christina Roman doubled in a run and set up the game's first run for Wayne Valley (18-7), which will seek its first county title.

"I've been waiting four years for this,"said Roman, a senior second baseman. "I'm so excited for this team. I hope we can finish it today."

In the fifth inning of a scoreless game, Michelle Mariconda of Wayne Valley led off with a double to right-center field and went to third on a sacrifice bunt by Deanna Cornell. Roman followed with a bunt single with Mariconda staying at third. Toni Verneeck then grounded to short, and a throwing error allowed Mariconda to score. In the seventh, Jen Eng singled and scored on Roman's double.

Winning pitcher Lauren Shaw took a no-hitter into the seventh inning before giving up a two-out single by Eileen Smith. Shaw struck out four and walked one.

Hawthorne (19-1) was led by pitcher Michele Graham, who struck out eight and walked two, while yielding four hits.

Passaic Valley's winning pitcher, Marisa Romeo, threw a two-hitter, striking out five, including the side in the seventh inning, while walking three. Rebecca Paulhas came through with the winning hit, a run-scoring single in the sixth that broke a 2-2 tie.

"I had some trouble in the first inning finding the strike zone," Romeo said. "My teammates picked me up a little and I felt a lot stronger as the game went on."

Passaic Valley (17-6), which last won the title in 1988, scored unearned runs in the third and fourth innings to tie the game after West Milford (19-5) had taken a 2-0 lead in the first on a two-run single by Justine Richardson.

In the sixth, Passaic Valley broke the tie when Jenna Munem hit a two-out single, moved to second on a walk to Angela Bianco and scored on the single by Paulhas.

"Anytime you can beat a team like West Milford, it is pretty special," said Passaic Valley coach Marc Salvatore. "They are an outstanding team but I'm really proud of the way we came back after trailing 2-0. Our kids never quit."

Minervini, Losek, Jova propel Nutley, 7-2

Samantha Minervini and Michelle Losek each went 3-for-4 and Lia Jova hit a single and solo home run when Nutley defeated Montclair, 7-2, yesterday in Nutley.

Losek had three RBI and Minervini drove in two runs for Nutley (18-7). Kelly Rauco allowed five hits with 12 strikeouts and four walks against Montclair (13-12).

Caldwell 8, Westwood 0: Senior right-hander Lauren Ewing fired a two-hitter, striking out four and walking none, to power Caldwell in Westwood. Reggie Douglas has two hits and an RBI, while Alexa Ferrara added three hits, including a double and an RBI, for Caldwell (23-2). Westwood is 8-12.

JIM WRIGHT/FOR THE STAR-LEDGER

Seton Hall Prep's Matt Kenney waits for the throw as Vincent Valerian of West Essex tries to steal second base in last night's Greater Newark Tournament championship game. West Essex won, 5-2.

West Essex takes crown behind Raimondo, Baab

GNT BASEBALL FINAL

BY GREGG LERNER
FOR THE STAR-LEDGER

Dom Raimondo admitted he wasted nearly every ounce of gas driving around yesterday in an effort to kill time before the biggest start of his high school career.

While his Toyota Camry may have been running on fumes by day's end, the West Essex ace was quite the contrary on the mound.

The junior right-hander built a noticeable confidence with each pitch. And, his growing assuredness transcended to his teammates' approach at the plate, giving way to a late-game rally that no one associated with the North Caldwell program will soon forget.

Raimondo shook off some early jitters and threw lights out over the final five innings, while batterymate John Baab delivered a clutch hit in the top of the sixth that snapped a tie and sent 15th-seeded West Essex, No. 19 in The Star-Ledger Top 20, to a 5-2 triumph over top-seeded and defending champion Seton Hall Prep, ranked No. 2, in the final of the 74th Greater Newark Tournament before nearly 1,000 last night at Bears and Eagles Riverfront Stadium in Newark.

"This is unbelievable," Raimondo said of West Essex's first GNT title. "Like a dream come true."

Raimondo yielded two runs and four hits over the first two innings before settling into a groove. From there, he nibbled on the outside corners with a steady mix of offerings and quietly retired 16 of the final 18 batters he faced, including the last 10 in a row.

"It was a matter of Raimondo and the performance he gave us on the mound," West Essex coach Scott Illiano said. "He had excellent command and mixed speeds. He competed and went after hitters and kept his poise under pressure."

JIM WRIGHT/FOR THE STAR-LEDGER

Joe D'Annunzio of West Essex gets ready to throw to first base after forcing out Seton Hall Prep's Nick Natale at second last night.

"I just threw," said Raimondo (6-1), who threw a five-hitter with two strikeouts and no walks. "I never put my head down. I knew my team would pick me up. It was meant for us to win."

Raimondo's premonition came to light in the form of a fifth-inning uprising against Seton Hall Prep (20-3-1) that resulted in two runs and then a three-run sixth keyed by a big blow from Baab to break it open.

Anthony Dalonges and Steve Zurawiecki singled to start the sixth. Joe D'Annunzio attempted to sacrifice the runners, but his bunt was fielded by relief pitcher Mike Ness (7-2), who fired to third to get the force. Mark Ruggiero followed with a grounder to short that resulted in another force at second base. However, the relay try to complete the double play failed to get the hustling senior at first.

Baab followed with a drive into the right-field corner for a two-run triple that gave West Essex (19-5) a 4-2 lead.

"That was probably the biggest hit of my life," said Baab, a junior catcher. "I knew I had to come through in that spot."

Nick Santamauro tacked on an insurance run by grounding a single up the middle to score Baab.

The first inning gave the impression it would be a long night for West Essex. Rick Porcello, Seton Hall Prep's fireballing junior right-hander, struck out the side and then notched two more in the second. Nick Natale put Seton Hall ahead, 1-0, with an RBI single in the second and a second run crossed one batter later on a throwing error.

However, West Essex showed signs of awakening in the top of the fifth. D'Annunzio drew a leadoff walk and Ruggiero's single to right was misplayed, allowing the runners to advance to second and third. Baab's run-scoring groundout was followed by Santamauro reaching on another error that brought in the tying run.

"They did a great job. They got base hits and did whatever they had to to get on base," said Porcello, who hit the mid-90s with his fastball before being lifted after five innings with seven strikeouts, three walks and four hits. "They just outplayed us."

Newark A wins Prep B crown, 4-0

BASEBALL

Dave Hardin went 3-for-3 with a double and two RBI as Newark Academy claimed the State Prep B Division title for the third year in a row with a 4-0 triumph over Montclair Kimberley yesterday in Livingston.

Stater Dave Ulrich (5-1) yielded two hits in four innings and Andrew Del Colle allowed just one hit in three in combining for the shutout for Newark Academy (19-3).

Greg Harbeck had two of the hits for Montclair Kimberley (12-11).

Meyer stars, boosts Millburn past Madison

David Meyer went 4-for-4, stole three bases, scored three runs and had two RBI as Millburn rallied from a four-run deficit to defeat Madison, 9-4, yesterday in Millburn.

Mike Dasti (1-0) earned the victory in relief for Millburn (13-11), shutting out Madison and yielding just two hits over the final 5⅔ innings. Dave Chiaroiarro pitched a complete game with six strikeouts and two walks for Madison.

Barringer 10, Weequahic 0: Sophomore righty Dauti Perez threw his first career no-hitter to lead Barringer (9-12) in the first round of the Newark Public Schools Tournament in Newark. Junior center fielder Nandi Reyes led the offensive attack for Barringer, going 2-for-4 with three RBI.

Clifton triumphs, 7-3, advances to PCT semis

Lakeland junior John Slootmaker was feeling great yesterday and that proved to be painful for Wayne Hills.

The right-hander allowed eight hits, struck out nine, gave up two earned runs and, importantly, did not issue a walk as defending champion and second-seeded Lakeland, No. 12 in The Star-Ledger Top, defeated seventh-seeded Wayne Hills, 8-2, in the quarterfinals of Passaic County Tournament in Wanaque.

Lakeland (19-4) will take on 11th-seeded Clifton in a semifinal game Saturday at 10:30 a.m. at Passaic Tech, while ninth-seeded Passaic Tech will meet Paterson Catholic at 1 p.m. at the same site.

Slootmaker, who won the county final last season, had been experiencing back spasms. But he felt much better against Wayne Hills (13-12).

Clifton 7, Hawthorne 3: Eleventh-seeded Clifton (13-10) tied it at 3-3 with two runs in the top of the seventh inning on Ryan Gorney's two-run double and won it with a two-out, four-run rally in the eighth in the Passaic County Tournament quarterfinals in Hawthorne. Kyle Terry laced a two-run single, Mike Urciuoli hit an RBI single and another run scored on an error. Mike Vinciguerra pitched an eight inning seven-hitter with seven strikeouts and two walks for Clifton. He has two victories this season, both complete game victories in county play.

Paterson Catholic 4, Passaic Valley 2: Andrew Collazo pitched a one-hitter with 10 strikeouts and six walks for fourth-seeded Paterson Catholic (11-8) in the Passaic County Tournament quarterfinals in Little Falls. The game was originally scheduled for Larry Doby Field but was switched because of a wet field. Paterson Catholic snapped a 2-2 tie with a run in the fifth. Marvin Elias, who had four singles, singled and later scored on Mike Castro's single. Joe Wassel doubled in the fourth inning for Passaic Valley (12-14), seeded 12th.

Passaic Tech 4, DePaul 3: Ninth-seeded Passaic Tech (14-11) knocked off top-seeded DePaul (16-9) for its fifth straight victory in the Passaic County Tournament quarterfinals at DePaul in Wayne. Passaic Tech grabbed a 4-2 lead with a run in the fifth inning. Onix Ortiz had an infield hit and went to third on a sacrifice bunt down the third-base line when no one covered the base. Pete Ross followed with a sacrifice fly.

"Now, we're hitting with guys on base and we're more relaxed," Passaic Tech coach Jim Lentine said.

Bryan Gambuzza hit a home run and three singles for DePaul.

CHAPTER 27

Good Luck, Mr. Gorsky

The pleasure would be winning, not trying to prove
anyone wrong. Criticism comes with the job. I've
never made it personal. Maybe I should've.

—Terry Francona
Boston Red Sox Manager
Prior to 2004 ALCS game seven against New York Yankees

IT WAS ABOUT 7:00 a.m. when I woke the next morning.

I had gotten home from Renshaw's at 5:00 a.m. He had scheduled an all-day pig roast months earlier, not realizing or expecting us to even reach the GNT finals. With the pig roast still technically in session, we arrived in his backyard around 1:00 a.m. to a round of applause from the people who still remained.

Despite my night's sleep of two hours, I was still too excited to rest. Call it adrenalin. I lit a cigar, picked up the New Balance sneaker, and walked outside. A garbage can sat against the wall of my garage. I took the New Balance sneaker and stared at it for a second. I thought about what it had done for me, thought about the qualities that it had brought out in me, and then tossed it like a basketball into the garbage can. It had served its purpose. It had brought me back from the lowest point in my career, but I didn't need it anymore, and I never wanted to see it again. It sits today presumably in a landfill near the Meadowlands across from Giants Stadium. Then I walked to the end of the driveway and picked up my copy of the *Star-Ledger*. I walked down the street and sat on a bench. As the smoke from my cigar cleared, the headline appeared in front of me. It read: "West Essex Takes Crown behind Raimondo, Baab"

I looked into the sky and wondered if it had really happened. Then I looked back down at the paper just to make sure that I wasn't dreaming.

Later that day, I received a call from Al Williams. He apologized to me, admitted that he was wrong, and asked permission to come and take a photo of the team and do a story. I felt that he owned up as a man, and I granted him permission to do the photo and the story.

We lost the following day, Monday, to Mendham in a game that clinched the Iron Hills Conference Championship for them. They were incredibly hungry. We were still talking about the Seton Hall game moments before the game began. Perhaps that was my fault, or perhaps that was a prime example of human nature.

West Essex Baseball's GNT Title
Certainly Had Historic Proportions

By Steve Tober

Scott Illiano has had that rare opportunity to both play and coach for a Greater Newark Tournament championship team.

He played first base and batted third for the legendary Jack Lynch on the 1988 Cedar Grove team that beat Glen Ridge, 7-1, to cop a GNT title and this past Saturday night he guided his 15 th-seeded West Essex team to its first GNT crown with a stunning 5-2 victory over top-seeded and defending champion Seton Hall Prep before a crowd in excess of 1,000 at Bears & Eagles Riverfront Stadium in Newark.

Even with Monday's 5-2 loss to a good Mendham team in regular-season, Iron Hills Conference, Hills Division action, it's hard to conceive that anything could take away from the miraculous weekend that was for Illiano's Knights.

On Tuesday, I walked into the deli for lunch. I picked up the *Star-Ledger*, walked over to the counter, and sat down. I couldn't help but smile as I read the headline of a story about our team by Bob Behre: GNT Champ West Essex Inspired by *Miracle*.

George came over.

"Congratulations. The big winner. These guys are sayin' you're a lock for Coach of the Year," he said.

"Thanks, George."

"Finally, you got my name right," said George. "Ya' know, Coach, I've been wondering. How come you're always calling me Mr. Gorsky and wishing me luck?"

"Do you remember back in '69 when Neil Armstrong and *Apollo 11* landed on the moon?" I asked. "As legend has it when Armstrong landed, he said 'Good luck, Mr. Gorsky.' For years, no one even knew who Mr. Gorsky was. He wasn't an astronaut, and he wasn't even a cosmonaut. Whenever

Armstrong was asked who Mr. Gorsky was, he would just smile. But then, twenty-six years later, in July 1995, after Mr. Gorsky had died, Armstrong finally revealed the mystery. As a young boy back in 1938, he was playing baseball, and he hit the ball into his neighbor's yard. As he picked up the ball near the neighbor's window, he heard Mrs. Gorsky telling Mr. Gorsky, 'Sex, you want sex? You'll get your sex when the kid next door lands on the moon!'"

George laughed. Then he made good on the free lunch that he owed me.

234

Mike Sheppard always emphasized to his players to be "humble in victory and gracious in defeat." His actions backed up his words. I walked into the mailroom at school, and to my surprise, a letter from Mike sat in my mailbox. He congratulated me and our program on winning the GNT. His letter was one of the classiest gestures that I've ever witnessed in sports.

"Legends Field" Mike Sheppard Jr. and Rick Porcello.
Photo by Richard Morris

Our season ended that Friday against Bernards in the first round of the state tournament. Raimondo was feeling a little under the weather and wasn't particularly sharp. Their pitcher kept us off stride all day long with an array of fastballs, curveballs, and changeups that he threw anytime in the count. Bernards would later lose to Hanover Park, who won five straight en route to capturing the Group II State Championship.

A lot of people asked what happened. We were coming off a win against a national power, and our season ended with two straight losses. The teams that we lost to were good teams, certainly worthy opponents, but neither was ranked in the top twenty in New Jersey. What happened? The simple answer is that I don't know. I do think that it took every fiber of our being to win the Greater Newark Tournament. The five-week run that we went through was such a mental grind. Maybe it had taken so much out of us that we had nothing left in the tank.

West Essex's Historic GNT Title
Was Essex Baseball's Top Story
By Steve Tober

After a 5-4 start, West Essex baseball was not exactly on anyone's radar screen as far as being given even a fighting chance of reaching the quarterfinals of the 74 th Greater Newark Tournament.

On the contrary, Seton Hall rebounded in resounding fashion and did not lose again for the remainder of the season. They won out all the way to the Parochial A State Championship, the most difficult field in all of New Jersey. In doing so, they captured the 2006 *Star-Ledger* Top 20 Trophy as New Jersey's number-one team for the fourth time in six years. We were not ranked in the final Star-Ledger Top 20. We finished the season ranked second in Essex County behind Seton Hall.

Within months of the conclusion of the 2006 season, Seton Hall became the number-one ranked team in the nation in four 2007 preseason polls: *Baseball America, USA Today, Rise Magazine/Sports Illustrated*, and *Baseball News Easton Sports*. They held this distinction as the number-one team in the nation for the entire 2007 season.

Part V

Chapter 28

The Journey Is Better Than the Inn

It was the best day of my life, four weeks in a row!

—Mark Ruggiero
2006 West Essex Shortstop

In his book *Wooden*, John Wooden quoted Cervantes, who said, "The journey is better than the inn."

"Your journey is the important thing," said Wooden. "A score, a trophy, a ribbon is simply the inn. You know where you'd like to go, whether it's a national championship or a particular goal in your business or life. You must also realize that this goal will be simply a by-product of all the hard work and good thinking you do along the way—your preparation. The preparation is where success is truly found."

Saint Anthony basketball coach Bobby Hurley commented in the Newark *Star-Ledger* about a tradition within his program. Only those who can expect to play in the next game wear maroon jerseys in practice, and any player can lose his jersey immediately for slacking off, displaying a poor attitude, or even a minor discrepancy. "I think the shirt is a reminder of the frailty of success in life," Hurley said. "Success can be a temporary thing, but you can assure more success by really working with passion every day."

These two basketball Hall of Fame coaching legends have won as much as any coach alive, yet they still point out the fact that success is fleeting. I have found that the journey really is better than the inn, because your stay at the inn is very short-lived.

The whole world now knows Rick Porcello. If they didn't know him prior to the summer of 2009, they do now after he was seen on *Baseball Tonight* throwing Boston Red Sox first baseman Kevin Youkalis to the ground during a bench-clearing incident. By that season's end, he became a household name after winning fourteen games and being selected by Detroit Tigers manager Jim Leyland to be the starting pitcher in a one-game elimination playoff against the Minnesota Twins during his rookie season in the major leagues.

Nick Santomauro is giving his best to get a chance to face Porcello again, as he is currently attempting to climb the professional ladder as a minor leaguer with the New York Mets.

However, the world does not know Dom Raimondo. He no longer pitches. He recently graduated from Essex County College and while he is pursuing further education, he currently works for an electrical union and runs his own painting business. But on that one magical evening, in May 2006, Raimondo, a five-foot-seven, 160-pound kid from Belleville, who wore a red glove and a crooked cap, did something that he will undoubtedly tell his grandchildren about. His red glove currently sits in a trophy case in our gym lobby next to a small GNT trophy. On his glove, it indicates that he tied a Greater Newark Tournament record with six consecutive wins, along with the date and score of the Seton Hall game.

A banner also hangs in our gym, but most students walk by every day and don't really know about it, nor do they know many of the players on that team, if any at all.

Nick Santomauro (above) went on to star at Dartmouth College where he was the 2009 Ivy League Player of the Year. On the next page he is seen crushing a pitch as a member of the Brooklyn Cyclones (New York Mets Class A affiliate).

After signing the richest contract for any high schooler in the history of major league baseball ($7.3 million), Rick Porcello impressed the Detroit Tigers at spring training in March 2008.

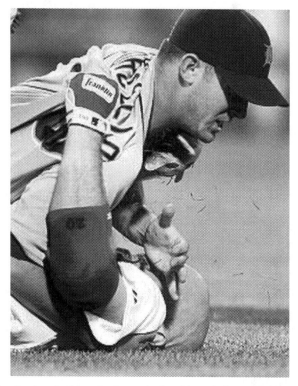

After hitting Boston Red Sox Kevin Youkalis with a pitch, Porcello held his own.

As a twenty-year-old in his first full major league season, Rick Porcello won fourteen games with the Detroit Tigers in 2009. In the process, he became the youngest pitcher to win five starts in a row since Dwight Gooden had won seven in a row in 1985. He was also the first Tiger age twenty or younger to win five consecutive starts since at least 1954. He finished third in the voting for American League Rookie of the Year honors.

Prior to Super Bowl VI in 1972, Duane Thomas of the Dallas Cowboys was asked what he thought about playing in the "ultimate game." He replied, "If it's the ultimate game, how come they're playing it again next year?"

The students in our program today have an awareness of what our team accomplished back in '06. They have heard all the stories, but they are really only focused, as they should be, on the upcoming games that they have in front of them.

When the New York Rangers won the Stanley Cup in 1994, a man appeared in the crowd with a sign that read: Now I can die in peace!

But is that really true?

Winning the Greater Newark Tournament did earn me personal

recognition in the form of awards. I also gained an increased sense of credibility throughout the community and perhaps more respect from opposing coaches, which happens to be a fraternity of people that I am honored to say I am a part of. Most importantly, winning that tournament saved my job! It also allowed me to continue doing what I set out to do in the first place—be a teacher and a coach, rather than wait on tables. But in reality, my life hasn't changed that much. In many ways, I maintain a sense of humility over it and often wonder what if Picardo's base hit at Montclair Kimberly was hit a fraction of an inch lower into the second baseman's glove, or what if there was a fence at Verona when Manny Melendez hit a four-hundred-foot bomb that Dalonges caught for an out? To this day, I realize just how close we were to being eliminated. Would I be any less of a coach then?

I used to think that if we could only win a championship, I would live happily ever after! I could then live a life void of any stress or any headaches. That is not true! That is something that has been written a lot about Alex Rodriguez. Many people now claim that since he played on the 2009 World Champion Yankees, he no longer has that burden to win a championship, but people are fickle and people forget! Experience has taught me that when he comes up to bat next postseason, he will again feel the burden of having to win a championship. Trust me when I say that happily-ever-after doesn't last that long.

I have found this to be true as my journey continues. Parents of a student who was not a part of your program when you won a championship, are not going to care about what you accomplished when their son was not involved in your program. However, if at some point their son's role in your program becomes less than what they expect it to be, they won't hesitate to call you and tell you about your business.

Six years, count them, six years after her son had graduated, I received a disparaging e-mail from Mrs. Cartwright. She was still "restrategizing." It was just before Christmas, and she was not writing to spread any holiday cheer or to share any blessings of the season. What she wrote was very nasty and condescending. Rather than share my reply, I will point out that I was polite in the process of putting her in her place.

Others since then have resorted to the standard disgruntled parent playbook, attacking my integrity, ability as a coach, and my overall human decency on the NJ.com online chat forum. I have received several phone calls informing me of disparaging remarks, one of them stating, "Time will tell if Scott Illiano will ever win a state tournament game."

In 2009, we won our fourth state tournament game in two years and captured the North Jersey Section II Group II State Championship. Time has told.

"Don't call it a comeback," Trongone would later say. "We've been here for years!"

HIGH SCHOOL SPORTS

W. Essex wins championship behind Rechten

BASEBALL

BY BOB BEHRE
FOR THE STAR-LEDGER

Moments after West Essex clean-up hitter Ryan Rechten used his bat to do his talking, he put into perspective what makes his team so successful.

"We play for we, not for I," Rechten said. "It's says WE right on our jerseys and that is what we play for, our team."

Rechten capped yet another complete effort by his team with a three-run, walk-off home run in the bottom of the sixth inning to give West Essex an 11-1 victory via the 10-run mercy rule over Bernards in the NJSIAA/Star-Ledger North Jersey, Section 2, Group 2 final yesterday in North Caldwell.

The victory gave West Essex's 14th-year coach Scott Illano his first sectional championship and first 20-victory season and sent the team to the Group 2 semifinals. It will oppose Section 1 champion Pequannock on Tuesday at William Paterson University in Wayne.

West Essex (20-4) broke the game open in the bottom of the fifth inning, striking for six runs, and finished the job in the sixth when Andy Santomauro (3-for-3) singled, P.J. Lawless (2-for-3) doubled and Rechten latched onto the 1-1 victory.

"I was sitting dead red and the ball couldn't have been in a better spot," Rechten (2-for-4, four RBI) said.

It seems West Essex wasn't about to allow any opportunity to slip free in this one and that pretty much has defined its run in the sectional tournament.

Senior righty Nick Rafanello (5-2) and lefty reliever Rob Pezrutti, a junior, combined to limit Bernards (16-10) to one run on four hits. Pezrutti recorded the only three strikeouts and Rafanello issued the only two walks by the pair.

"I had a sense coming in that, regardless, we'd give them a combo look," Illano said, referring to the switch from his righty starter to his lefty closer. "It was just a question of when."

Rafanello permitted just one run in the first of the first two innings West Essex has allowed in the sectional tournament — and four hits.

"I didn't really have my break ball," Rafanello said. "I got through it by locating my fastball."

Illano did not hesitate to go to Pezrutti, who, remarkably, has not allowed a run all season while being used exclusively in the bullpen.

Pezrutti entered with one out in the fifth and West Essex nursing a 2-1 lead. Bernards' leadoff hitter Matt Decota had just singled off Rafanello. But Pezrutti needed just four pitches, a three-pitch strikeout and a one-pitch 6-4 forceout, to end the threat and the fifth inning.

West Essex blew it open in the bottom of the inning. It chipped away at first, scoring the first two runs on a pair of sacrifice flies by Joe D'Annunzio and Rechten. Then Pat Jennings followed with a two-out, two-run single and Dylan Cascino extended the lead to 8-1 with a two-run double.

Pezzutti threw just 11 pitches in the sixth, getting two strikeouts around a groundout to position Rechten's walk-off in the bottom of the inning.

West Essex extricated itself from jams in the first and fourth innings.

Third baseman Jennings made a fine throw home to get Decota trying to score on a groundball for the second out of the first after Bernards had gotten its first two runners on base Rafanello induced another groundball to get out of the inning.

In the fourth, Bernards loaded the bases on a double by Conner DeLeon, a single by Shaun Hanna and a walk to Jason Travaglini. But Rafanello induced a 6-4-3 double play that scored DeLeon and a fly-ball to right to get out of it with a 1-2 change-up on the out-side corner and sent it to left-center for a three-run home run. Shore never looked back, building an eight-run lead through six innings and holding on for an 11-6 victory over Gov. Livingston in the championship game of the NJSIAA/Star-Ledger Central Jersey, Group 2 tournament before 7-4.

After Jayme Hyndsman and C.J. Mayer led off the top of the first with singles, Juliano connected with a 1-2 change-up on the out-side corner and sent it to left-center for a three-run home run. Shore never looked back, building an eight-run lead through six innings and holding on for an 11-6 victory.

"Nick showed tremendous courage there," Illano said. "The 6-4-3 and the flyball gave us such a momentum swing. The game was hanging in the balance right there."

Newark A falls; Montclair K rolls

BASEBALL

Senior lefty Dan O'Neill pitched a four-hitter, struck out 11 and walked six, and Anthony Lubeiro (2-for-3) hit a solo home run as St. Mary edged Newark Academy, 5-4, in an NJSIAA/Star-Ledger North Jersey, Non-Public A semifinal yesterday in Rutherford.

Ryan Sharkey had a two-run single in the first inning and Kidane Rutty had two doubles and an RBI for St. Mary, which advances to face Montclair Kimberley in the final on Tuesday at Ivy Hill Park in Newark.

Pat McMahon (2-for-4) had an RBI double in the top of the seventh to drive Newark Academy (17-9) within 5-4. Dave Warner (5-3) took the loss.

Montclair Kimberley 13, St. Mary (J.C.) 3: Catcher Andrew Zage was 3-for-2 with three RBI and two runs scored for Montclair Kimberley in the semifinals of the NJSIAA North Jersey Non-Public B tournament at Caven Point in Jersey City. Pat Livesey and Mike

Delbarton defeats Seton Hall Prep, 7-3

Nick Donatello scattered seven hits and delivered a key RBI single to lead Delbarton, No. 11 in The Star-Ledger Top 20, to a 7-3 victory over Seton Hall Prep in the NJSIAA/Star-Ledger North Jersey, Non-Public, Section 1, Group 1 final at Brian E. Fleury Field in Morris Township.

Matt DeRenzi and Donatiello each hit RBI singles in the sixth and Paul Bello delivered a three-run home run when Delbarton (24-4) pushed across the runs to open a 5-2 lead. Bello, who finished with four RBI, drove in a run with a two-out RBI single to help Delbarton tie the game at 2-2.

Gov. Livingston topped by Shore

BASEBALL

BY CHRIS ORLANDO
FOR THE STAR-LEDGER

Todd Juliano of Shore Regional knew that a fast start was impossible this yesterday against Gov. Livingston.

"Anytime you can get an early lead it's huge," said Juliano, who entered the game with a Shore Conference-leading 10 home runs. "And I came into the game a little homer hungry."

After Jayme Hyndsman and C.J. Mayer led off the top of the first with singles, Juliano connected with a 1-2 change-up on the out-side corner and sent it to left-center for a three-run home run. Shore never looked back, building an eight-run lead through six innings and holding on for an 11-6 victory over Gov. Livingston in the championship game of the NJSIAA/Star-Ledger Central Jersey, Group 2 tournament before 7-4.

"It's always a great feeling to help your own cause," said Britton, who totaled 96 pitches. "I wasn't throwing that fast but I felt I was in a good rhythm."

Catcher Matt Marsh agreed.

"Mark was mixing up his pitches and getting it over," said Marsh, who was 1-for-1 with an RBI and two walks. "Anytime he got into a jam, he was able to battle through and get out of it."

Gov. Livingston, which was seeking its first sectional title since it reached the overall Group 2 final in 2006, used a two-run homer by the third from Jake Skinner and a solo shot in the fifth by Paul Mira-bell to cut its deficit to 8-3.

Shore, however, struck for three more runs in the sixth to take an 11-3 lead.

Shore has now defeated two straight Union County teams in two straight games. On Thursday, Rob Corel's one-out RBI single in the seventh forced a tie and Ju-liano added a ninth-inning home run as Shore defeated Cranford, 7-4.

"Union is a great county for baseball," said Shore head coach Jeff Karpell. "We needed to come back in that game, so it was nice to break the heat throughout here. But Gov. Livingston battled back as well."

Gov. Livingston scored three times in the bottom of the seventh, keyed by an RBI groundout by Mike Balboni and a two-run double by Andrew Cunningham. Reliever Anthony Okagaki got out of a bases-loaded jam, however, and induced a game-ending pop-up.

Ndu, Booker break records

NJSIAA GROUP TRACK

BY RICH BEVENSEE
FOR THE STAR-LEDGER

Ugonna Ndu, of Union and Dominique Booker of Montclair Immaculate seized the limelight by breaking meet records, while Trenton's Rolston Braithwaite and Washington Township's Tim Carey were the individual boys stars with thrilling performances on the final day of competition at the NJSIAA/Star-Ledger state group championships yesterday at Silver Eagle Stadium in Egg Harbor Township.

The program was halfway completed when several lightning strikes and the threat of a torrential storm forced meet director Ed Colona to halt the meet at 7:20 p.m. The meet is scheduled to resume today at 10 a.m.

Ndu, a senior at Union, improved upon her standing as the country's fastest 400-meter intermediate hurdler by winning the state Group 4 title in 59.36, a meet record and No. 7 in state history. The old Group 4 record was 59.66, set in 1997 by Mandee Dulin of Shawnee in Medford.

Booker, a junior at Montclair Immaculate, took out a special uniform to break her own Non-Public B meet record in the 100 dash.

Booker won her 100 trials best in 12.03, shaving .03 seconds off the mark she set two years ago. For good luck, she was wearing for only the second time in her career an alternative blue-and-white uniform with an "IC" on her singlet.

Booker wore the uniform for the first time two years ago when she first broke the 100 record at Egg Harbor.

The 100 final, normally on the same day as the preliminaries but pushed back to today because of the weather, is Booker's chance to lower the record even further.

"I definitely want to go 11.9," said Booker, who competed in a state-best 11.98 at the New Jersey Catholic Track Conference meet on Sunday. "I will definitely have to get out of the blocks better and use all of my speed. I didn't run as hard as I could in the trials, so I know I can do it."

Trenton's Braithwaite, a senior headed for Michigan State, won his second straight Group 4 triple jump title with a 49-14, No. 4 all-time in state history, on his sixth and final attempt.

Carey, a senior at Washington Township, won the Group 4 hurdles in 52.10, the second-fastest time in the nation this season and No. 17 in state history.

Bostwick said it was the first time this season Carey did not race the intermediates in the middle of the track.

Jorge Merino of Old Bridge and East Brunswick's Sam Mattia, the state freshman record holder in the discus, fashioned a 1-2 finish for the Greater Middlesex Conference in the boys Group 4 discus.

Merino threw 166-4 on his very first throw, while Mattia threw a 166-1 on his second throw of the finals to finish second.

Steimle wins javelin; Caruso soars in 100

NJSIAA GROUP TRACK

BY JIM LAMBERT
FOR THE STAR-LEDGER

Kevin Steimle of Mahwah got the state record he had been chasing all season in the javelin and Vicky Caruso of Wallkill Valley continued her remarkable comeback by scoring a victory on the first day of the NJSIAA/Star-Ledger group championships yesterday at Frank Jost Field in South Plainfield.

Steimle's day did not start off as if it would be anything special, but it sure ended that way when the 6-foot-5 Mawah senior came up with a mammoth launch of 206-5 on his first attempt in the Group 2 final to break the meet and state records.

Steimle's record toss of 206-5 is No. 9 in the nation this season and broke the meet and state records.

Junior right-hander Mark Britton (3-1), who throws sidearm, was effective, scattering seven hits, five earned runs and two walks while striking out two over the first six innings.

Britton also went 3-for-3 with three runs and hit a two-run home run to left-center that gave Shore a 5-0 advantage in the third.

Englese will be running the 200 and 4x400 today as she and Burke try to lead Cranford to its first state team title.

In the girls Group 3 1,600, Lanie Thompson of Voorhees passed Ajee' Wilson of Neptune with 60 meters left to win her third straight group title in the event with a meet-record 4:50.40. Wilson was second in 4:52.03, just off the state freshman record (4:51.4 by South-ern's Jill Smith in 2006) as six girls broke 4:59.

Thompson, the M of C winner in the 3,200 last year, is skipping that race in hopes of running a fast 800 today.

In the Group 3 boys 1,600, Liam Tansey of Morris Hills in Rockaway ripped a 58.1 last 400 to run away from the blue-hair race in 4:14.68 and a record eight runners dropped below 4:20.

Nick Vena of Morristown, known for his shot put dominance (he owns the state record of 72-2¼), flashed his running talent as he ran a major threat to win the discus at the M of C as well after he unleaded a 180-11 on his final attempt to win the Group 3 discus.

DuBois, in fourth place before her last attempt, It just the second girl from Irvington to win a state title. Thea Blandford won the Group 4 100 hurdles in 1982.

"To win a state title on my last try is pretty awesome," DuBois said. "My coach told me not to look down at the board and just get up and that's what I did."

SCOREBOARD AND SCHEDULE

I might add that Al Williams was on the field covering that game and was quite congratulatory to us for having earned our second title in four years.

Coach Itch Jones was perhaps only half-joking when he said, "I used to give my kids one schedule that was correct. Then, I'd give the parents another one so they would show up at different places."

Eventually, I decided to dissolve the baseball Booster Club altogether. That decision now prevents parents from thinking that their involvement in the organization would equal any amount of playing time for their son. In addition, it also prevents parents from ever accusing me of playing someone else's son based upon what his father had contributed to the Booster Club. Upon dissolving the Booster Club, I moved the funds into a student activities account controlled by our school business administrator and superintendent, and we now do our own fund-raising as a team. Today, I have far less attempted interference on behalf of the parents, and I have found that having the players do their own fund-raising fosters teamwork and a sense of accomplishment that they earned something.

CHAPTER 29

Swimming Upstream

It's kind of fun to do the impossible!

—Walt Disney

IT HAS BEEN SAID that "success breeds success." Four years after our magical tournament run of 2006, our program had grown significantly. Many of our new players had been in attendance the evening that we defeated Seton Hall Prep at Bears and Eagles Riverfront Stadium as members of our seventh- and eighth-grade team. Prior to that, they had attended my West Essex Knights Summer Baseball Camp as elementary students. They all loved baseball, and they had dedicated much of their adolescent lives to developing themselves into the best players that they could possibly be. Many of them had also committed themselves to developing their speed, agility, and strength under the expert tutelage of our school strength coach, Bill Wosilius. And talk about street dogs!

Those little boys who I had first met at my camp as elementary students had now grown into the young men who comprised our varsity team. After winning the North Jeresy Section II Group II State Championship in 2009, we returned five starting-position players for the 2010 season. More importantly, we now had pitching depth that we had not previously seen in my fifteen-year coaching tenure. One of our pitchers was a third-team All-State selection as a sophomore and was now a year older. Two other junior pitchers, who had torn it up on our JV team in '09, also showed great promise pitching for our team over the summer. By the time March rolled around, they had already hit growth spurts. Their bodies had filled out, and they seemed athletically more mature. These three pitchers looked like college prospects, and there were a few others behind them on our roster who were more than capable of giving us quality innings on the mound. It may have taken us fifteen years, but our team had made a transition—from an underdog type of program that was hoping to play competitively, to a team that was now a favorite and expected to win.

Being a favorite was a role that we were not used to, and one that places an entirely different type of pressure on you. I think I spent more time in the 2010 season on mental training. I had to teach our players to think exclusively about playing and executing, rather than thinking about results or winning. Much of what I taught, I had learned from studying the teachings of Ken Ravizza in his book *Heads-Up Baseball* and from speaking with him in person at clinics. Ravizza's wisdom provides players with specific methods and strategies for how to live in the process of playing the game of baseball "one pitch at a time" while reducing the burden of thinking about the results or outcomes of your performance.

The 2010 season would also be the single best season in West Essex baseball history. Witnessing how our teenage players encountered and overcame the pressure and expectations from being ranked favorably by the news media and being seeded highly for tournaments would ultimately make it one of our most memorable and enjoyable. Some of the players had to fight like mad to bring their confidence levels to a point in which they could overcome their fears. Watching them mature in that way was incredibly gratifying for me as their teacher.

Our team finished with a 28–3 record and completed a very rare "Triple Crown" sweep of three different championships—winning the SEC Conference, our second Greater Newark Tournament, and our school's first-ever Group II State Championship. We also set a school record for wins, shattering the former mark of twenty-two set in 1993. For our efforts, our team won the *Star-Ledger* Top 20 Trophy as the number-one ranked team in New Jersey. However, I was quickly reminded that no amount of success could ever exonerate a coach from having his detractors.

When we won the overall Group II State Championship it was a special moment in our program. Many of the parents were on the field, hugging, kissing, and celebrating. By now Al Williams was not just taking our picture on the field, he had become a full-blown fan! I'm told that one set of parents in particular had scowls on their faces and seemed genuinely disinterested in the accomplishment since their son had not participated in that game.

At our annual team banquet held the very next day after the state championship final, a parent approached me and shared his excitement about our season. Then he explained that another parent was very upset with me and had been sounding off.

"What's the matter?" I asked. "He's mad that we won the state championship?"

The parent shook his head and said, "I guess you can't please everybody. I just figured that I would warn you before he gets here."

MAY 16, 2010 THE SUNDAY STAR-LEDGER EX SECTION FIVE PAGE 9

HIGH SCHOOL SPORTS

For additional coverage, go to **nj.com/hssports**. *For photos, go to* **nj.com/hsphotos**. *For videos, go to* **nj.com/hsvideos**.

No. 8 West Essex takes GNT championship, 5-4

BASEBALL

By Bob Behre
FOR THE STAR LEDGER

It was the West Essex way.

Mike Rafanello led off the bottom of the seventh inning with an infield single. Dan Gautieri's exquisite bunt moved him to second and, naturally, Lee Holzman singled hard to right field to score the speedy Rafanello with the run that gave West Essex a thrilling 5-4 victory over gritty Columbia and the Greater Newark Tournament championship.

"It's a hit that's altered Lee's life forever," said West Essex coach Scott Illiano, never one to understate a big event. It was a big event before 1,000 or so fans in the county's biggest baseball venue, Bears & Eagles Riverfront Stadium in Newark.

But it was how top-seeded West Essex (19-13), No. 8 in The Star-Ledger Top 20, put together that winning rally that will keep providing this team joy in years to come.

Rafanello is the No. 2 hitter and, perhaps, ideal for that role. He had already beat out a bunt for a single in the first inning and faked a bunt then lined a shot through the left side for another single in the third. In the seventh, the senior shortstop hit the first pitch he saw from reliever Robert Buchner deep into the 5-6 hole and beat out the long throw by shortstop Armand Spears.

"Anyway on," Rafanello said. "I was busting it down the line. I knew I'd beat it out."

Gautieri, who had relieved starter P.J. Lawless in the sixth, had been used sparingly at the plate this season.

"Definitely less than 10 at bats," Gautieri said.

The junior righty laid down a beautiful bunt to the first-base side that was so good he very nearly beat it out. But the sacrifice moved Rafanello into scoring position with West Essex's No. 4 and 5 batters getting a shot to win it.

Buchner hit clean-up hitter Jimmy Kenny with his first pitch and, after a conference on the mound, Holtzman, the West Essex catcher, stepped in.

Buchner threw a first-pitch change-up that Holtzman lined into right field for a single. Right fielder Matt McGriff picked up the single on the run as Rafanello charged around third base. But Rafanello's speed proved the difference as he slid across home, beating McGriff throw and setting off a wild celebration at home plate.

"I tried to take everything out of my head," said Holtzman about his approach at the plate. "The pitch was middle-away and I just went with it to right field."

That West Essex was still alive in the game to that point was a credit to Gautieri's relief work.

ED MURRAY/THE STAR-LEDGER

West Essex players pour out of the dugout as Mike Rafanello scores the winning run in the seventh inning yesterday. West Essex defeated Columbia, 5-4, in the Greater Newark Tournament championship game at Bears & Eagles Riverfront Stadium in Newark.

Columbia, in its typical fashion, battled back from a 4-0 deficit with three runs in the fifth and one in the sixth. Stephen Tamayo hit a two-out, three-run home run over the fence in the left to draw Columbia (15-8), the sixth seed, to within 4-3.

"That was huge," Columbia coach Larry Busichio said. "We showed once again that we are never out of a game."

Lawless had gotten the first two outs of the inning, but surrendered a walk to Spears and a single to Andrew Rigassio.

"P.J. lost a little command at that point, but held an incredibly dangerous lineup to three runs over five innings," Illiano said.

Gautieri started the sixth and surrendered an unearned run on a pair of infield errors that tied the game at 4-4 for Columbia. But Gautieri minimized the damage in dramatic fashion when he struck out the No. 3 hitter Rigassio looking at a nasty curveball for the second out and got Tamayo on the very next pitch via a forceout at second base.

"It was an incredible performance by Gautieri to get Rigassio in that spot, then to get that bunt down when we asked him to bunt toward first base," Illiano said.

But Gautieri (5-0), who seemed shaken emotionally by he and his teammates' performance, remembered his strikeout in the seventh more clearly. He retired Columbia in order and closed it out with a 3-2 curveball that Buchner could only wave at.

Columbia starter Jimmy Murphy did a nice job keeping his team in the game, limiting West Essex to four runs, two earned, over four and a third innings on seven hits. He struck out one and walked two.

Rafanello was 3-for-4 and scored twice, Holtzman had two singles, a double and two RBI, and Kenny delivered two runs on a pair of sacrifice flies for West Essex. Buchner had two hits and scored a run for Columbia.

Seton Hall Prep 9, Montclair 1: Jonathan Bujtas connected for a two-run double in the second inning and Shane Nolan delivered a three-run triple in the third inning as Seton Hall took a 5-1 lead in West Orange. John Norwood was 2-for-2, knocked in a run and scored three times for Seton Hall (17-6). George Steuart had an RBI single in the second inning for Montclair (14-8).

Belleville 4, Glen Ridge 3: Keith Everett scattered six hits over seven innings, striking out five and walking one to steer Belleville in Belleville. Everett, Angel Colon and Jonathan Caraballo each collected hits in a four-run fifth inning for Belleville (9-15). Glen Ridge is 6-14.

Bloomfield 21, Millburn 1: Jared Guglielmino, Patrick Bollotta, Chris Goodwyn and Anthony Giamo each hit home runs to power Bloomfield in Bloomfield. Giamo was 2-for-3 with five RBI and Guglielmino connected for a double, drove in three runs and scored four times for Bloomfield (12-12). Peter Han singled and drove in the run for Millburn (12-12).

Passaic 2, Clifton 1: Passaic, the ninth seed, used an error and a ground out to score the winning run in the top of the seventh inning in the first round of the Passaic County Tournament in Clifton. Clifton (10-11) was the eighth seed. Passaic meets top-seeded West Milford at 11 a.m. this coming Saturday at Westbrook Elementary School in West Milford.

Shabazz 14, West Side 6: Christopher Gomez, TyShaun Christian and Rudy Martinez each went 2-for-3 for West Side, but Shabazz (1-9) prevailed in the first round of the Newark Public Schools Tournament in Newark. Christian drove in a run and Gomez doubled for West Side (5-11).

Hackensack 6, Glen Rock 1: Tim Swatek spun a six-hitter for Hackensack (18-6) in the second round of the Bergen County Tournament in Emerson Boro.

ED MURRAY/THE STAR-LEDGER

Ralph Velardi of West Essex holds onto the ball to force out Joe Meola of Columbia yesterday in the Greater Newark Tournament championship game. West Essex won, 5-4.

Castelli-led Cedar Grove tops West Essex in ECT final

SOFTBALL

By Mike Lamberti
FOR THE STAR LEDGER

Cedar Grove's Gabby Castelli and Austin Leigh of West Essex provided the fans at Ivy Hill Park in Newark with a classic pitching duel in yesterday's Essex County Tournament championship game.

Neither allowed an earned run and both yielded four hits while striking out six and walking one. But in the end, Cedar Grove's defense and its ability to capitalize on two miscues was the difference in a 2-0 victory before 500.

It was the first championship for third-seeded Cedar Grove, No. 9 in the Star-Ledger Top 20, in 26 years and fourth overall. Seventh ranked West Essex, the top seed, was seeking its fourth championship in the tournament's 33-year history. It last won in 2007 and had never lost in a county title game before.

Castelli, a freshman right-hander, worked out of a few early jams, including the second inning, when she gave up consecutive singles to Leigh and Candice Travis to start the frame. Castelli then rallied back to strike out the side and didn't allow another hit until Alexa Ramos singled with two outs in the seventh.

"I knew they were a good-hitting team," Castelli (21-2) said. "I also knew I needed to shut them down in that spot and pitched a little harder. Our defense was incredible today. They deserve all the credit. I don't know what to say. I'm bouncing around here, just trying to calm down."

Cedar Grove (22-3) could muster little offense against Leigh, who scattered two singles through the first six innings to Lisa Stacevicz and Kaitlin Sinisi. But in the sixth, Cassidy Trause, a freshman third baseman, drew a one-out walk, then came around to score when Gianna Cuffari hit a grounder which resulted in an overthrow to the outfield and moved Cuffari to third.

"When I got that walk, I thought maybe it could lead to something," Trause said. "Leigh was pitching great, but any time there's a walk, especially in a close game, it creates opportunities. When Gianna hit the ball, I remember running to second and looking over at Coach (Rob Stern) and he's waving like crazy at third and saying 'get here' and before I knew it, I had scored."

Leigh retired the next hitter on a groundout, but a second miscue on a Stacevicz grounder allowed Cuffari to score.

"I figured it was going to be a low-scoring game," Leigh (16-3) said. "I thought I pitched well and Castelli was tough, too. It's a difficult loss, but we'll regroup. We've got a good team and we'll get ready for states."

West Essex (17-3) also threatened in the fourth inning when Allissa Kerr reached on an error and Leigh walked to start the frame. But once again, Castelli worked out of it by getting the next two hitters to ground out, which erased the lead runner at third each time, then retired the side on a groundout to second.

In the sixth, Jackie Branco led off with a hard line drive that seemed headed to left field for a hit, but Trause dove and caught the ball on the fly at third.

"When she hit it, I felt like I had a good jump and could catch it," Trause said. "We had just taken the lead and didn't want to give them a chance to start a rally."

Stern, whose teams had lost in the last two county finals to Mount St. Dominic, credited both teams with a good game.

"West Essex is a great team," Stern said. "But our kids have been playing great defense all year long and today it was probably the difference. Gabby showed what kind of competitor she is, too. She's one of the best pitchers in the state and has been outstanding all year long for us."

Secaucus 13, Lyndhurst 3: Tara Roarty, Shannon Waters and Andrea Innis each went 2-for-2 and scored two runs in the fifth inning when Secaucus erupted for 13 runs in Lyndhurst. Waters collected four RBI, Innis three and Roarty one for Secaucus (16-6). Lyndhurst is 7-12.

Bishop Ahr 6, Mount St. Dominic 3: Jill Popek's two-run double polished off a five-run second inning as No. 16 Bishop Ahr went on to knock off No. 13 Mount St. Dominic in Edison.

Becky Hilliard (8-2) and Jessica Gomez combined on a nine-hitter for Bishop Ahr (19-3), which has won 17 of its last 18 games. Hilliard gave up two runs in three innings, striking out two and walking none. Gomez went four innings, giving up one run on a solo homer to Rebecca Gormey, striking out two and walking one. In the second, Gabby Elvina led off with a single and moved to third when Mt. St. Dominic made an error on a sacrifice bunt. Julie Braun then drove in the first run with a single. After another error plated a run, Alexis Herrman drew a bases-loaded walk before the power-hitting Popek lined a double to drive in her 37th and 38th RBI of the season.

Mount St. Dominic (16-6) was led by Rebecca Gorney, Cora Ianiro and Jamie Purcell, who each drove in a run. Popek had two of Bishop Ahr's five hits against two Mount Dominic pitchers, who combined on nine walks.

St. Dominic 10, Memorial 0: Stephanie Bolger pitched a five-inning two-hitter, striking out 10 and walking one to lead St. Dominic in the quarterfinal round of the Hudson County Tournament in West New York. Kelisa Matias was 2-for-2 with two doubles and three RBI and Jamie Leale was 3-for-3 with a double and drove in three runs for St. Dominic (14-7). Caolanny Melo doubled for Memorial (15-5).

North Arlington 2, St. Mary (Ruth.) 1: Michelle Chiamese had an RBI double in the bottom of the 10th inning to snap a 1-1 tie and lead North Arlington in North Arlington. Kerrin Dys scattered 12 hits over 10 innings, with 20 strikeouts and two walks, and went 3-for-5 at the plate with a double and scored on Chimaese double in the 10th for North Arlington (10-10). Vanessa Romero singled and scored for St. Mary (Ruth.) (13-8).

Millburn 5, Mountain Lakes 0: Kaitlin Zampino pitched a five-hitter with 12 strikeouts and one walk for Millburn (13-9) in Mountain Lakes. Charlotte McCaffery singled twice and Lauryn Fiore had a single and two RBI. Carson Mehl was 3-for-4 for Mountain Lakes (10-14).

West Milford 10, Pompton Lakes 5: Sara Zambelli was 2-for-2 with two home runs, four RBI, and four runs scored to lead West Milford over Pompton Lakes, 10-5, in the championship game of the Passaic County Tournament last night at Main Memorial Park in Clifton. Erin Withersoon was 3-for-4 with four RBI for West Milford (23-2), which has captured the PCT championship six out of the last nine years. Pompton Lakes (16-7) was led by Steph Pasquale, who went 2-for-3 with a home run, a double, and a pair of walks. It was Pasquale's sixth straight game with a home run, giving her 11 home runs on the season.

Morristown 1, Chatham 0: Tara Lopez hit an RBI double with two outs in the third inning for Morristown (13-8).

Union 3, Rahway 2: Danielle Reilly singled in the tying run and Heather Baumann singled in the winning run as Union (19-4) scored twice in the bottom of the eighth inning to rally for the victory in the Union County Tournament quarterfinals.

Note—The GNT changed to a two-pitcher format in 2010.

I immediately thought back to our team banquet held ten years prior when Brian's mother dug her nails into me, puncturing the skin of my arm. *How upset is he?* I wondered. *Am I going to have to drive home from a formal school banquet with blood on my shirt again?*

I looked around to my left and right, but no one from the school was present in the event that an incident were to happen with an irate parent. I was on my own. Then again, with very few exceptions, I always had been! If I wasn't a man on the day I took this job, then the job had made a man out of me. I prepared myself to deal with any type of conflict head on.

I wondered if this parent would really have the nerve to confront me here in front of all these other people after such a magical season for our team. The euphoria from the previous day's accomplishment of becoming state champions had not yet even slightly diminished. It was then that I realized that not even in supreme success is a coach ever shielded from a disgruntled parent.

As the parent entered the dining area he looked miserable and appeared to be very angry. He immediately walked toward me. Was he just going to give me a piece of his mind? Was he going to take a swing at me? Sadly, I had seen and heard too much over time to feel any measure of security in this situation. I braced myself and expected the worst while hoping for the best. As it turned out he was not there to hit me. Instead, he chose to convey his disdain for me by greeting me with a cold shoulder that went along with a few grunts and some mumbling. I was happy that was all that it was and that it didn't escalate any further.

Within days of our banquet, I received an e-mail from another disgruntled parent expressing disdain over his son's role within our team. Another parent grabbed Trongone's ear at a graduation party and verbally shredded me to pieces over my playing-time decisions, prompting him to leave the party abruptly.

I had helped the boys of both of those parents become part of something very successful. In the process, I also taught them some valuable lessons that they will use in their life long after they leave high school. However, their parents hated me because it didn't go exactly as they wanted it to go.

HIGH SCHOOL SPORTS

*For additional coverage, go to **nj.com/hssports**. For photos, go to **nj.com/hsphotos**. For videos, go to **nj.com/hsvideos**.*

ONLINE BRACKETS *For up-to-date brackets in the baseball, softball and lacrosse state tournaments go to **nj.com/hs-brackets***

Randolph tops Livingston, 7-3, for section title

BASEBALL

By Bob Behre
FOR THE STAR-LEDGER

Professional and college scouts may not be fawning over the Randolph pitching staff, but the team's alleged liability is doing just fine — thank you.

Right-hander Thomas Travaglia limited Livingston to two runs on three hits over six innings and the vaunted Randolph lineup provided its usual fireworks display on the way to a 7-3 victory and its second straight NJSIAA/Star-Ledger North Jersey, Section 1, Group 4 championship yesterday in Randolph.

Randolph, which lost to Hunterdon Central in the Group 4 final last year, advanced to the Group 4 semifinal and will oppose the North Jersey, Section 2 champion, Bridgewater-Raritan, at Demarest on Tuesday.

Travaglia (8-1) struck out one and walked one and threw just 57 pitches, allowing just one base runner, on a walk, after the first inning. Closer Robbie Berger gave up a lead-off home run in the seventh to John Beaubien before finishing off the tidy one-hour, 28-minute contest.

Second-seeded Livingston (18-11) sure looked good from the start as Jimmy Napolitano and Frank Schwindel launched back-to-back solo home runs with one out in the top of the first inning.

"I found out they are free swingers," said Travaglia. "They were jumping on fastballs out over the plate. I started to mix it up and get the ball down in the zone."

Top-seeded Randolph (26-3) gave Travaglia all the support he would need in the bottom of the third when it exploded for six runs on seven hits to open up a 6-2 lead.

"We can hit the ball," said Travaglia. "I knew the bats would wake up."

A typical slumber for Randolph is one trip through lineup.

Livingston opened the door by committing a pair of infield fielding errors to begin the third and Randolph followed with seven consecutive hits to chase Livingston starter Brian Drapeau (3-2).

Five of those hits were doubles and all of them where of the noisy variety. Mike Rampone's one-out double sent Mike Zavala to third and set the stage for the rally.

Alex Guerra, the No. 3 hitter, singled home the first two runs to tie the game at 2-2 and Brett Zaziski followed with a double down the line in right field to put Randolph in front, 3-2.

Chris Reynolds and Travaglia then came through with RBI doubles and Chris Hugg singled hard through the left side for another run that boosted the lead to 6-2. That finished Drapeau, who had thrown just 12 pitches to the eight batters he faced in the inning.

Rampone, Guerra, Zaziski, Reynolds and Travaglia, in fact, each ripped the first pitch they saw from Drapeau.

"He threw me two curveballs my first at bat," said Guerra, who hit into an inning-ending double-play in the first. "He threw me a hanger the next time and I rocked it.

"We weren't worried when we fell behind. Thomas is a great pitcher. I think our pitching is a lot better than people think. We have great depth."

Randolph scored an unearned run in the fifth when Livingston committed its fifth and sixth errors of the game. Chris Lowery singled home Reynolds, who had reached on an error.

Livingston relievers Ryan Sullivan and Sean Rucker did a nice job shutting down Randolph the rest of the way but Travaglia and Berger made sure the Essex County school would not rally.

"Our problem has been that we are not consistent," said Livingston coach Scott Schroeder. "We were confident coming up here. It's a tough road game but we had a plan and felt good."

Randolph had defeated Livingston, 13-3, in a regular-season contest on May 11.

"You can hold this team down one time through the lineup but they learn something," said first-year Randolph coach Oscar Zavala. "I told the guys from day one that if we get any kind of pitching this season, we will win. When you win championships it's with pitching."

Moore, Gray steer Mo-Beard by Newark A

Tom Moore doubled twice and drove in four runs and Zach Gray went 3-for-4 with a double and three RBI to lead Morristown-Beard to a 15-9 victory over Newark Academy in the NJSIAA/Star-Ledger North Jersey, Non-Public B semifinals yesterday in Morris Township.

Moore doubled to right-center with one out in the fifth to bring in two runs and give Morristown-Beard (20-8) an 11-5 lead. Ryan Kinsella had a hit, walked three times and drove in three runs and Adrian O'Connell earned the victory with 3-2/3 innings of one-hit ball in relief for Morristown-Beard, which will face St. Mary of Rutherford on Tuesday at Don Bosco Prep. Brian McHugh went 2-for-5 with a triple for Newark Academy (10-20).

St. Mary (Ruth.) 7, Dwight-Englewood 2: Brian Cuevas had three RBI for St. Mary (18-9), which took a 4-2 lead after one inning in the semifinals of the North Jersey, Non-Public B tournament in Rutherford. St. Mary will take on Morristown-Beard in the sectional final on Tuesday. Max Leventhal had an RBI for Dwight-Englewood (11-13).

No. 14 Seton Hall tops No. 2 Don Bosco, 7-5

Sophomore right-hander Mike Sheppard got himself out of a bases-loaded, none-out jam in the bottom of the seventh inning to give Seton Hall Prep, No. 14 in The Star-Ledger Top 20, a 7-5 upset of No. 2 Don Bosco Prep in the NJSIAA/Star-Ledger North Jersey, Non-Public A semifinals yesterday in Ramsey.

Seton Hall advances to face No. 15 Immaculata in the final Tuesday at Diamond Nation in Flemington.

Sheppard surrendered a double, walk and an infield single to open the seventh. He then got a strikeout, pop up to first base and a strikeout to end the game.

Sheppard entered the game with one out in the sixth after Don Bosco (24-4) had scored twice and he walked the first batter to load the bases. He then induced a pop up and got the final out by strikeout to strand three runners.

Junior lefty Steven Silvestri (8-1) out-dueled Don Bosco's Eric Stevens (5-3). Rob Fonseca's two-run triple capped a five-run fourth that gave Seton Hall a 7-3 lead. Stevens was 3-for-5 with a two-run double for Don Bosco.

Immaculata 8, Pope John 6: Cody Silverman had a dream game that included two doubles before a walk-off home run in the bottom of the eighth inning when Immaculata (20-5), No. 15 in The Star-Ledger Top 20, stopped 10th-ranked Pope John (24-5) in the semifinals of the NJSIAA/Star-Ledger North Jersey, Non-Public A tournament in Somerville.

SARAH RICE/FOR THE STAR-LEDGER

Randolph's Alex Guerra slides into third base just before the throw to Livingston's Greg Gamba in yesterday's NJSIAA North Jersey, Section 1, Group 4 final. Randolph gained a 7-3 victory.

W. Essex takes crown behind Gautieri, 5-0

BASEBALL

By Mike Wellamann
FOR THE STAR LEDGER

West Essex pitcher Dan Gautieri is a sophomore, and yesterday he went up against a junior who had yet to lose a decision in his varsity career.

No problem.

Gautieri pitched a four-hit shutout with one walk and three strikeouts to lead West Essex to a 5-0 victory over Hackettstown and starter Matt Reynolds for the championship of the NJSIAA/Star-Ledger North Jersey, Section 2, Group 2 tournament in Hackettstown.

It was the first shutout of the season for Gautieri (6-0).

"This is unreal," Gautieri, who finished with a tidy 76 pitches, said. "This was my lowest pitch count all season. Coach (Scott Illiano) always says two pitches (working) wins games. Three pitches means shutouts. Everything came together today. This is an unbelievable feeling."

West Essex (26-3) advanced to meet Ramsey, who defeated North Warren, 9-7, for the North Jersey, Section 1 title, 4 p.m. Tuesday in a Group 2 semifinal at William Paterson University in Wayne.

Hackettstown (21-5), the section's top seed, seemed to have the deck stacked coming into the contest. West Essex arrived just 10 minutes before the scheduled game time after a 1½-hour bus ride and had to face Reynolds.

But Reynolds (8-1), now 13-1 overall, never got a chance to settle in as speedy leadoff batter Andy Santomauro tripled to open the game. He eventually scored on an error, one of two in the first that led to two runs for West Essex.

Mike Rafanello added an RBI single in the third before West Essex gave itself some breathing room with a two-run fifth. Back-to-back doubles by Santomauro and Rafanello set the tone. Santomauro, who also singled in his final at-bat, was 3-for-4 on the day. Rafanello, who drove in Santomauro with his double, finished 2-for-4 with two RBI. P.J. Lawless drove in the second run in the fifth with a single.

Jimmy Kenny, who came up after Lawless, was hit in the face with an errant pitch by Reynolds. After lying on the ground face down for several moments, Kenny got up and stayed in the game. The right fielder also made two outstanding catches, as did Santomauro in center.

"We have a lot of respect for Hackettstown. They are a good club," said Illiano, whose team lost in the Group 2 semifinals last year to eventual Group 2 champion Pequannock. "(Reynolds) was as good as advertised. He was outstanding. It just feels great to get the opportunity to get back to William Paterson."

Hackettstown, which was seeking its first sectional crown since 2007, never got the bats going against Gautieri. In its previous three playoff games, Hackettstown, which hadn't been held to fewer than three runs in its first 25 games, outscored the opposition by a combined margin of 34-1. Center fielder Kirby Neuner had two of the team's four hits, which were all singles.

"Matt had trouble with his location and wasn't throwing his off-speed stuff for strikes," Hackettstown coach Gary Poyer said. "They made some great plays and never really opened the door for us. We didn't show any patience at the plate."

Cranford topples Morristown, 9-8

In a showdown between two county champions — and with a sectional title at stake — Cranford outlasted Morristown to once again assert itself as one of New Jersey's top programs.

Eric Walano, who was 3-for-4 with three runs and two RBI, singled, stole second and scored as Rob Ghiretti's grounder to short was misplayed with two out in the bottom of the eighth inning to lift Cranford, No. 16 in The Star-Ledger Top 20, to a 9-8 victory over No. 20 Morristown in the championship game of the NJSIAA/Star-Ledger North Jersey, Section 2, Group 3 tournament yesterday at Memorial Field in Cranford.

The sectional title is the first since 2007 and seventh since 1997 for Cranford, which will face Lakeland in a Group 3 semifinal at Kean University on Tuesday at 4 p.m.

Cranford won its first Union County Tournament title and sixth overall this spring when it rallied from a five-run deficit to defeat Westfield, 6-5, on May 15. Morristown won its second straight Morris County Tournament crown when it defeated Delbarton, 2-0, on the same day.

Morristown took an 8-6 lead in the top of the seventh on Rafe Shupe's leadoff homer, but Cranford scored twice — on a Ghiretti ground out and Sean Feeney's RBI single — to knot the score, 8-8, in the bottom of the inning.

"The kids fought the whole time," said Cranford head coach Dennis McCaffery, who was The Star-Ledger Baseball Coach of the Year in 2007. "Nick Cook came in and did a great job for us. This team works extra hard and our success is the result of that hard work."

Feeney, who was 3-for-4, was one of three freshman starting yesterday for Cranford, which took a 3-0 lead in the first. Morristown answered back with three runs in the third and four in the fourth to take a 7-4 lead. P.J. Jennings was 2-for-2, including a two-run single in the fourth.

Cranford had also rallied to reach the sectional final. It trailed No. 17 Scotch Plains-Fanwood by a run before scoring four runs in the sixth and holding on for a 6-5 victory on Tuesday in Scotch Plains.

"We played a very good Morristown team today," said McCaffery, who has guided Cranford to six sectional crowns. "But we stuck with it and stayed on track."

— *Chris Orlando*

Whippany Park wins on Falkman's RBI, 6-5

Gary Falkman's RBI single in the bottom of the eighth inning gave Whippany Park a 6-5 victory over High Tech in the NJSIAA/Star-Ledger North Jersey, Section 2, Group 1 final yesterday in Whippany.

Winning pitcher Matt Mantione, who went the distance and struck out five while allowing three earned runs, finished 2-for-2 with a double and Joe Labracio went 2-for-3 with two RBI for Whippany Park (19-4). Jose Aresmendi, who hit a two-run home run in the fourth, tied the game at 5-5 with a two-out RBI single in the seventh for High Tech (19-5).

Pace lifts Spotswood over Gov. Livingston

Cody Pace of Spotswood has come through when his team has needed him the most this season time after time.

Yesterday was no exception.

Pace, a senior right-hander, delivered a gutsy effort on the mound and hit a big two-run home run in the sixth inning to lift Spotswood to a 7-5 victory over Gov. Livingston in the championship game of the NJSIAA/Star-Ledger Central Jersey, Group 2 tournament yesterday at Gov. Livingston in Berkeley Heights.

Spotswood (14-12), which last won a sectional title in 2007, will meet Audubon in a Group 2 semifinal on Tuesday at Rutgers at 4 p.m. Gov. Livingston (23-9) was also seeking its first sectional title since 2007.

Spotswood, which struck for five runs in the top of the first, held a 5-4 edge before Pace hit a two-run home run to left-center with two out in the top of the sixth to push the lead to 7-4.

Gov. Livingston's Mike Rielly led off the seventh with a single but was erased from the base paths on a 1-6-3 double play. Pace then issued a walk to Billy Worswick and Joey DiSarno reached on an error before an RBI single to right to cut the Union County school's deficit to 7-5.

VIDEO

*Take a look back at Spotswood's victory over Governor Livingston in the Central Jersey, Group 2 baseball final only at **nj.com/hsbaseball***

SCOREBOARD

BASEBALL

NJSIAA TOURNAMENT
CHAMPIONSHIPS
NORTH JERSEY, SECTION 1
GROUP 4
Randolph 7, Livingston 3
GROUP 3
Lakeland 4, Northern Highlands 2
GROUP 2
Ramsey 9, North Warren 7
GROUP 1
Emerson Boro 5, Butler 2
NORTH JERSEY, SECTION 2
GROUP 4
Bridgewater-Raritan 2, Edison 1
GROUP 3
Cranford 9, Morristown 8
GROUP 2
West Essex 5, Hackettstown 0
GROUP 1
Whippany Park 6, High Tech 5
CENTRAL JERSEY
GROUP 4
Jackson 5, Manalapan 1
GROUP 3
Hopewell Valley 12, W. Windsor North 2
GROUP 2
Spotswood 7, Gov. Livingston 5
GROUP 1
Robbinsville 5, Henry Hudson 4
SOUTH JERSEY
GROUP 4
Washington Township 7, Lenape 4
GROUP 3
Ocean City 9, Highland 2
GROUP 2
Audubon 4, Buena 3
GROUP 1
Pitman 12, New Egypt 0
SEMIFINALS
NORTH JERSEY
NON-PUBLIC A
Seton Hall Prep 7, Don Bosco Prep 5
Immaculata 8, Pope John 6
NON-PUBLIC B
Morristown-Beard 15, Newark Academy 9
St. Mary (Ruth.) 7, Dwight-Englewood 2
SOUTH JERSEY
NON-PUBLIC A
Bishop Eustace 14, Red Bank Catholic 0
St. Joseph (Met.) 18, Notre Dame 5
NON-PUBLIC B
Gloucester Catholic 15, Sacred Heart 2
St. Rose 2, Holy Cross 1

SOFTBALL

NJSIAA TOURNAMENT
CHAMPIONSHIPS
NORTH JERSEY, SECTION 1
GROUP 4
Morris Knolls 1, Montclair 0
GROUP 3
Paramus 11, Pascack Valley 0
GROUP 2
Indian Hills 1, Pequannock 0
NORTH JERSEY, SECTION 2
GROUP 4
J.P. Stevens 2, Hillsborough 1
GROUP 3
Nutley 2, South Plainfield 1
CENTRAL JERSEY
GROUP 4
East Brunswick 4, West Windsor South 2
GROUP 2
Gov. Livingston 5, Raritan 1
SOUTH JERSEY
GROUP 1
New Egypt 6, Pennsville 0
SEMIFINALS
NORTH JERSEY
NON-PUBLIC A
Paramus Catholic 10, Pope John 0
NON-PUBLIC B
Lodi Immaculate 3, Gill St. Bernard's 1
Mont. Kimberley 5, Newark Academy 4
SOUTH JERSEY
NON-PUBLIC A
St. John Vianney 7, Red Bank Catholic 2
NON-PUBLIC B
Gloucester Catholic 1, Holy Cross 0
Sacred Heart 1, Mater Dei 0

GIRLS LACROSSE

NJSIAA TOURNAMENT
CHAMPIONSHIP
GROUP 3
Mendham 12, Shawnee 6

BOYS VOLLEYBALL

NJSIAA TOURNAMENT
CHAMPIONSHIPS
NORTH JERSEY 1
Fair Lawn d. Wayne Valley 25-22, 25-21
NORTH JERSEY 2
St. Peter's Prep d. Bayonne 25-14, 25-15
CENTRAL JERSEY
St. Joseph (Met.) d. Old Bridge 25-15, 25-19
SOUTH JERSEY
Southern d. Cherry Hill East 25-18, 23-25, 25-23

PAGE 10 SECTION FIVE — THE SUNDAY STAR-LEDGER — JUNE 6, 2010

HIGH SCHOOL STATE BASEBALL CHAMPIONSHIPS

For additional coverage, go to **nj.com/hssports**. *For photos, go to* **nj.com/hsphotos**. *For videos, go to* **nj.com/hsvideos**.

Pitman defeats Whippany

GROUP 1

By Everett Merrill
FOR THE STAR-LEDGER

Steve Schuler abandoned his curveball three weeks ago because he couldn't get left-handed batters out with it.

In its place, the senior left-hander from Pitman replaced the curve with a slider.

And it was the slider that Schuler relied on yesterday when he struck out 13 to lead Pitman to a 5-0 decision over Whippany Park in the NJSIAA/Star-Ledger Group 1 final at Toms River East.

The victory gave Pitman (23-4) its first group state title. The Gloucester County school claimed four straight South Jersey Group 1 titles from 1963 to 1966 before the NJSIAA tournament was expanded and played down to group state champions in 1971.

Whippany Park was appearing in the Group 1 final for the fourth time. The Morris County team had lost in 1996, 2002 and 2005.

VIDEO
Check out the highlights from Pitman's victory over Whippany Park at: **nj.com/hsbaseball**

Schuler (10-1), who scattered seven hits, walked one and hit a batter, finished the season with a school record of 110 strikeouts. He was challenged in the fifth and sixth innings when Whippany Park (20-4) put runners on in each inning. Both times he ended the threat with strikeouts.

"We couldn't put the ball in play," said Whippany coach Barry Russomano, "that was the difference in the game. You can't win a state championship striking out 13 times."

Whippany Park starter Matt Mantione (7-1) matched Schuler for the first four innings, striking out seven and limiting Pitman to only an infield single from Dylan Colgate in the second inning.

Colgate, who would double in a run in Pitman's two-run sixth, came home when Mantione overthrew third on a ball hit back to him. Colgate was at third after a wild pitch and fielder's choice moved him around. That run in the second inning gave Pitman a 1-0 lead.

Whippany Park, which left eight runners on, had its best opportunity in the fifth and sixth. Joe Catanzaro singled with two outs in the fifth and Alex Coriddi followed by getting hit by the pitch. Schuler struck out the number-three hitter, Vincent Allocco, for the third time on a slider.

With one out in the sixth, Pasquale LaBracio singled for Whippany and advanced to third on a double to right by catcher Matt Bizzarro. The runners were left stranded there when Schuler eliminated C.J. Winkler and Joe LaBracio (Pasquale's brother) on strikeouts.

Schuler dominated the lower third of the Whippany Park lineup, striking out seven of the nine plate appearances by Winkler, Joe LaBracio and Gary Falkman.

"I gave up on my curveball because I was missing up and away," said Schuler. "The slider will break more and farther away from a lefty, so that's what I concentrated on."

Pitman moved ahead 3-0 when shortstop Nick Capelli launched a two-run homer deep over the fence in left in the fifth. Pitman tacked on two more runs in the sixth for the final margin.

Pasquale LaBracio and Coriddi each went 2-for-3 for Whippany Park.

"Today doesn't diminish what they have accomplished," Russomano said about his Whippany Park team that had outscored its previous four opponents in the state tournament, 33-11.

THE FINALS

GROUP 4
Randolph 8, Jackson 4
GROUP 3
Cranford 15, Ocean City 3
GROUP 2
West Essex 2, Audubon 1
GROUP 1
Pitman 5, Whippany Park 0
NON-PUBLIC A
Immaculata 7, St. Joseph (Met.) 5
NON-PUBLIC B
Gloucester Catholic 7, Morristown-Beard 5

MITSU YASUKAWA/THE STAR-LEDGER
Cranford players celebrate yesterday's 15-3 victory over Ocean City in the NJSIAA Group 3 championship game.

Rutmayer, Ghiretti, Walano help Cranford roll to crown

GROUP 3

By Chris Orlando
FOR THE STAR-LEDGER

This wasn't so much a state final for Cranford, but a coronation.

Led by solid starting pitching by Kurt Rutmayer, an early defensive gem by Rob Ghiretti and one of the team's biggest offensive displays in its illustrious history, Cranford, No. 16 in The Star-Ledger Top 20, rolled to a 15-3 victory over Ocean City that lasted just five innings in the championship game of the NJSIAA/Star-Ledger Group 3 tournament yesterday at Toms River North.

The state group crown is the third overall for Cranford (26-5) and first since it captured the Group 3 title in 1997. Cranford, which ended its season with a season-high nine-game winning streak, won the state's inaugural Group 4 title in 1971.

The Union County school had lost in its last three trips to the Group 3 title game, including in the 2007 final to Seneca. Ocean City (21-9) was seeking its first state group title.

"That was our goal here all year — to win a state title," said junior right fielder Eric Walano, who was 2-for-3 with three runs and two RBI. "Today we got it done. It's an amazing feeling."

Cranford pounded out 11 of its 12 hits during the first three innings, scoring twice in the first and six runs each in the second and third.

Greg Matlosz brought home the first run with an RBI triple in the first with two outs and then scored as Mark Osofsky's grounder to short was misplayed.

Ocean City, which was making its first appearance in a group final, loaded the bases against Rutmayer in the second on a single, a walk and a hit batsman with two outs, but Ghiretti made a great play at second, snaring a hard-hit grounder by Connor Ortolf. Ghiretti quickly ran to second to get the force and end the threat.

"The ball really exploded off the bat, but it took a good hop and I was able to get it," said Ghiretti. "This is a great way to end my senior year."

Ghiretti then reached second on a two-base error to start the bottom of the second for Cranford, which would send 11 men to the plate. Freshman third baseman Sean Feeney lined an RBI single, and after Marc Linger walked, the next five Cranford batters delivered base hits.

Sean Trotter and Nick Pace each hit an RBI single, Walano delivered a two-run single and, after Matlosz singled, Mark Osofsky smacked an RBI single to give Cranford an 8-0 advantage.

"This is one of the greatest feelings ever," said Rutmayer, a sophomore right-hander, who improved to 7-1. "Rob made a great play to keep them off the board and then we went and got six runs."

And Cranford would add six more in third, sending 10 more batters to the plate.

After Pace's RBI triple and Osofsky's bases-loaded RBI single, Nick Cook put an exclamation point on Cranford's offensive surge, crushing a 1-1 fastball well over the 390-foot sign in center field for a grand slam and a 14-0 advantage.

"I knew it was gone right off the bat," Cook, a senior first baseman, said. "This has just been tremendous."

Cranford's superb freshman left-hander Ryan Williamson relieved Rutmayer with one out and two on in the third. Williamson, as he's done so many times this spring, got out of the jam, getting the final two outs of the inning on a strikeout and a fly out to right.

The only negative for Cranford happened in the fourth when the fifth batter of the inning for Ocean City — Villanova-bound Tyler Reich — lined a shot that caught Williamson right on his pitching hand. He came out, replaced by Rutmayer, who got the last out of the inning.

"I'm not sure if it's broken," Williamson said of his hand. "And I'm not complaining. Today was a great day for us. This season has been unbelievable."

Pat Gilstrap pitched a perfect fifth inning, ending the game with a strikeout.

This spring, Cranford won its sixth Union County Tournament championship and its seventh sectional title — the North Jersey, Section 2, Group 3 crown — before winning its first state title in 13 years.

"This team had focus and commitment, which is what you need if you want to be successful," said Cranford's 12th-year head coach, Dennis McCaffery, who was The Star-Ledger Baseball Coach of the Year in 2007. "Today, Rob made a big play early, Kurt gave us another strong effort, and the offense was great. We got to this point and finally finished it off."

Jackson falls to Randolph, 8-4

GROUP 4

By Gregg Lerner
FOR THE STAR-LEDGER

Presented with a golden opportunity to supply an early spark as Randolph loaded the bases in the top of the first inning, Chris Hugg embraced the moment.

"That spot is unlike anything you can ever imagine," the senior left fielder said. "It's the best position you can be in."

The moment unfolded in an at-bat that Hugg, his teammates and the Randolph faithful will not soon forget.

After missing a fastball, Hugg got another and unloaded a line-drive grand slam to right field that ignited Randolph, No. 7 in The Star-Ledger Top 20, to an 8-4 victory over No. 4 Jackson in the NJSIAA/Star-Ledger Group 4 championship game yesterday at Toms River East.

Starter Thomas Travaglia pitched a gritty six innings for Randolph in a triumph that was not only the perfect culmination to a 28-3 campaign but also an end to a spate of heartbreaking late-season losses. The Morris County power bowed in three of the last four Group 4 championship games, including a 7-3 setback to Hunterdon Central a year ago, but this year won its first state title.

Hugg's homer highlighted a five-run first and was set up by an epic at-bat from Travaglia. The senior right-hander, who allowed 10 hits while

VIDEO
For highlights of yesterday's Group 4 championship game featuring Randolph vs. Jackson, go to: **nj.com/hsbaseball**

fanning two and walking two to wrap up an 11-0 campaign, worked a full count against Jackson starter Dan Falvo (6-2) before fouling off three straight pitches. He took the ninth offering to draw a walk with the bases loaded that forced in the game's initial run and set the table for Hugg.

"I knew I had to battle," said Travaglia, who finished 2-for-2 with a single, double and two RBI. "I'm not a great hitter but I knew I had to get on base somehow, some way. I kept fouling off fastballs until he walked me."

"We were just trying to continue to hit spots and he fouled some pitches off where we missed spots," Jackson coach Frank Malta said. "It was a great at-bat. He lengthened their inning and gave (Hugg) an opportunity and they took advantage of it."

Jackson (25-7), which was shooting for its first state crown since winning Group 3 in 1972, methodically fought back. Leadoff batter Matt Meleo, who went 2-for-4, started the bottom of the first with a single and eventually scored on a sacrifice fly by Brandon Adams.

In the fourth, designated hitter Ian Booth followed a single from Alex Herceg with a two-run homer to narrow the deficit to 5-3.

Travaglia countered with an RBI double to deep center in the fifth and Randolph, which pounded out 12 hits, added two more runs in the sixth on a run-scoring double from Brett Zaziski and a throwing error to build an 8-3 cushion.

Mike Folk and Matt Thaiss delivered two-out singles for Jackson in the sixth and Meleo backed them with an RBI base hit to center to make it 8-4 before Travaglia induced a fly out to avoid further damage.

"That was the best feeling in the world," Travaglia, who capitalized on an effective changeup, said of being staked to a sizeable early advantage. "All you have to do is pump strikes the whole time and, even if they do put up three or four runs, you still have the lead and our team will keep hitting."

"Their guy had pretty good command and was throwing strikes," Malta said of Travaglia. "We just got to that spot where the five-run first was tough to overcome. We got opportunities, but give them a lot of credit because he made pitches when he had to make pitches. They are a very good club. We couldn't catch them."

Right-hander Robbie Berger took over for Travaglia and struck out two in the seventh before getting a game-ending fly out.

Junior second baseman Mike Rampone, who initiated the first-inning rally with a one-out double, was 3-for-4 with two runs for Randolph.

Gautieri steers W. Essex

GROUP 2

By Bob Behre
FOR THE STAR-LEDGER

West Essex's offense is predicated on beating an opponent at all the little things, including capitalizing on an opposing team's mistakes.

Audubon made two mistakes in the second inning and, as if by second nature, West Essex pounced.

The North Caldwell school scored two unearned runs in the inning and rode junior right-hander Dan Gautieri's four-hitter to a 2-1 victory over Audubon and the NJSIAA/Star-Ledger Group 2 championship yesterday at Toms River South.

Gautieri was sensational in outdueling Audubon's Wade Gies. He struck out seven, walked two and retired 13 of the final 14 batters he faced to deliver to West Essex (28-3), No. 3 in The Star-Ledger Top 20, its first group championship.

Gautieri struck out the side in the top of the seventh inning around a one-out walk to No. 5 hitter Tom Dyer. West Essex coach Scott Illiano strode to the mound, though, to chat with Gautieri after the walk to Dyer.

"Nope, it was my game," said Gautieri when asked if he thought Illiano was going to lift him for P.J. Lawless, who was warming up in the bullpen.

Gautieri (7-0) bore down and struck out Joe Furlong and Tyler Urban, both on 3-2 pitches, to end the game and set off a wild celebration. He did not allow a hit to the numbers four-through-nine batters in the Audubon lineup in a 107-pitch grinder.

"I had to step off before the last strike and clear the emotions from my head," Gautieri said.

Gautieri had held a one-run lead since Brett Phillips' two-out RBI single in the third inning drew Audubon (21-6) to within 2-1. That's because Gies (8-3) was equally sensational. The right-hander limited West Essex to two runs, both unearned, on three hits. He struck out eight and walked none in his six innings of work.

Gautieri owes an assist to center fielder Andy Santomauro, who robbed Audubon leadoff hitter John Flacco of a home run in the sixth.

Flacco, the brother of Baltimore Ravens quarterback Joe Flacco, had doubled in his first two at-bats and scored his team's only run. Flacco led off the sixth by rocking an 0-2 pitch to straightaway center. Santomauro raced to his left, leaped and snared the ball above the 351 mark as he crashed into the wall.

"I caught an 0-2 curveball and thought it had a chance," Flacco said. "When I rounded first, I saw the kid make a great catch. It was a great play."

Gies and Audubon fell victim to West Essex's opportunistic play in the second inning. West Essex, in fact, forced some of its own luck in one sequence.

Sophomore clean-up hitter Jimmy Kenny led off and reached on a throwing error by the third baseman. Kenny then stole second on a curveball to Vin Consenzo.

Consenzo then struck out swinging at a curveball in the dirt and made off for first base. As Consenzo broke from home, so did Kenny, from second. Catcher Derek Wickersham peaked at the breaking Kenny then fired toward first.

Wichersham's throw glanced off Consenzo and into right field as Kenny charged home with the game's first run. Consenzo reached second on the play.

Gies struck out Ralph Velardi for the second out, but Tim Perrotta (2-for-2), the No. 8 hitter, laced a double into right-center field to score Cosenzo and give West Essex a 2-0 lead.

Audubon nearly struck for a couple runs in the first inning.

Flacco led off the game with a double and Phillips drew a walk before junior Brian Flacco sent a seed through the right side that appeared to deliver his older brother with the game's first run. Phillips, however, was clipped by the ball as he broke from first base and was called out as John Flacco returned to third and Brian Flacco took first.

Gies then popped out to shortstop for the second out. John Flacco was then caught in a rundown between third and home as Audubon tried to pull off a double steal. Catcher Lee Holtzman faked to second to draw John Flacco off third and hung him up.

On June 18, 2010, the *Star-Ledger* published a story honoring us as the 2010 State Team of the Year and recipient of the *Star-Ledger* Top 20 Trophy for being the number-one ranked baseball team in New Jersey. In the paper that day, I was also personally honored as the New Jersey State Coach of the Year.

Trongone and I were chatting briefly about the naysaying parents.

"I just can't get over these people, Moose," said Trongone. "I mean, look at the year that we just had!"

The year to which Trongone was referring was a year in which we had actualized a vision that I had for our program that began as far back as the day that I walked down the path on the way to my car, half in disbelief that I had just become the new head baseball coach. During some of those tough years, Suit Number Two had mocked me, calling our program "the Milwaukee Brewers of high school baseball." Fifteen years in the making, but we had done it. We were the best team in the state of New Jersey!

"We'll never escape it, Steve," I said. "It's like death and taxes. No matter what, we will always swim upstream!"

The 2010 Knights put together the best season
in the history of West Essex baseball.
Photo by Tim Perrotta

Scott Illiano

➔ BASEBALL/SOFTBALL   2010 SPRING HIGH SCHOOL HONORS   2010 SPRING HIGH SCHOOL HONORS

West Essex players celebrate after defeating Audubon, 2-1, in the NJSIAA Group 2 championship game.

PATTI SAPONE/THE STAR-LEDGER

Attention to details carried West Essex

NO. 1 BASEBALL TEAM

By Bob Behre
FOR THE STAR-LEDGER

To illustrate how fragile the prospects for a baseball team can be, West Essex coach Scott Illiano explained to his players how the malfunction of an O-ring, two-and-a-half inches in diameter, led to the tragic explosion of the Space Shuttle Challenger in 1986.

Baseball, like life, is chock full of moments and opportunities that, Illiano explained in his analogy, if not handled properly can lead to much bigger problems.

"If you're not doing the little things, a game can quickly implode on you," he said. "If a two-and-a-half inch O-ring can take down a Space Shuttle, something comparatively small can destroy a baseball game."

West Essex did all of the little things correctly this season, whether it was a perfectly executed squeeze bunt, moving a runner over, taking an extra base on a bad relay or simply delivering a timely hit.

The attention to details seemed to cause huge problems for West Essex's opponents as the North Caldwell school won its division in the Super Essex Conference, captured the Greater Newark Tournament championship, a second straight NJSIAA North Jersey, Section 2, Group 2 title and, finally, the school's first-ever Group 2 championship.

For that impressive revenue and a 28-3 record, West Essex is The Star-Ledger Top 20 Trophy winner as it concludes the 2010 season as the No. 1 team in the state.

"Our pitching is the obvious thing you look at," Illiano said.

A high school pitcher at Cedar Grove in the 1980s, Illiano was blessed with one of the state's top staffs, a trio of junior right-handers — P.J. Lawless (7-0), Dan Gautieri (7-0) and Dave Jesch (8-0) — who combined to go 22-0.

West Essex also boasts center fielder Andrew Santonarro, an All-State selection, who ignited the offense from the leadoff spot with a .469 average and was 17-for-17 in his steal attempts for a team that thrived on its running game.

Gautieri registered victories in the GNT semifinals and final, the sectional final and pitched a four-hitter in a 2-1 victory over Audubon in the Group 2 final.

But this team was so much more than a compilation of statistical achievements.

"There were so many little things that you can't attach an average to," Illiano said. "We had the speed that pressures defenses, but that speed was combined with an ability to run the bases real well. Six of our nine hitters were legitimate base-stealing threats."

Then there is the defense.

"We had the ability to keep the routine play routine, then went beyond that to make the above-average play," Illiano said.

COACH OF THE YEAR

Scott Illiano of West Essex is The Star-Ledger Baseball Coach of the Year. Read the story at nj.com/hssports

Hun's Ford bounced back

PREP BASEBALL

By Mike Berg
FOR THE STAR-LEDGER

Player of the year: Mike Ford's 1-6 record in 2009 did nothing to discourage the senior pitcher from bouncing back for a dominant performance in 2010.

A hard-throwing right-hander, struck out 110 batters while walking 11 and limited opponents to 30 hits and seven earned runs in 59 innings this season. He finished with a 0.83 ERA and a 6-1 record to lead Hun to the Mid-Atlantic Prep League title.

"Last year, I knew we were young and inexperienced and had to fight through a lot of hard times," said Ford, who lost five one-run games last spring. "I knew we gave it everything we had last year, and I knew we'd come back with

everyone having an extra year of experience."

At the plate, the 6-1, 200-pound Ford drove in 32 runs and connected for eight homers while compiling a .481 batting average and .681 on-base percentage. He'll continue his career at Princeton University next season.

"Mike's in the gym all the time and, because of that, everyone looks up to him. All of a sudden, you'll start seeing freshman and sophomores in there, too, because of Mike," coach Bill McQuade said. "He's so big that he gives off the impression of a lumberjack coming out of the woods, and he has that mentality that he expects to beat you. If you get a hit and wind up on base, he's coming right at the next guy. He thinks to himself, 'This is my mound and you're at the wrong plate.'"

A year later, Indian Hills soared to crown

NO. 1 SOFTBALL TEAM

By Sean Reilly
FOR THE STAR-LEDGER

Joe Leicht has been the head softball coach at Indian Hills for the 13 seasons. He's also been a math teacher at the Bergen County school for 36 years. And at certain times, the two positions blend together for a singular purpose.

One instance came late in the afternoon on May 29, 2009. The Indian Hills season had just ended with a 1-0 home loss to Pequannock — the eventual state champion — in the NJSIAA North Jersey, Section 1, Group 2 final, despite a one-hitter from pitcher Katie Enright.

Before everyone went home, Leicht made sure to speak with his team in the school gym. The purpose of the meeting was to start thinking toward 2010.

"I told the team that day that the two best teams in Group 2 had just played," Leicht said. "And our job was to figure how to get one run better. We needed to touch that fourth base."

Once the players departed, Leicht stayed at the school with assistant Phil Lomenzo three additional hours to commence the planning process. The players bought in, and worked throughout the summer, fall and winter in preparation for what figured to be an exciting season, especially with Enright back for her senior season in the pitching circle.

Flash forward to May 28, 2010, and Indian Hills was again playing as the host to Pequannock in the sectional final. And this time, center fielder Perri Goldberg hit a solo home run, Enright scattered five hits and the team played excellent defense to preserve a

1-0 victory.

Indian Hills was, in fact, one run better against Pequannock, and then it followed with a 8-2 triumph over West Essex in the state semifinals. Indian Hills capped a season that included championships in the North Bergen Interscholastic League and the 31-team Bergen County Tournament by defeating Overbrook, 1-0, for the school's first Group 2 state title on June 5 at Toms River East.

Indian Hills ended 33-2 — tying the 2004 St. John Vianney team that was 33-0 — for the winningest season in state history. The county and state titles were the first for Indian Hills, which receives The Star-Ledger Top 20 Trophy as the top-ranked team in the state.

"They all worked like crazy in the offseason," Leicht said. "We were solid 1-through-9 in the lineup, we had a great

pitcher and we could field."

Indian Hills offered a glimpse of its season-long success in the seventh inning of its victory against Overbrook in the state final. No. 9 hitter Carey Houston doubled with one out. It was her first extra base-hit of the season. Leadoff batter Kelly Strittmatter popped up, but on the 14th-pitch of her at-bat against highly-touted Jen Metzger, Goldberg was hit by a pitch, then Ashley DeYoung walked. Enright ended the game by drawing a walk on full count to score Houston with the winning run.

COACH OF THE YEAR

Luann Zulla of Nutley is The Star-Ledger Softball Coach of the Year. Read the story at nj.com/hssports

Klemmer's hard work about to pay off in big way

PREP SOFTBALL

By Mike Byrne
FOR THE STAR-LEDGER

Player of the year: When Aly Klemmer was around 12 years old she came to a grown-up conclusion.

"Playing sports can pay," she realized. "I could get a college education."

And that is what has happened for Hun's first baseman.

The Prep Player of the Year has a full scholarship to play for Marist in New York next year, principally because of her prodigious hitting ability.

As a child, she first started

playing baseball, but as she got older, she switched to softball.

"It was quite a change to see a big ball coming at me instead of a little one. I still think that," she said.

Klemmer transferred to Hun in her junior year from Notting-ham High School in Hamilton.

This year, Klemmer batted .419 with a home run, two triples, four doubles, 15 RBI and 14 runs scored.

In an April 28 game against rival Lawrenceville, Klemmer belted an RBI double in the top of the ninth to give her team a 3-2 victory over the eventual Prep A champion.

Peddie coach Tim O'Reilly called Klemmer "one difficult out."

Peddie took a 1-0 victory over Hun in the Mid-Atlantic Prep League Tournament.

"We thought we figured her out," O'Reilly said. "We shut her down."

The teams squared off a couple of days later in the Prep A tournament.

"She had made an adjustment and crushed three or four balls to right center for big hits," O'Reilly said. "She's a tough competitor."

Hun won that game, 9-2, and Klemmer went 4-for-4.

Klemmer was impressive on defense as well.

"She always made our infielders look good with her stretching abilities to get the out at first base," Hun coach Kathy Quirk said.

Klemmer said she doesn't know where she gets her athletic prowess, but she credits the support of her parents and grandparents with her success.

"Without them being there for me, I wouldn't have made it," Klemmer said.

She approaches academics with the same passion as for sports.

"When I transferred from Nottingham, my grades suffered at first," she said. "But then I realized at Hun there were teachers available and the library was available and I could work to bring (my grades) up. At Hun, I had several free hours a day to do that, which I didn't have at Nottingham."

As a senior, her grades were mostly As, and she plans a pre-med major in the fall.

840 Bloomfield Avenue
Clifton, NJ 07012
973-777-BATS (2287)
www.leftyssportsacademy.com

Star-Ledger writer, Bob Behre, presents us with the 2010 *Star-Ledger* Top 20
Trophy as the number-one ranked team in New Jersey. From left to right, Steve
Trongone, Bob Behre, myself, Athletic Director Damion Macioci, and Jim Whalen.
Photo by Tim Perrotta

The *Star-Ledger* Top 20 Trophy is the "Holy Grail" of New Jersey high school
baseball, coveted by more than four hundred schools. In 2010, it was ours!
Photo by Tim Perrotta

West Essex Baseball Handled Pressure
To Emerge As A Champion For Ages

By Steve Tober
For sidelinechatter.com

West Essex was a heralded team long before it achieved the rare triple crown of high school baseball (conference, county and state championships) that very few programs are ever able to achieve in a single season.

There was pressure indeed for the Knights (28-3) since they were expected to challenge for top honors from the very start of the spring, but they withstood the rigors of a scholastic campaign and emerged a true champion for the ages in Essex County baseball.

Last Saturday's well-earned 2-1 triumph over Aububon for the overall Group 2 state championship on a hot afternoon at Toms River South sealed the deal as far as veteran head coach Scott Illiano's Knights being one of the state's very best teams in 2010.

Now, with the Essex County American Legion season already well underway, other travel team commitments in the process of being met and post-season awards commencing, there is still time to look back and remember just how sweet it was, especially since such diligence by all went into the process to build a champion.

"I'll remember how hard our kids worked," said Illiano. "The 5-hour practices, and how they routinely came early and stayed late. They even stayed after home games for extra reps, and pitchers ran on the track. I'll remember how incredibly well they handled pressure. The pressure that comes from state rankings, tournament seedings, and just how well they performed under 1-run pressure in elimination games.

West Essex Won Every Possible Title
As Essex County's No. 1 Baseball Team

By Steve Tober
For sidelinechatter.com

Baseball is full of superstitions, everything from not walking on the chalk line to the various rituals batters go through before stepping into the box and prepare to hit. For West Essex, it was the feeling that no one could beat the Group 2 champions in their home white uniforms.

Superstitions aside, even those regarding one's collective rise in confidence regarding what uniform was worn, didn't really seem to matter to the general high school baseball ban populace which watched the Knights put together a proverbial season for the ages, setting a new school single-season record for victories with 28 while copping the Super Essex Conference-Liberty Division regular-season title, a second Greater Newark Tournament crown, a second straight North 2, Group 2 state sectional title and a first-ever overall Group 2 state championship.

The rare quadruple crown of high school baseball in the Garden State was achieved by a West Essex team that was pitching-rich with stellar defense and timely hitting in addition to being blessed with one of the state's best coaching staffs headed by Scott Illiano, the 2009 Sideline Chatter Essex County coach of the year, who would be a leading candidate for top coaching honors in any season. Plus, he appreciates the nuances of the great sport of baseball, including the aforementioned superstitions, or perceived touches of good luck, that players and teams may adhere to for whatever comfort or joy that can be engendered.

For West Essex, our 2010 "Team of the Year" in Essex County baseball, the ability to be the county's best team from start to finish included completing a 28-3 season with 13 straight wins to end the campaign, while bettering the previous school-best 22-5 mark of 1993. The season not only made history, but also produced plenty of fun for Illiano and company despite the inherent pressure that was there for a ball club predicted to be very good back in March and wound up being a true champion while regarded in many circles as the state's No. 1 team.

CHAPTER 30

It Will Be Difficult. It Will Be Worth It!

"For 42 years I made small regular deposits of education, training,
and experience, and the experience balance was sufficient that
on January 15th I could make a sudden large withdrawal."
—Captain Chesley Burnett "Sully" Sullenberger III
US Airways Pilot - Flight 1549 January 15, 2009

IF MY EXPERIENCE QUALIFIES me to give young aspiring coaches any advice
it would be this: There is a difference between a person who sings a song and
a singer, a person who tells a joke and a comedian, a guy who coaches a team
and a baseball coach.

Ron Polk said, "There is a difference in being 'a' coach and being 'the'
coach. You want to be 'the baseball coach' in your respective community."

Rob Gilbert once asked our class of graduate students, "What is the single
most important decision you will ever make? Is it where you'll go to school?
Where you'll work? Who you'll marry? All of these are important, perhaps
life-changing, but what is the most important decision you can make?"

Gilbert explained that the most important decision that we would ever
make would be if we were going to be "in it" or "into it."

"Will you be in school or into school? In a job or into a job? If you're in
school, you're passively enrolled. If your into school, you're actively involved. If
you're in a relationship, you are headed for trouble. If you're into a relationship,
you're happy. That's the most important decision you'll ever make!" Gilbert
exclaimed.

"The world's most powerful preposition is *into*. The difference between
success and failure in coaching, as well as other endeavors, is often the
difference between those two words: *in* and *into*. *In* equals frustration, but
into equals fascination."

"*Into* beats *in* every single time!" Gilbert continued.

Are you going to be in coaching, or are you going to be into coaching?
The majority of what you do in coaching will be thankless, but that does not

diminish the value in what you are doing. If your goal is to make everyone happy, you will be better off selling ice cream—even then someone might complain that they didn't get enough sprinkles. There will be days when you will suffer losses so tough that you will feel like you can't even eat. You can also take it to the bank that you will get berated by a disgruntled parent. He or she will push you to a point where you don't think that you can take it for a minute longer. Do not quit!

Joyce Meyer once said, "The most important question that you will ever ask of yourself is 'How do I behave during hard times?'"

It is at those times that you must not lose sight of the enthusiasm that you had the day you first signed on the dotted line and accepted a position in which young men are trusting you to be "the" baseball coach, not just "a" coach. Remember, you are always just one play away from swaying the outcome of an entire game. You are also always just one win away from changing your coaching legacy.

Teach your kids about commitment. In today's society, words such as *mandatory* and *commitment* have basically just become words that are in the dictionary but have no meaning. Both players and their parents won't hesitate to sign up for two different teams comprised of different sports during the same season. They won't hesitate to book a vacation during your season either, and they will expect their son to be back in the lineup the very day that they return, "booming" tan included.

Teach the parents about this commitment too, and teach them about being into something rather than just in it. When you explain yourself, make eye contact. Rest assured, what you say will not be popular, but it will be right.

If you ever happen to be invited to a graduation party, be sure to ask the parents in advance if alcohol will be served to minors. It might surprise you to discover that there are parents who will allow this illegal behavior. Perhaps the best "Yogism" that I ever heard Yogi Berra say was, "Little League baseball is really great because it keeps the parents off the streets and the kids out of the house."

There will, in all likelihood, be a time when an administrator does not support you, especially if a big-name parent in your community is involved. If an administrator remains neutral in an unreasonable conflict between you and a disgruntled parent, he or she is on the side of the parent. Think your plan of action through very carefully. Be sure that with whatever decision you come to, you can put your head on your pillow with a clear conscience if the worst possible scenario plays out. Again, know that the grass is not greener elsewhere. In all likelihood, the grass is just different. Most of these problems are universal. Never leave a place unless you have somewhere better to go to.

As the late George Steinbrenner once told Billy Martin, who had asked him for a contract extension after winning two consecutive American League pennants, "No one is ever indispensable. Even in success!"

Try to not fall into the mentality of "if this happens" or "if that happens" I can be happy. Be happy today and exude that happiness toward your players. The days and seasons go by far too quickly.

San Francisco 49ers quarterback Steve Young once said, "The road to success is paved through criticism. Brick by brick, each person adds one."

If you don't honestly think that you can handle being criticized, then don't involve yourself in the field of coaching.

But if you do, know that even though you will not make a million dollars, you will feel like a millionaire; you will feel it was worth every bit of criticism that you took when a senior walks up on that final day, folds his uniform, offers his hand to you, and says, 'Thanks, Coach!'"

Teach your kids great character. Itch Jones once joked, "Most kids have parents, and you have to put up with what the parents raised."

Former Indianapolis Colts coach Tony Dungy told his team, "We have to become uncommon men."

Look around and see what has now become common in society. Developing uncommon people will be far more lasting—and better than any trophy or state championship you could ever win. It was just as rewarding for me to see one of my former players, Montville High School Coach Joe Cardinale be named Morris County Coach of the Year by the Star-Ledger in 2011. Common was never satisfactory to Joe. His work ethic continues to demonstrate this.

Auggie Garrido was once asked why he does not leave the University of Texas and move on to coach at the professional level. Garrido explained that at his level he uses the game for the betterment of the player. At the professional level, they use the player for the betterment of the game, and he doesn't think the game is that important.

Perhaps the best explanation of how meaningful baseball can be came from Ravizza in his book, Heads-Up Baseball. Ravizza wrote, "Trying to find the meaning in baseball brings to mind the Greek story of Sisyphus." As the story goes Sisyphus was caught eavesdropping on a conversation between the gods about the meaning of life. For his wrongdoing, he was given a sentence in which he would have to push a large rock up a long steep hill until he reached the top. Then, when the rock would roll to the bottom of the hill, Sisyphus would have to start all over again. He was ordered to do this for eternity. The gods watched Sisyphus take many different approaches. Sometimes he would go fast, other times very slow, and sometimes he appeared very graceful. He also maintained his intensity, stayed focused on his task, and showed a strong sense of purpose. Ravizza compared the game of baseball to the process of Sisyphus pushing the rock up and down the hill because each day you must begin again with the same rules and the same score, 0–0. "What is the meaning of baseball?" asked Ravizza. "The meaning comes from you. You decide what you put into it and what you get out of it. You have to push a lot of rock to play the game well, so work to develop some sense that what you are doing makes a difference to you. The more meaning you bring to playing baseball, the more you get out of it."

The West Essex players from the 2006 team have all gone their separate ways. Some will stay local, some will move out of state or perhaps out of the country. Some may go on to be great businessmen, accountants, or lawyers. Some will be great fathers. Raimondo, Valerian, and Zurawiecki are all currently studying to be teachers and want to be coaches too. One day, ten or so years down the road, they will walk into a bar and bump into one another, and they'll know that they are still walking together. They won't have to say it. They'll just know it. The expressions on their faces will say more than words could ever describe, because they took something from the game that no one can ever take from them. Their experience provided them with a meaning that only they can understand.

I don't always see the players from that team, but I am reminded of them often. Perhaps the best reminder occurred on April 29, 2009. I walked to my car with Whalen, who had replaced Renshaw as my assistant coach in 2007. Renshaw had resigned after the 2006 season to devote more time to graduate school and his football coaching position at Westwood High School.

We had just returned from a tough loss at Morris Hills. With the tying run on third base and one out, one of our players failed to get a safety squeeze bunt down that could have tied the game in the seventh inning. Then, he struck out. The game ended after the next hitter was retired. We failed to do a little thing right. We lost by one run.

I threw my bag into my trunk and slammed it.

"I'm tellin' ya, Moose. He gets that bunt down, we're still playing right now," I said to Whalen.

Whalen nodded and got into his car. I started my car and slammed my hand against the steering wheel.

"Dammit, get the bunt down!" I yelled.

As I drove home, I glanced across Route 46 at the same restaurant where I had once waited on so many tables.

I was a kid back then, I thought. It felt like a lifetime ago. Yet, as a grown adult I was still acting like an immature kid, because I felt like putting my hand through my car windshield. I just couldn't let go of the loss that we had just suffered. For a second, I was reminded of that tiny little three-by-one-inch ad, which has since turned a yellowish brown and still sits on my desk in my office at home.

Then, I turned my car radio on. New York Yankee radio broadcaster John Sterling's voice echoed through my car: "And Porcello deals. Jeter is called out, strike three. Jeter doesn't like the call, but the young flamethrower Rick Porcello catches Derek Jeter looking."

Rick Porcello's mom was a big fan of Derek Jeter. Her son had just struck out her favorite baseball player.

As I sped down Route 46, my frown turned into a smile as I remembered.

In my mind, I pictured Raimondo removing an ice pack from his swollen elbow. Anthony Tundo and Anthony Cerza were standing in the gym with their arms in slings. Mike Cordasco was wearing a neck brace. Kevin Picardo winced as he held his shoulder. Mark Ruggiero took two extra shuffle steps before throwing the ball. Joe D'Annunzio made a spectacular play up the middle. Anthony Dalonges put down a great bunt. Lawrence Caprio poured drops into his bloodshot eyes. Santomauro rifled a throw from the outfield wall. Baab screamed, *"This is our time, guys. This is our time!"* The players in the dugout rose up, *"Hold onto the rope, John. Hold on!"*

By now, I couldn't stop smiling.

"We didn't have it altogether," I said out loud to myself. "But together, we had it all!"

Around the Horn:
Seton Hall Preparatory School

- After losing to West Essex in the 2006 GNT final, Seton Hall rebounded to win their next five games en route to becoming Parochial A state champions and the *Star-Ledger* Top 20 trophy winner as the number-one-ranked team in New Jersey for the fourth time in six years.
- At the conclusion of the 2006 season, Seton Hall became the number-one-ranked team in the nation in *Baseball America, USA Today, Rise Magazine/Sports Illustrated*, and *Baseball News Easton Sports* 2007 preseason rankings.
- During Rick Porcello's senior season, Seton Hall finished 31–1. They won four different titles, including their third consecutive Parochial A state title and their fifth of seven *Star-Ledger* Top 20 trophies as the number-one-ranked team in New Jersey.
- Seton Hall Prep maintained their "number one in the USA" distinction for more than a year after *USA Today, Rise Magazine/Sports Illustrated*, and *Baseball News Easton Sports* rated them number one in the nation in their final 2007 rankings.
- From 2003 to 2007 Seton Hall's record was 143–12–1.
- In May of 2007, Rick Porcello was selected as the Gatorade National Player of the Year, a prestigious honor once held by major leaguers Gary Sheffield (1986) and Alex Rodriguez (1993).
- In June of 2007, the Detroit Tigers selected Rick Porcello with the twenty-seventh pick in the first round of the Amateur Players Draft. Porcello was the second player from Seton Hall Prep to be drafted in the first round of the Major League Baseball draft. (Eric Duncan was the first, selected by the New York Yankees in 2003.)
- On August 13, 2007, it was announced that Porcello had agreed to a major league contract with the Detroit Tigers. It was the richest contract ($7.3 million) for a high school pitcher in Major League Baseball history.
- Eight players from the 2006 Seton Hall baseball team were recruited to play Division I baseball.

- Six of those players earned Division I scholarships:
  1) Rick Porcello (North Carolina)
  2) Mike Ness (Duke)
  3) Evan Danielli (Notre Dame)
  4) Steven Brooks (Wake Forest)
  5) Nick Natale (Rice)
  6) Joe Jamison (Wagner)
- Two other players were recruited to play Division I baseball.
  7) Tim Shoenhaus (Delaware)
  8) Ryan Vander May (Delaware)
- To date, four players from the 2006 Seton Hall team were drafted by major league teams. Two (Porcello and Danielli) were drafted during their senior year.
  1) Rick Porcello, 2007 (first round, Detroit Tigers)
  2) Evan Danielli, 2007 (twenty-third round, Minnesota Twins) and in 2010 (twenty-fourth round, Atlanta Braves)
  3) Mike Ness, 2009 (forty-seventh round, San Francisco Giants) and in 2010 (thirty-third round, Houston Astros)
  4) Steven Brooks, 2010 (seventeenth round, Chicago Cubs)
- Mike Ness, Rick Porcello, and Evan Danielli earned *Star-Ledger* First Team All-State honors.
- Rick Porcello, Steven Brooks, and Evan Danieli earned Aflec All-American honors.
- Rick Porcello, Steven Brooks, Nick Natale, and Evan Danielli earned Rawlings/ Perfect Game First Team All-Northeast honors
- In 2006, Seton Hall coach, Mike Sheppard Jr. was elected to the NJSCA (New Jersey Scholastic Coaches Association) Hall of Fame. In 2007, he was named ABCA National Coach of the Year for the second time in five years (2003 and 2007). Coach Sheppard has won eight Parochial A State Championships, twelve Greater Newark Tournament championships, twelve Iron Hills Conference Championships, and two SEC American Division Championships. His teams have also won five Star-Ledger Top 20 trophies as the number-one-ranked team in New Jersey. Coach Sheppard has produced over forty Division I players. Fourteen of his players have been drafted by major league teams, while one signed a free-agent major league contract. He remains an exemplary role model for young people and a most reliable friend to me and other area coaches.
- Rick Porcello made his major league debut for the Detroit Tigers against the Toronto Blue Jays in April 2009, where, as a twenty-year-old rookie, he won fourteen games.

West Essex High School

- None of the players from the 2006 West Essex baseball team earned a scholarship.
- Nick Santomauro went on to star at Dartmouth College. In 2009, he was named Ivy League Player of the Year and was drafted in the tenth round by the New York Mets.
- Mark Ruggiero played college baseball at Division III Ramapo College of New Jersey.
- Nick Santomauro and Dom Raimondo earned 2006 *Star-Ledger* First Team All-Essex County honors.
- John Baab, Mark Ruggiero, and Vin Valerian were named to the 2006 *Star-Ledger* All-Essex County Second Team.

Glossary

Area Code Game: Major league scouts invite prospects to showcase their skills by playing in a game they have organized. Participation is by invitation only.

Came Set: The action of the pitcher coming to a full stop prior to delivering a pitch when men are on base. He does this in an attempt to keep the base runner nearer to the base. Otherwise known as the stretch position, it has become a standard form of delivery for most relief pitchers, whether men are on base or not.

Fungo Bats: This is an especially light, thin bat used by coaches, managers, and sometimes players to hit fly balls and ground balls to outfielders and infielders during regular or pregame practice and drills.

Go Ahead Run: This refers to any runner on base when the score is tied. Should he score, his team would be ahead. This changes if the score is tied, and the home team has a runner on in the bottom of the ninth or an extra inning. The runner then becomes referred to as the winning run.

Hat Trick: The same player scoring three goals in a hockey game.

Mercy Rule: This rule is applied to high school baseball games in New Jersey. It means that if one team is ten runs ahead of the other team, the game may be called by the umpires provided the requisite number of innings are played: four and a half if the home team is ten runs ahead, five full if the home team is losing by ten. Thus you get the concept of mercy being shown the team on the short end of the score.

Numbers: Count Versus Score: The count is simply the number of balls and strikes on the batter. The appropriate accounting is to always state the balls first. Thus a count of 0 and 1 means no balls, one strike; 3 and 2 means three balls and two strikes, etc. The score is simply the number of runs one team has amassed as opposed to the other team. A score can be 0–0, 5–4, 10–6, etc.

Pickoff Attempt: A throw by a pitcher or catcher to a base already inhabited by a legal base runner in order to get the runner out, thereby picking him off.

Pitchout Signal: A covert signal given by a catcher. He does this with the aspiration that the following pitch will be thrown to him outside of the strike zone, and he will thus more easily be able to handle the pitch and throw out a runner attempting to steal a base. In giving such a signal, the catcher is gambling that the runner will attempt to steal and he will therefore be an easy out.

Putout: In baseball this word is never used alone. One who catches a fly ball or pop-up, who steps on a base a runner is forced to go to before the runner arrives, who tags a runner off the base with the ball, or who catches a third strike is credited with a putout.

Sacrifice Fly: A fly ball hit a sufficient distance which enables a runner at third base to touch the bag (concurrently with the ball touching the fielder's glove) and score a run. The batter is credited with a sacrifice fly.

Steal of Home Sign: A sign given by the third-base coach telling the runner that he should attempt to steal home.

Warning Track: This is a dirt track located at the farthest extremities of the outfield. It is there because its different footing warns the outfielder chasing a fly ball that he is nearing the fence.

Wiffle: A lightweight plastic sphere, safer than a baseball, designed to allow the wind to penetrate it and move it in various directions, emulating curves, sliders, knuckle balls, etc.

List of Quoted Sources

1. John Feinstein, <u>A Year with Bob Knight and the Indiana Hoosiers- A Season On the Brink</u>, Published by Fireside/Simon and Schuster, copyright by John Feinstein, 1989.

2. Pat Riley, <u>The Winner Within</u>, The Berkley Publishing Group, Copyright by Riles and Company, 1993.

3. Jerry Kindall and John Winkin, <u>The Baseball Coaching Bible</u>, Human Kinetics Publishers, copyright by Human Kinetics Publishers, 2000.

4. Adrian Wojnarowski, <u>The Miracle of St. Anthony- A Season with Coach Bob Hurley and Basketball's Most Improbable Dynasty</u>, Published by Penguin Group, Gotham Books, copyright by Adrian Wojnarowski, 2005.

5. VHS Tape- <u>Winning the Big One With Skip Bertman</u>, Teamwork LLC, 1998.

6. John Wooden with Steve Jamison, <u>Wooden- A Lifetime of Observations and Reflections On and Off the Court,</u> Published by Contemporary Books, Copyright by Steve Jamison and John Wooden, 1997.

7. VHS Tape- <u>New York- A Documentary Film, The Center of the World- Episode Eight 1946-2003</u>, PBS Home Video, A Steeplechase Films production for American Experience, 2003.

8. DVD <u>Miracle- The Story of the Greatest Moment In Sports History</u>, Walt Disney Pictures, 2004.

9. Rick Carpinello, <u>Messier Hockey's Dragon Slayer, Published by McGregor Publishing,</u> Copyright by Rick Carpinello, 1999.

10. DVD <u>Inning By Inning - A Portrait of a Coach-Auggie Garrido</u>, A Film by Richard Linkletter, Virgil Films, 2009.

11. Ken Ravizza and Tom Hanson, <u>Heads Up Baseball- Playing the Game One Pitch At Time,</u> Published by McGraw-Hill Books, copyright by Ken Ravizza and Tom Hanson, 1995.

Please Note- Every effort has been made to determine and acknowledge copyrights and sources, but in some cases copyrights could not be traced. The author offers apologies for any such omission and will rectify this in subsequent editions upon any notification.

About the Author

Scott Illiano

Following the 2006 season, Scott Illiano was named Essex County Coach of the Year by both the *Star–Ledger* and sidelinechatter.com. In 2009, following his team's winning the North Jersey Section II Group II state championship, he was again selected by sidelinechatter.com as Essex County Coach of the Year. In 2010, after his team won the SEC Liberty Division championship, the schools' second Greater Newark Tournament championship, a second consecutive North Jersey Section II Group II title, and West Essex's first ever New Jersey State Group II championship, his team was awarded the Star-Ledger Top 20 Trophy as the number 1 ranked team in the state of New Jersey. Illiano was also chosen by the *Star–Ledger* as the New Jersey State Coach of the Year. In addition, he was named the 2010 New Jersey State Coach of the Year by the New Jersey Scholastic Coaches Association, and was chosen as the 2010 Northeast Region Coach of the Year by the National Federation of State High School Associations. In his career Illiano has coached the Knights to more than 250 wins. In 2011, his team won a second consecutive SEC Liberty Division championship, their third consecutive North Jersey Section II Group II championship, and their second consecutive North Jersey Group II title. Prior to the start of his teaching career, Illiano graduated from Ramapo College where he served as a co-captain of the baseball team during his senior year. He holds master's degree in educational administration from Montclair State University, and continues as a teacher of special education, head varsity baseball coach, and assistant hockey coach at West Essex High School in North Caldwell, New Jersey.

Acknowledgments

I would like to thank the many coaches who I have met and gotten to know over the years. I have taken something from all of you and benefitted from our encounters.

I would like to thank the many teachers, administrators, board of education members, and parents, who have shared their insight, supported our program, and offered help along the way.

I also want to thank Dr. Rob Gilbert, Coach Mike Tully, David Denotaris, and Ed Agresta. What you have given of yourselves and generously passed on has touched my life, as well as the lives of countless other people.

I would like to thank my editor A.T. Jones for her expertise and assistance.

A special thanks to Steve Tober of sidelinechatter.com, Richard Morris of Seton Hall Preparatory School, and Tim Perrotta for generously sharing photo images and/or copyrighted material.

I thank Bob Behre of the Star-Ledger and Steve Tober for their professionalism, dedication, and outstanding overall coverage of high school athletics.

I thank Matthew Lutts and the Associated Press, and Giovanna Pugliese and the Star-Ledger for licensing both photo images and copyrighted material.

I thank Nick Santomauro for sharing photo images, and Mark Ruggiero for sharing photo images and also for writing the forward to this book. Mark's words accurately set the tone for what we were about to embark on and provided a perfect history of the GNT, which provided a valuable understanding of reverence and tradition behind this significant event.

To the 2006 Seton Hall Prep baseball players, you are as classy as you are talented, and you rank amongst the best teams in the history of New Jersey baseball. To Coach Mike Sheppard Jr., Coach Frank Gately, and the Seton Hall Prep baseball community, you have set a standard of excellence for all other coaches and high schools to model and emulate.

To all of my players, both past and present, the game has given you the knowledge and skills that you need for each and every moment in your future. All the ability that you need is already inside of you. All you have to do is figure it out. There is nothing in this world that that a Knight can't do. Believe!